Louisiana
LEGAL
Advisor

Louisiana
LEGAL
Advisor
Fifth Edition

Stephen E. Covell, J.D.
Lauren K. Covell, J.D.

PELICAN PUBLISHING COMPANY
Gretna 2012

First edition, April 1987
Second edition, June 1989
Third edition, April 1993
Fourth edition, May 2005
First Pelican edition, August 2012

*The word "Pelican" and the depiction of a pelican are trademarks
of Pelican Publishing Company, Inc., and are registered in the
U.S. Patent and Trademark Office.*

ISBN 9781455617159
E-book ISBN 9781455617166

IMPORTANT: Laws change constantly. The reader is therefore responsible for finding out the most recent changes and additions to the law. Laws and the material in this book can also be subject to different interpretations. If the reader intends to use this book as a substitute for competent legal advice, the reader must accept all responsibility for the consequences. The authors and the publisher assume no liability for the uses to which this book may be put.

Printed in the United States of America

Published by Pelican Publishing Company, Inc.
1000 Burmaster Street, Gretna, Louisiana 70053

Contents

Your Family

Your Property

Your Business

Your Rights

Do It Yourself

How to:

Introduction

Everyone seems to be interested in the law. This is probably because our daily lives are touched by laws that we do not always understand. Most of us face legal problems with a sense of helplessness because we do not understand the laws that affect us. People in Louisiana seem to be especially interested in the law because they have heard that our law is different and wonder why.

Louisiana law is distinctly different from the other 49 states because all of the other states have their roots in the English common law. The common law tradition is based on the interpretation of law by judges who rely on precedent for their decisions. Our law descends from the civilian tradition that is based in Roman law through the French Revolution and the Code Napoleon. Civilian law is created by scholarly research and the drafting of legal code which is passed into law by the legislative branch of government. It then becomes the judge's task to interpret the legislative intent more than to follow judicial precedent. This is the theoretical difference between common law and civilian law. As a practical matter, our Louisiana law is a mixture of common and civilian law that is impossible to distinguish at times.

Since the law can be so complicated, people rarely are aware of what their rights actually are. Or, they think they know what the law is only to find out they were wrong. For example, most people are aware that Louisiana has a joint custody law. Very few people, however, understand exactly what this law means. We are always having to explain to clients that this does not mean that each parent has the children fifty percent of the time. We also have a hard time convincing fathers that an award of joint custody does not relieve them of the obligation to provide child support.

The rules that fill up our law books are not always relevant to our modern society. Some laws may be outdated by hundreds of years or by just a few years, and may seem to be a lesson in history rather than rules to govern our modern society. Seven pages of our statutes are devoted to the advertising and sales of fallout shelters. These laws even specify how shelters can be advertised and how they can be classified as "blast resistant" or "limited blast resistant." The seller cannot advertise that the shelter is guaranteed as blast resistant if he does not "promptly and scrupulously fulfill his obligations under the guarantee." In other words, if your shelter does not last through a nuclear war, you can have the satisfaction of suing to get your money refunded.

Until now, there has never been a book to explain to the layman some of the basics of Louisiana law. The first purpose of this book, then, is to give you enough information so that you understand some of the basics. If you have this knowledge, you may be able to recognize a potential problem and do something about it before it becomes a real problem.

Most people also have a tendency to see a lawyer only after a problem becomes serious or even hopeless. If you know some of the basics, you may find that you can take a problem to a lawyer while it can still be solved. The second purpose of this book is to help you recognize problems that need a lawyer's attention.

Some laws grant us rights, other laws restrict our rights. If life is a game, then the laws created by our Legislature and courts are the rules of that game. The person who has some knowledge of those rules has a distinct advantage over the person who does not have an understanding of the rules.

The third purpose of this book is to help give you an understanding of some of the rules that control your life.

The case examples given in italics in this book are based on actual Louisiana cases that have been heard in one of the five Circuit Courts of Appeal or in the Louisiana Supreme Court. The results of these cases should not be used to assume that a similar case would be decided in the same way. There are three reasons for this: 1) every case is decided by the court based on its own unique set of facts, another case has to be slightly different; 2) in many of these cases the court was not unanimous in the decision and a similar case could be decided by the minority next time; and 3) the law is constantly changing. What was decided by one court may be reversed or altered by another court. Or, the Legislature may change the law because it is not happy with a line of court decisions. Although the facts contained in these cases are a matter of public record, we have changed the names of the parties involved in the suits.

And now a few words about what this book cannot do for you: it cannot act as a substitute for a lawyer just as a medical encyclopedia cannot act as a substitute for a doctor. The Louisiana Statutes comprise 94 volumes which contain nearly 47,000 pages. The Louisiana cases that interpret these statutes are contained in over a thousand volumes containing close to a million pages. Obviously a book this size is not intended to offer specific advice about a particular legal problem. Our intent is to give an introduction to Louisiana law which may give you a general idea of where you stand. We give many examples of how our courts have resolved problems based on a particular fact situation. Do not make the mistake of assuming that because your problem is similar to the cases discussed in this book, a judge in your case will come to the same conclusion.

We hope this book will help you recognize those situations in which a lawyer's representation can be bypassed because you simply cannot afford it or because you are the sort of person who likes to do things for yourself. Representing yourself, however, is never advisable if there is any possible way to retain the services of a lawyer. This book, or any book, cannot fully prepare you for all the potential legal problems that can arise in even the simplest case. Keep in mind the old saying that is so often quoted because it is so true: "The person who acts as his own lawyer has a fool for a client."

About the Authors

Steve and Lauren Covell met and were married while they were students at Louisiana State University Law School. Steve graduated in 1975 and Lauren graduated a year later. After graduation, Steve worked for a Baton Rouge law firm doing general civil practice, although he also represented defendants in four murder cases. Lauren worked as an attorney for the Louisiana Department of Health and Human Resources in both the family law and administrative law sections. In 1979 they decided to start their own law firm in Baton Rouge under the name Covell & Covell.

It has been an interesting thirty years practicing law together, raising children, and participating in community affairs. Steve began concentrating his practice in estate planning early on. Because estate planning is so closely linked to financial planning, he became a Series 65 registered investment advisor and spends a good deal of time helping his clients with their financial planning. Lauren has found that she spends most of her legal time helping clients with dividing assets after divorce. This is especially important, and complicated, when it comes to dividing pension and other retirement related assets. Both speak frequently to civic organizations on topics ranging from divorce to estate planning and have participated in radio and television talk shows that invite listener questions.

It was while participating in these speeches and talk shows that Steve and Lauren realized the need for a Louisiana law book written for non-lawyers. People were interested in the law, but there was nothing in the book stores or libraries to answer their questions. That led to the first edition of the *Louisiana Legal Advisor.*

Part 1

Your Family

Marriage

Marriage has been described as not a word but a sentence. Perhaps that is why nearly one-half of all marriages end in divorce. Despite this fact, there seems to be no decline in the number of people who want to get married. As we shall see, there is more to getting married than choosing the right mate and showing up at the church on time. The institution of marriage carries with it many legal rights and responsibilities.

Getting Married In Louisiana

Who can get married? Anyone can, as long as one of them is domiciled in Louisiana, they are male and female, the right age, not too closely related, not currently married, and have a marriage license that was issued not sooner than 72 hours prior to the marriage. Well, maybe getting married wasn't as easy as you thought.

In recent years the issue of same-sex marriage has captured the headlines. Civil Code Article 89 states that: "Persons of the same sex may not contract marriage with each other." Civil Code Article 3520 then goes a step further and talks about same-sex marriages performed in states that do allow the practice: "A purported marriage between persons of the same sex violates a strong public policy of the state of Louisiana and such a marriage contracted in another state shall not be recognized in this state for any purpose..."

To apply for a marriage license, the woman must be at least sixteen years old (with parental consent if not yet eighteen) and the man must be at least eighteen. The applicant can prove his or her age with a certified copy of a birth certificate. If either party is under this age, he or she and the parents must appear before a judge to determine whether it is in the child's best interest to get married. The requirements for marriage by minors is now contained in the Children's Code which became law in 1992. A marriage license is only good for thirty days.

An example of how this procedure works was our client's daughter, Belinda, whose advanced physical development belied her tender age of 14 years. Belinda was dating John, age 21. Belinda and John decided that they wanted to get married and Belinda's parents, who were having a difficult time controlling their daughter, gave their approval in the hope that marriage would help her mature. Before a marriage license could be issued, Belinda and John had to present a court order authorizing the marriage. One judge, who was approached by us as attorneys for Belinda's family, refused to consider authorizing the marriage and stated that it was his policy never to approve a marriage when one party was so young. We presented the case to another judge who decided to grant approval since Belinda made it clear that she would run away from home and live with John anyway.

John and Belinda were married. Within a few months John left Belinda, and a suit for divorce was filed. The same judge who granted approval for the marriage happened to be assigned the divorce trial. The look on his face made it clear that he was not pleased. Undoubtedly he will take a dimmer view of approving marriages for 14 year old girls in the future.

The law also forbids marriage between men and women who are too closely related. Louisiana law prohibits the marriage between a brother and sister (whether whole or half), an aunt and nephew, an uncle and niece, first cousins, and anyone related to each other in the direct ascending or descending line. Before a marriage license can be issued, one of the parties to the marriage must submit an affidavit stating that they are not related within the degree prohibited by statute. Getting married in another state to avoid these prohibitions will not work either. The couple would actually have to move to the other state where the marriage is not prohibited and establish a domicile in that state in order to have a valid marriage.

Can an adopted child marry a sibling or other related party who is not a blood relation? Prior to 1987 there was no provision in the law to allow marriages between adopted siblings and other members of the family. Now there is a new law that would allow the marriage (except between parents and children), but only with a specific written order from a judge. The judge must consider whether family harmony would be advanced or impeded by the proposed marriage. There are no guidelines for the judge to follow, so the decision as to what best serves "family harmony" might vary greatly from one judge to another.

A couple who wants to get married must first obtain a marriage license from the clerk of court. This is done by presenting certified copies of the birth certificates. It was always required that the couple also present a certificate from a doctor stating an examination revealed no venereal diseases. The 1987 Legislature added the requirement that the parties also be tested for AIDS. The entire statute requiring AIDS and other tests was revoked by the Legislature, so that left us currently with no requirement for any type of medical certificate to get married.

If all is in order, the clerk of court issues a marriage license. At the same time, the clerk must give the couple a printed summary of the current matrimonial regimes law of Louisiana. This summary must inform the couple that they can enter into a marriage contract before the marriage is performed.

Once the marriage license is issued, the couple has to wait 72 hours before getting married. This waiting period can be waived if a judge or justice of the peace attaches a certificate to the license stating that there are good reasons to perform the marriage immediately. Once issued, the license is only good for thirty days. The marriage must be performed before a person authorized to celebrate marriages and in the presence of two witnesses.

The "Tourist" Marriage. There is also our new "no-wait" law for Orleans Parish. This is only available for tourists, not residents of Louisiana. If a couple domiciled outside of Louisiana wants to get married while taking in Mardi Gras, the waiting period can be waived as long as the marriage takes place in New Orleans.

Of course, people who are already married cannot legally get married to someone else because the law forbids a bigamous marriage. But what happens if one of the parties is already married, and the other does not know about it? The law calls this a "putative marriage" and if contracted in good faith, the innocent spouse is afforded some protection. For example, the innocent spouse will still have inheritance and community property rights, and any children born of the putative marriage will be considered legitimate. At one time, the benefits of a putative marriage ended when the innocent spouse discovered the impediment to the marriage. Now, the benefits of marriage continue until the marriage is declared null. *"When the cause of the nullity is one party's prior undissolved marriage, the civil effects continue in favor of the other party, regardless of whether the latter remains in good faith, until the marriage is pronounced null or the latter party contracts a valid marriage."*

There are even cases where both spouses are in good faith and believe that they are validly free from a prior marriage. This can happen when one party obtains a divorce that is overturned later because of a technicality. If the belief that the former marriage was dissolved is reasonable, a putative marriage exists in favor of the spouse who was free to marry and all of the civil benefits of marriage are still enjoyed by the couple and the children of their union. The only cure once the defect in the prior divorce is discovered is to remarry. Why would the couple have to remarry? Because a married person is prohibited from getting married. Therefore, the second marriage could never have been valid, regardless of how much good faith the couple had.

> *Arthur and Judy were living together even though Arthur was still married to his first wife Janet. Arthur and Judy decided to combine a vacation and divorce in one trip to the Dominican Republic. The formalities of Dominican law were observed; a notice of intent to divorce Janet appeared for three weeks in the Santo Domingo newspaper; and the Dominican court granted Arthur a final divorce from Janet. The happy couple returned to Louisiana and were married two weeks later. The following year, Arthur obtained a Louisiana divorce against his first wife, Janet, just to make sure that he was really divorced. A few months after the second divorce, Arthur sued to have his marriage to Judy declared null based on the invalidity of Arthur's first divorce decree.*

Are Arthur and Judy married, or not? If they are not married, is it at least a putative marriage? Judy made the argument that even if the divorce were not valid, Arthur should not be allowed to worm his way out of the marriage, since he was the one that obtained the divorce in the first place. Judy also argued that she should at least be considered a putative wife and therefore entitled to her share of community assets.

The court decided that the Dominican divorce was null since it was apparent that Arthur and Judy were domiciled in Louisiana and never intended to live in the Dominican Republic. It was also decided that since the marriage to Judy was prohibited, Arthur was not prevented from pointing out its invalidity, even though he was the person who sought the invalid divorce.

Was it at least a putative marriage? There was enough evidence presented at trial to indicate that Judy had some suspicions as to the validity of the Dominican divorce. The court concluded that Judy was not in good faith since she didn't investigate her suspicions and that she, therefore, could not be a putative wife. Since the divorce from Janet was invalid, there was no marriage between Arthur and Judy. The invalidity of their marriage was not altered by Arthur's Louisiana divorce, since the divorce was not obtained until after the marriage between Arthur and Judy.

This case might be decided differently today in one respect. In 1987 the Legislature gave more protection to the spouse who marries a person who has a prior undissolved marriage. Whether in good faith or not, the innocent spouse continues to benefit from the civil effects of the marriage until the marriage is pronounced null. This provision only applies to cases where one spouse has a prior undissolved marriage, not to cases where there is another type of impediment.

The marriage between Arthur and Judy was an absolute nullity. In legal terms, "absolute nullity" means that the marriage never existed. There are three circumstances in which a marriage can be considered absolutely null:

- When the marriage is done without a marriage ceremony.

- When contracted by procuration.

- When contracted in violation of an impediment.

Marriage by procuration is typically a mail order bride situation where one party is not present or is represented by a third party at the ceremony. In Arthur and Judy's case, the marriage was an absolute nullity because Arthur was still married to Janet. The marriage to Janet was an impediment to marrying Judy.

A marriage can also be relatively null. This means that the marriage is still valid but can be declared null by a judge. A marriage is relatively null when the consent of one of the parties was not freely given. Only the party whose consent was not freely given can ask that the marriage be invalidated. Examples of a lack of free consent would be mistaking the identity of the person you are marrying and being coerced into the marriage.

It is difficult to imagine a situation where you could be mistaken as to the identity of the person you are marrying. In 1889, a novel approach was tried. A young man discovered that his bride was not a virgin. In attempting to get the marriage annulled, he made the argument that she was not the chaste woman he thought she was. The court did not buy this argument and decided that the statute only covered a mistake as to the person, not as to some quality of the person. Similar unsuccessful arguments were made in later years when a young man found out his bride was insane and when a young lady found out her husband had married her under an assumed name.

A suit for nullity based on coercion is raised more frequently, especially by young men who have to face the angry father of their pregnant girlfriend. But when a young man was told by a father that marrying his daughter would be "the manly and decent thing to do," the court held that this was not enough of a threat against the young man to nullify the marriage.

Jimmy and Pat were married and three months later, Pat had a baby and Jimmy found out that he was not the father. He sued Pat to nullify the marriage based on two grounds: that she was not the girl he thought she was, and that he was coerced into marrying her because she was pregnant. He also added to his suit the fact that he was not even dating her at the time she conceived and demanded that blood tests be performed to determine paternity.

We saw that claiming a person is not the person you thought she was because she was not chaste didn't work in 1889, and it didn't work for Jimmy when this case went to the appeals court. Jimmy's argument that he was coerced into marrying Pat because she was pregnant also didn't work, although he made a valiant attempt to convince the court that she induced him to marry her by fraudulently convincing him that the baby was his. In any event, the court reasoned, Jimmy continued living with Pat after discovering the "mistake" and Louisiana law clearly states that you lose an action for nullity if you continue to live as man and wife after discovering the reasons that give you an action for nullity.

Covenant Marriage

A covenant marriage in Louisiana is different than a regular marriage in that you are pretty much saying "I really mean to abide by my marriage vows." So, you also agree when you enter into a covenant marriage that you will make it more difficult for yourself to get divorced in case it turns out that you really didn't mean to abide by your marriage vows.

To enter into a covenant marriage, the couple first have to both sign a declaration of intent that must contain, among other things, a statement that "We have chosen each other carefully and disclosed to one another everything which could adversely affect the decision to enter into this marriage. We have received premarital counseling on the nature, purposes, and responsibilities of marriage. We have read the Covenant Marriage Act, and we understand that a Covenant Marriage is for life. If we experience marital difficulties, we commit ourselves to take all reasonable efforts to preserve our marriage, including marital counseling."

A couple that enters into a covenant marriage is not allowed to divorce under the no-fault six month waiting rules available for regular marriages. A covenant marriage is normally only dissolved after first going through a judicial separation. The covenant marriage laws have not exactly been a success and only account for about 1% of the total in Louisiana. Out of 40,561 marriage licenses issued in a recent year, only 469 were covenant.

Community Property

From the time you marry, Louisiana law will determine what property is yours and how the property will be divided in a divorce or upon your death. This determination can only be changed by a valid contract between the husband and wife.

There are only a few community property states in the U.S.: Arizona, California, Idaho, Louisiana, Nevada, New Mexico, Texas, Washington, and Wisconsin. Naturally, in what seems to be a continuing effort to be different, Louisiana is one of them. Without a marriage contract, all property owned by a husband and wife is presumed to be community property. That is, each spouse owns an undivided one-half interest in the property accumulated during the marriage. It does not matter that one spouse has a large income that has paid for the house, the retirement plan and everything else the couple owns. If the couple should divorce, the spouse who had no income is still entitled to 50% of everything, including the bills.

So, assuming you haven't prepared a marriage contract prior to your marriage, Louisiana has made one for you. It might look a little bit like this:

MATRIMONIAL REGIME CONTRACT

WHEREAS, the party of the first part plans to marry the party of the second part, and

WHEREAS, the parties hereto wish to enter into a partnership and wish the terms hereof to control all of their financial dealings and responsibilities,

NOW, THEREFORE, it is hereby agreed as follows:

1. This agreement is binding and irrevocable until the decision of a judge terminates it or one of us dies.

2. It does not matter who makes the money. When our partnership ends, we will split everything we've made down the middle. "Everything" includes any tangible benefits an employer gives either of us (such as stock options and retirement plans), regardless of who actually contributed to the plan.

3. Everything we own will be presumed to be community. If you had property before we married, or were given or inherited something after we were married, you will have to prove it.

4. Any property you prove to be separate may be considered community regardless if you mingle those funds with community funds.

5. Any debts I run up will be half yours.

Wendy Wife   *Harold Husband*

Our law therefore presumes that when a couple marries they intend to create not just a social or spiritual relationship, but a business partnership. This partnership is called the "community of acquets and gains," and the marital partners are treated virtually the same way as the partners in a shoe store. There is only one significant difference —the partners in the shoe store probably consulted a lawyer and executed a partnership contract that spelled out every detail of their relationship.

The married couple entered into a partnership contract as well, but the details of their partnership were decided in volumes of statutes. The married couple probably wasn't even aware they entered into a contract, and certainly, they had nothing to say about the terms. If your fiance's lawyer had prepared a contract for you to review on the morning of the wedding, it might look something like our example.

Would you reconsider marriage if your fiancee presented you with this document as a condition to the ceremony? Do you think there ever would have been a shoe store if one of the partners had prepared a contract with terms like this one?

This contract is, of course, intended to be tongue-in-cheek. But it does point out some basics that you agree to when you marry. In the absence of a marriage contract, the State of Louisiana determines the status of property belonging to a married couple. Our Civil Code spells out in very great detail your contract, starting with the definition of Matrimonial Regime: "A Matrimonial regime is a system of principles and rules governing the ownership and management of the property of married persons as between themselves and towards third persons."

The Code then goes on to say that there are two major types of matrimonial regimes: the legal regime and the contractual regime. Contractual regimes are those which are governed by a marriage contract. Legal regimes (community property regimes) operate automatically when no contract is prepared prior to marriage. Most people end up with the legal regime, as in our example, since very few people actually enter into a marriage contract prior to the marriage. A marriage contract can also be entered into after marriage. This usually involves more trouble than executing the contract prior to marriage, as we shall see later.

Let's look more closely at this contract, this legal regime, that you didn't know you had:

Part 1 of the contract states that you cannot revoke the terms of the contract without either getting a judgment or dying (we'll discuss the details of this later in the section on termination of the community).

Part 2 states the underlying concept of community property regimes: virtually everything acquired by either spouse during the marriage is owned equally by the spouses regardless of where it came from. The Civil Code states that each spouse owns a "present undivided one-half interest in the community property." The Code then defines community property as "property acquired during the existence of the legal regime through the effort, skill, or industry of either spouse."

The community presumption. The Code adds further that all income from separate property, property donated to the spouses, and generally all things not specifically classified by law as separate, are also community property. So, if property isn't specifically defined by law as separate, then it must be community. The presumption that property is community is very hard to overcome in many cases.

This leads to some interesting court battles when a marriage hits the skids and two people first discover that they entered into a financial contract on their wedding day. The battle is often over whether a particular asset is community or separate property. If the asset is community, both contestants get half of its value. If the asset is separate, one contestant may be entitled to the whole thing.

People do not always understand that in a community property regime, all income from either spouse is community. Let's look at the case of Fred and Alice for an example of how this works. They have been married fifteen years during which Fred has been an executive earning $90,000 per year. Alice has stayed at home raising the children and has no income. Fred pays all the household expenses and invests the remainder in stocks and a savings account. The stocks are registered in Fred's name alone and the savings account requires only Fred's signature for withdrawals. Does Alice have any interest in these investments that have been made with Fred's earnings? Of course she does. All income belongs to both spouses regardless of who actually brings home the pay checks. The fact that Fred put the money in an account and in stocks in his name does not matter. Alice is still the owner of an undivided one-half interest in the account and in the stocks.

People frequently make the mistake of assuming that the title to a car determines who owns the car. In fact, how you decide to title your car does not affect its status as community property. Whether the title is made out jointly to the spouses or whether it is the name of one spouse alone, the car will be community property unless there is some reason otherwise, like a marriage contract.

The Civil Code says nothing about pensions or other deferred company benefits which may not be withdrawn until the job is terminated. Is a pension a community or separate asset? What if the pension is not payable until the spouse who earned it retires 20 years after the divorce? In cases where the

Code does not spell out the result of a particular situation, a judge will have to interpret what was intended by the Legislature. Such interpretations of law tend to lead to a sort of legal evolution. One judge frequently bases his decision on the decision of another judge in a similar case. This decision may then be reviewed by a higher judge in a court of appeal or by the Louisiana Supreme Court.

This evolutionary process led the courts to conclude that a pension or retirement fund was indeed community. At one point it was decided by some courts that the non-working spouse was entitled to one-half the vested value of the fund for the years the marriage existed. If the working spouse had been married twenty years at the time of the divorce, but his company benefit plan allowed no payment until retirement, the other spouse received nothing. At least that is the way it used to be.

During the middle 1970's a further legal evolution took place. The courts decided that a pension was a *right* that was created during the existence of the community. A non-working spouse is therefore now entitled to a portion of the retirement proceeds at the time the working spouse retires, regardless of whether there were any retirement rights that could be withdrawn at the time the community ended. Whether community money was contributed to the fund or whether the employer completely funded the retirement is immaterial. This line of reasoning started with a very famous case named *Sims v. Sims* and is still frequently used as a basis to determine spousal rights to retirement plans.

Part 3 of the contract states the law as it exists: all things in the possession of either spouse during the existence of the community property regime are presumed to be community, but either spouse may prove that they are separate property. The burden, as we said earlier, would be on a spouse to prove that a particular piece of property was separate if the other spouse claimed that it was community.

"The burden rests upon the one claiming that the property is the separate property of either of the spouses to show that it was acquired and paid for with separate and paraphernal funds and in commenting on the character of proof that is required, the court has used, among others, such absolute terms as 'affirmative', 'strict', 'certain', or 'positive', indicating how convincing it should be."

The Civil Code defines separate property to include property owned by a spouse prior to the community property regime, and property acquired during the community property regime with separate funds. Property acquired with a combination of community and separate funds can still be separate if the community funds used were inconsequential in comparison to the separate funds used. Property can also be separate if the spouse received it as an inheritance, as a gift made to that spouse individually, or as part of a damage award.

Let's say that Alice received a $10,000 gift from Aunt Minnie which she deposited in the bank in a special account. After the divorce, Fred claims these are community funds and Aunt Minnie is no longer around to back up Alice's story that it was a gift to her alone. Fred may be entitled to $5,000 if Alice cannot prove the origin of these funds.

The spouses can also turn community property into separate property by a donation of community property. That is, Fred can donate his undivided interest in the house to the separate estate of Alice. This would make the house entirely the separate property of Alice. Likewise, the spouses can also turn separate property into community property by donation.

There is a peculiar twist in Louisiana law that can cause serious problems and that should be kept in mind when attempting to divide the assets of the community or to donate to a spouse's separate estate. It is generally the law that income from separate property is community. In other words, If Alice had a house before marriage, any rentals from that house received during the marriage would be community assets. It would be the same for any dividends she receives from her separate stock or interest on separate bank accounts. However, if during the marriage Alice donates her interest in the community house to Fred, the income from that house is his separate property. So keep in mind that income from separate property is generally community, but if the separate property is created during the marriage by division or donation of a community interest, the income or fruits from the separate property will be separate as well.

Let's change our earlier example about the $10,000 gift to Alice and say that good old Aunt Minnie is still around. She can testify that she made the gift to Alice which means that it is now separate property. But Alice deposited the money in an account that Fred and Alice both use to make the house payment and pay other community debts. Part 4 of the contract says that this gift has been commingled in a community account and may therefore no longer be Alice's separate property.

Part 5 points out that each spouse is responsible for community debts. When the community ends, each spouse is entitled to one-half of the assets, but only after all community debts are subtracted. Like assets, debts are also presumed to be community. It is possible to show that a particular debt is the separate responsibility of a spouse, but the burden of proof is often difficult.

The Marriage Contract

If you don't like the contract our state has provided, you are perfectly free to draw up your own contract either before or after the marriage. The contract can make any provisions you wish as long as they are not against public policy or do not attempt to circumvent other laws, such as forced heirship. Most marriage contracts state that the parties simply wish to renounce the community regime entirely and that all income and property acquired by either spouse belong to that spouse alone and that each spouse will manage his or her own affairs without the concurrence of the other spouse.

"A matrimonial agreement is a contract establishing a regime of separation of property or modifying or terminating the legal regime. Spouses are free to establish by matrimonial agreement a regime of separation of property or modify the legal regime as provided by law. The provisions of the legal regime that have not been excluded or modified by agreement retain their force and effect."

A marriage contract can be limited and is often done for a specific reason. A spouse who goes into a marriage with oil producing property, for example, may want to specify that all royalties mineral rights and bonuses from that property are separate property. All other property would still be community.

The marriage contract entered into before marriage must be in writing and must be signed by the intended spouses before a notary and two witnesses. No marriage contract is effective against third parties, such as creditors, until it has been recorded in the conveyance records of the parish where the couple resides and in each parish where they own real estate.

You can enter into a marriage contract after marriage, but it is more trouble. The contract must be approved by a judge who must be satisfied that the contract is in the best interest of the parties and that they understand what they are doing. This must be done by filing a petition and having a hearing, usually a simple meeting of the parties in the judge's chambers.

A married couple can enter into a marriage contract at any time without court approval if the purpose is to accept the legal regime. In other words, you could renounce the community regime in a contract before marriage and re-establish it in a contract after marriage without going to court either time.

A couple who has been married and later moves to Louisiana can enter into a marriage contract without court approval as if it were being done before marriage. It must, however, be done within one year of locating in this state. (See the Do it Yourself section for an example of a marriage contract).

There is another way to be certain that income gained from separate property stays separate. In our earlier example, the spouses had a marriage contract stating that all income from oil producing property will be separate . The same thing could be accomplished at any time during the marriage without a marriage contract and without court approval. Instead of a marriage contract, the spouse who owns the separate property could execute an act of reservation of separate fruits and income. Besides not needing court approval after a marriage, there is another big advantage to this: unlike a marriage contract, the reservation of separate fruits does not need your spouse's approval. To insure that revenue from your separate property is separate as well, the reservation must be an authentic act and must be filed in the parish where you live and where any immovable property subject to the reservation is located.

These types of agreements should always be prepared by an attorney to be sure that they are done properly. Although the reservation can be done without the spouse's approval, a copy must be provided to the spouse prior to recordation.

Ending the Community

As we have seen, the community property regime is created automatically by the act of marriage unless there is a marriage contract to the contrary. While marriage is the most common way to create the community, there are only four ways to end it: death of a spouse, judgment of divorce, marriage contract, and judgment terminating the community regime.

The death of a spouse automatically terminates the community as of the date of death. A succession would then be opened in which a judge would recognize the surviving spouse as owner of one-half of the community property (and responsible for paying one-half of the community debts). If your spouse was considerate enough to have made a will leaving the other half of the community and all separate property to you, it would make the transition much easier. Without a will, and depending on the relationship of the heirs and whether the property is community or separate, you could end up watching your spouse's nephew Morris inherit assets that you had assumed would be yours.

A judgment of divorce ends the community retroactively to the day the successful petition for divorce was filed. In those cases prior to 1990 when separation was still allowed, if you got a judgment of separation but reconciled with your spouse, the judgment of separation was automatically terminated. Also, the community property regime was reinstated automatically unless the spouses filed an act stating that they did not wish to resume the community. Since there is a court record showing that you separated, third parties are not bound by your automatic re-establishment of the community unless you file a notice that the community has been re-established.

If the parties reconciled after a judgment of separation rendered prior to September of 1985, the re-establishment of the community property regime was done in exactly the opposite manner. If you were legally separated prior to that date, but went back to your spouse, the effect was the same as having a marriage contract that chose a regime of separate property. To reinstate the community property regime, you and your spouse had to sign a statement before a notary and two witnesses to that effect and it had to be filed in the conveyance records of the clerk of court in the parish where the couple resides.

A marriage contract entered into after marriage can also terminate the community. The married couple can choose to terminate the existing community in the contract just as they could have rejected the community in a contract before the marriage. Court approval is required before the spouses can validly enter into a marriage contract once the marriage takes place. An important (and only) exception is for married couples who enter into a marriage contract within one year of moving to Louisiana.

The community property regime gives each spouse, with some exceptions, the right to manage and dispose of community property. If a husband or wife feels that his or her spouse is depleting the community or is not managing community funds correctly, that spouse can petition the court to have the community property regime terminated even though the parties remain married. The termination is retroactive to the date the petition is filed.

Dividing the Community

At any time during the community property regime, spouses may voluntarily, without court approval, partition the community in part or in whole. This means that the spouses can make a list of the items that will belong to each party. For example, Mr. and Mrs. Jones could decide that they wanted to make the house the sole property of Mrs. Jones and the automobiles and bank account the sole property of Mr. Jones. The property thus divided becomes the separate property of each spouse and the division is effective towards third parties when recorded in the conveyance records of the parish where the parties are domiciled and in each parish where there is real estate. Mr. and Mrs. Jones can even elect to divide all of their assets. However, this does not end the community —property and debts accumulated after the division are still community.

In most cases, people are only interested in dividing their assets and debts after the community terminates because of a divorce. This can be done on a "friendly" basis between the spouses or it can be done through a court proceeding. We will look at both ways of dividing community assets after the community is terminated.

If the owners of community property wish to agree on how the assets and debts will be divided, the agreement is called a Community Property Settlement or Partition Agreement. We refer to this as a "friendly" division, but from experience we know that these really should be referred to as a "grudging" division. The parties usually agree to the division because they know that a court battle will be long, expensive, and that both will end up with less. At least they should know this if the attorneys on both sides explain the reality of how the court will divide their property if they do not reach an agreement.

A community property settlement agreed to by the parties should divide the community assets and liabilities so that each spouse receives property of an equal net value. When property cannot be equally divided, one spouse will frequently end up with more assets than the other spouse. In that situation, the spouse with more assets will find it necessary to pay the other spouse cash or something else of value to make up the difference. It is not unusual for one spouse to give a promissory note that provides for monthly payments to the other spouse. A promissory note to pay for part of a community property settlement obligation should always be secured by a valid recorded mortgage on property. If it is not secured, a bankruptcy by the debtor spouse can leave the other spouse with nothing.

It is important to make sure all assets and debts are described in the settlement agreement. Any debts or assets not included may continue to be the joint obligation or joint property of the spouses. This happens frequently when debts such as tax deficiencies show up years later.

A community property settlement agreed to by the parties should be executed before a notary public and two witnesses. This is mandatory if the division includes any real estate. Although this type of settlement is done without the necessity of going to court, there is one exception —pensions or other company deferred benefits. As we will discuss later, a Qualified Domestic Relations Order should be obtained through a court proceeding when deferred benefits are involved.

You have to be careful when entering a partition agreement. The law assumes that the basis for any partition agreement is that each party should receive equal value. If the party transferring the property receives less than three-fourths of the value of his share, that party may be able to sue for lesion. Lesion is a remedy peculiar to Louisiana law that allows the party who transfers property to get out of an agreement to sell, exchange, or partition immovable property under certain circumstances. One element of lesion is that one party to a contract did not receive close to a fair amount. A fair amount for purposes of lesion can be one-half the actual value that should have been received by the transferring party in some situations, or even three-fourths of the value that should have been received. When co-owners divide property, as in a community property partition, the three-fourths rule applies. (See the section on contracts for a more complete discussion of lesion.)

As we said earlier, the "friendly" community property settlement usually isn't friendly. There are arguments over who gets what item of property and there are arguments over how much the items are worth. If Alice gets the grandfather clock, she will say it is worth $100 while Fred will insist it is worth $2,000. We often suggest that the parties agree on a list of values for all the property before they attempt to divide the assets. The proper values are not what the items cost new, nor even what the replacement values would be. The proper values are the amounts that the items could be sold for in their present condition to a disinterested third party —a sort of garage sale value. Once values are established, the parties can take turns choosing items that they wish to keep. If both parties want an item, they can auction it to each other. The high bidder gets the item and the other party gets a credit for the amount bid.

Even when the spouses can agree on a division of assets and debts, there can still be problems. When property is divided in a community property settlement, it is common for the spouses to stipulate which debts shall be the responsibility of each spouse. This can be binding between the spouses, but will not be binding on the creditor to whom the debt is owed. For example, when one spouse gets the house, that spouse usually agrees to assume all responsibility for the mortgage. As far as the mortgage holder is concerned, however, both parties are still liable on the mortgage. If the responsible spouse defaults, the mortgage holder is going to sue both.

If the spouses cannot reach a "friendly" agreement, there is no alternative other than going to court and letting a judge divide the assets and liabilities. Once the spouses are divorced, either can bring suit to partition the community. Each party must prepare a list of assets, values and liabilities which must be signed under oath. Each party has an opportunity to traverse the other party's list. This means that a spouse can disagree with the value that the other spouse has given an asset and it means that the spouse can even deny that the item is community property.

If the descriptive list is traversed, the judge will decide the proper values for the disputed items. The judge can appoint experts to help determine values and the spouses can have their own experts testify as to particular items of community property. As you can see, the process gets more and more expensive. Who pays the court costs, fees and attorneys for all of this? These costs are paid by the parties and there will be less to divide if the spouses cannot be reasonable with each other.

Once the judge decides the values for disputed items of community property, the assets and liabilities are then divided so that each spouse receives an equal net value. The judge may divide a particular asset or liability equally or unequally, or it may be allotted entirely to one spouse. The judge has to consider the nature and source of the asset or liability, the economic condition of each spouse, and any other relevant circumstances. For example, the judge may allot the house to the husband because he has enough income to pay the mortgage notes. However, the husband will probably be allotted the mortgage obligation as well, and he will be obligated to satisfy the mortgage.

This would be a good time to go back to the issue of deferred company benefits. The Louisiana courts decided many years ago that a pension or other deferred company benefit was community property. The real problem, however, was in determining the interest the non-employed spouse had in the pension.

The courts had to devise a formula to establish exactly how this interest could be determined. One early formula worked roughly like this: you divide the total years worked by the spouse during the marriage by the total number of years the spouse worked before retirement, and multiply this figure by half. The percentage figure you get is the portion of each retirement check to which the other spouse is entitled.

The current formula actually used by the courts is more complicated and uses phrases such as "portion of pension attributable to creditable service during the existence of the community." The early formula is easier to understand and allows you to come close enough to an estimate of the interest a spouse would have in the other spouse's pension.

As an example of how our simplified formula works, let's say that Fred and Alice get married at about the same time that Fred begins to work for Monolith Industries. Monolith has a pension fund that matches any contribution that Fred makes. After 15 years, Fred and Alice decide to divorce, but Fred must work for Monolith for at least 30 years before he is entitled to full retirement benefits. At the time of the divorce, Fred's company statement estimates the current value of his pension at $16,000. What is Alice entitled to?

Alice is entitled to more than one-half of Fred's current value of his pension. She is entitled to one-half of the pension which is attributable to the time she was married to Fred, payable at the time Fred retires. Since Fred and Alice were married for one-half the time Fred worked for Monolith, she gets one-half (her community interest) of one-half (the percentage of time he worked at Monolith while married to Alice), or one-fourth of each of his retirement checks when he retires. Of course, using our simplified formula will result in an inaccurate estimate of Alice's share if more of Fred's share is attributable to his service after the termination of the community.

The right to receive a portion of the spouse's retirement or other deferred company benefit is not automatic. The non-employed spouse must include the claim in a suit to divide the community so that the interest, if any, can be determined by the court. That interest could then be received directly by the non-employed spouse (the "Alternate Payee" in plans governed by the Employee Retirement Income Security Act (ERISA)) from the company benefit plan administrator at the appropriate time. In order to have an enforceable right to the work benefits of the employed spouse (the "Participant" in ERISA plans), a Qualified Domestic Relations Order must be rendered by the appropriate Court.

This is referred to as a QDRO by plan administrators and attorneys who specialize in this area of law (and pronounced "Quadrow" by them). Among the basics contained in a QDRO are a recognition of the rights of the alternate payee; the amount or percentage of payments due the non-employed spouse; the duration of the payments; the forms under which the benefits are available; and the names, social security numbers and addresses for all parties. The QDRO should also include provisions as to survivor's annuities and a designation of beneficiaries, if appropriate. Once obtained, the QDRO should be sent immediately to the employer to be certain there are no problems with its acceptance. It may also be appropriate for the employer to set up a separate benefits account for the alternate payee at that time.

It is important to understand that any QDRO should be pre-approved by the plan administrator of the company's benefit plan. If it is not pre-approved, any judgment ordering a division may not be binding on the plan. So, you could get a judgment, wait twenty years for retirement, and then find out the judgment was worthless.

Certain deferred work benefit plans are not governed by ERISA and thus are not subject to division pursuant to a

Qualified Domestic Relations Order. However, all of these plans do require a court order which complies with the plan requirements and often must comply with other laws, both federal and/or state, to partition those benefits as community property between former spouses. These division orders require the payment of benefits made to the parties directly by the Plan Administrators themselves at the applicable times as stated in the Order and permitted by the Plan. Examples of such non-ERISA deferred work benefits are governmental plans such as Federal and State benefits, including military retirement, teachers' retirement through the Teachers' Retirement System of Louisiana (TRSL), state civil service pension through the Louisiana State Employees' Retirement System (LASERS), church benefit plans, and many other plans governed by law other than ERISA. In Louisiana, the majority of deferred work benefit plans which are community property to be divided between former spouses are either ERISA plans from employers such as ExxonMobil or Dow or for state employees or teachers.

If Fred and Alice want, they can settle Alice's claim against Fred's retirement at the time the community is divided instead of waiting until he retires. This is usually done by estimating how long Fred will live after retirement and discounting the total retirement he is likely to receive to today's dollars. One-fourth of this amount might be a fair cash settlement to give Alice. However, Fred cannot force Alice to accept this or any cash amount for her interest. Also, Alice cannot force Fred to pay a cash settlement. If Fred buys out Alice's interest completely so that no division of his retirement benefits are necessary, then a QDRO would usually not be required.

However, division of deferred work benefits at the time a couple separates is more beneficial and timely than waiting until retirement of the Participant. The passage of time without division of these benefits can itself create problems. These include the Participant's termination of employment by resigning or retiring without a recognition of the rights of the former spouse which can be lost without a QDRO. Further, the removal of funds from certain savings plans by the Participant or the disability of the Participant can also cause problems if the benefits have not been divided. Most importantly, the death of the Participant prior to a QDRO or other division Order causes major problems for the former spouse since it is then too late to obtain an order acknowledging his/her rights to benefits which might otherwise be payable to a subsequent spouse. From the Participant's point of view, if there is an injunction prohibiting the removal of any community asset and you wish to retire, you may not be able to do so until this asset is divided. The moral to this story is: don't wait. Divide your deferred work benefits through the applicable court order as soon as possible.

Divorce

The best news for couples facing the prospect of splitting up is the drastic change in Louisiana's divorce laws. Prior to 1990, a couple usually had to obtain a legal separation based on fault before a divorce could be granted. A suit for separation had to allege grounds, such as: the other party was an habitual drunk; physically or mentally abusive; a convicted felon; or guilty of abandonment. Now, there is no such thing as a legal separation in Louisiana (except for covenant marriages).

The old grounds for fault can still be relevant, even though we no longer have separations. Fault is still in issue in deciding whether a spouse is entitled to final or final periodic support. To be eligible for final or final periodic spousal support, the spouse seeking the support must be relatively free from fault in the breakup of the marriage. The issue of fault, then, can be hotly contested in a hearing that has nothing to do with divorce.

We finally have a true "no-fault" divorce where a waiting period is the only issue. However, the traditional grounds for obtaining a divorce where no waiting period is involved are still with us:

- Conviction of the other spouse of a felony and his being sentenced to death or imprisonment at hard labor.

- Adultery on the part of the other spouse.

- The fact that the spouses have lived separate and apart in excess of six months without a reconciliation.

A divorce based on felony conviction is rare, although it does come up on occasion. One client of ours was married after a whirlwind romance of three weeks. Her new husband worked unusual hours, but seemed to earn a very good living for the new couple. A few months after the wedding, the police came to her door looking for her husband. It turned out that he was robbing banks and hiding the money in the garage. We obtained a divorce for her as soon as the robbery conviction was confirmed. Since this type of divorce is unusual, we will limit our discussion to the grounds that are most often used.

Adultery

Outside of the spouse being convicted of a felony, adultery is the only way to get a divorce without a waiting period of at least six months. Assuming you can prove adultery occurred, you can have a judgment of divorce the first time you go to court. The problem is one of proof. You will need the supporting testimony of one or more witnesses as well as your own.

How do you prove your spouse committed adultery? Private detectives taking pictures through the window of a cheap motel as it is portrayed on the late show may not be necessary. It will be up to the individual judge as to the amount of proof required, although the Louisiana higher courts have stated that you must at least show the time and place the adultery took place as well as the name of the other party, if known.

We have seen many divorces granted after a trial that proceeded like this: the petitioner takes the stand to present his or her testimony. This testimony includes the reason the petitioner suspected adultery had occurred followed by a recounting of how petitioner and two witnesses saw the defendant enter the one bedroom apartment of a person of the opposite sex at 8:00 p.m. on the ninth of January. At 1:00 a.m. the lights went out and at 9:00 a.m. the defendant left the apartment and drove to work. The two witnesses each take the stand and confirm the petitioner's story.

The law requires that you prove your case to the exclusion of every other reasonable explanation of what occurred. The mere fact that a man and a woman spend the night together at the same residence is not by itself necessarily enough proof that adultery took place. In this case, if the suit has not been contested by the defendant, the judge might assume that adultery took place. If the spouse contests the suit, he or she will have to come up with an explanation as to what did happen in that apartment which, under the circumstances, would not be easy.

Jim and his wife Nellie had been friends with Robert and Louise for several years. One day, Robert confided with Nellie that she believed Jim and Louise were having an affair. Nellie confronted Jim and a fight resulted after which Nellie moved out and filed for divorce based on adultery. At trial the judge heard testimony from Jim, Nellie, Robert, and Louise. Jim and Nellie denied they had been having an affair. There was evidence as to frequent phone calls between them, an unexplained hicky on Nellie's neck, and a meeting at Robert's camp -except Nellie and Robert's testimony did not match on most of the details. Based on the evidence presented, the judge found that adultery occurred and granted the divorce.

Nellie appealed and the higher court reversed the adultery judgment. The appeals court stated "The facts and circumstances must lead fairly and necessarily to the conclusion that adultery has been committed as alleged in the petition. In other words, the circumstantial proof in these cases must be so convincing that it establishes the guilt of the party accused to the exclusion of any other reasonable hypothesis."

You need to be very careful in presenting proof of adultery. There has been a recent trend in the higher courts to require very specific proof that adultery actually occurred.

Charles hired two private detectives to keep an eye on his wife, Rowena. The detectives followed her to a house that was being rented by two men. The detectives saw her enter the house with the two men and saw the lights go out at two in the morning. Charles sued his wife for divorce based on adultery, and she failed to file an answer contesting the case. At the trial, which was not attended by Rowena, the detectives testified as to what they had seen.

The court awarded Charles his divorce. However, Rowena appealed and claimed that Charles had not presented enough evidence that adultery had occurred. Even though she had not originally contested the suit, Rowena claimed that the judge was wrong in granting the divorce. The appeals court agreed and reversed the decision of the trial court. The higher court noted that spending the night in the same house with a man was not enough proof that adultery took place. The fact that two men were there, made it seem even less likely to the higher court that there was adultery.

Factors that helped convince judges in other cases that adultery occurred included: (1) proof that the man and woman spent the night in the same room; (2) proof that they were in a state of undress; (3) proof that they were behind a locked bedroom door; and, (4) proof that the adulterous affair was well known in the community. There is also a case that granted a divorce based on adultery where it was proven that oral intercourse had occurred. Former president Clinton would have not have been successful in our courts with his claim that oral sex is not sex.

In the cases we have discussed so far, the proof that adultery occurred had to be proven by circumstantial evidence. This was necessary because there was no direct evidence. Direct evidence would be the testimony of a witness who actually saw the couple in an act of intercourse. Obviously, this does not happen very often. Direct proof might also be the testimony of the person with whom the spouse was committing adultery. If the name of that person is known, he or she can always be subpoenaed to testify at the trial. If the adultery is admitted, there may be enough proof. Keep in mind that the admission of the spouse that he or she committed adultery is not enough proof. That sort of testimony is considered collusive. In other words, a judge will not allow a couple to get a divorce simply because they both claim that adultery has occurred.

Since no one is anxious for the job of witness in an adultery trial, the witnesses are often friends or relatives of the petitioner. You can hire private detectives to provide the necessary testimony. This will usually cost a minimum of $90 per hour per detective, plus expenses. The meter is running while the spouse under suspicion travels from bar to bar and finally, with some luck, to a stranger's apartment. It is not hard to see why this is done less often than most people think.

Six Month Separation

This type of divorce based on six month separation evolved from the twelve month separation, which evolved from the two year separation. The only requirement for filing this type of divorce is that the spouses were living separate and apart for at least six months prior to the filing of the petition. After at least six months physical separation, either spouse can file asking for a divorce.

The disadvantages are the six month wait and your unchanged legal status pending the final divorce. Unless you took some legal action to terminate the community, there still may be some responsibility for each other's debts during the required six month physical separation. To avoid potential responsibility, it is advisable to petition the court to terminate the community as soon as there is a physical separation, and then later file for a divorce after there has been six months of physical separation. This procedure would end the community obligations of both parties. This is frequently called a "103" divorce after the provisions of Civil Code Article 103(1): *"Except in the case of a covenant marriage, a divorce shall be granted on the petition of a spouse upon proof that: The spouses have been living separate and apart continuously for a period of six months or more on the date the petition is filed."*

"102" Divorce

The majority of divorces in Louisiana are now filed under the provisions of Civil Code Article 102: *"Except in the case of a covenant marriage, a divorce shall be granted upon motion of a spouse when either spouse has filed a petition for divorce and upon proof that one hundred eighty days have elapsed from the service of the petition, or from the execution of written waiver of the service, and that the spouses have lived separate and apart continuously for at least one hundred eighty days prior to the filing of the rule to show cause."*

Why the Legislature chose to define the waiting period for a 103 divorce in terms of months, while defining a 102 divorce waiting period in terms of days, is a mystery. It has led to a great deal of confusion and to many cases being delayed because of a miscalculation of exactly when the 180 days began and ended. This happens all too frequently when someone assumes that six months and 180 days are the same thing –they are not.

Divorce based on Civil Code article 102 is frequently referred to as a "102 divorce" by lawyers and judges. The 102 divorce has two stages: 1) the filing of a petition and service on the spouse; and, 2) the filing of a motion more than 180 days after the service asking that the divorce be made final. Once the 180 day period has elapsed, either party can file the motion to make the divorce final. If the divorce is granted, the community is terminated retroactive to the date the original petition was filed.

There must be a hearing on the motion and it must be proven that the spouses have lived separate and apart for at least 180 days since the service of the original petition. The difference between this type of divorce and the six month separation divorce is that there is no need to be physically separated before the petition is filed. In fact, a 102 petition for divorce can be filed while the parties are still living together. However, this may not be wise if there is a fear of abuse and the filing party is usually advised to be out of the house from at least the day before the filing. Further, in many courts no hearing is held on the issues of occupancy of the family home or support issues as long as the parties are still living together as those issues are deemed premature.

When a couple is seeking a divorce, there is usually a need to settle other issues that result from marriage. For example, who will have custody of the children? Who will pay child support and spousal support, and how much? Who will have the right to remain in the house? Although the six month separation (103) divorce and the 102 divorce are no-fault and usually uncontested, these other issues can be hotly contested and can involve the question of fault.

When a petition for divorce is filed, either spouse can ask that these questions be resolved. The typical 102 divorce contains not only a request for a divorce, it also asks that the court award custody, child support, interim spousal support, exclusive use of the family home and the use of certain other items of property such as a car. Although the waiting period for the divorce is more than 180 days, a hearing on these other matters can be scheduled within several weeks of filing. At the hearing, the court will decide whether custody should be sole, joint, shared, or split; whether one spouse should pay the other support; whether one spouse should have the exclusive right to occupy the family home; and whether a spouse should be prevented from using community assets. If the spouses can agree on these matters, a stipulation can be prepared and submitted to the judge without a court hearing. From experience, we can tell you that the more you can agree on things, the easier (and less expensive) the whole process will be.

Reconciliation

In all divorce actions, there must be no reconciliation between the parties or the cause of action is extinguished. If there is a reconciliation at any time before the judgment of divorce, the parties would have to start over again with a new divorce suit. In other words, a reconciliation can restart a waiting period and it even voids a pending divorce action. It can also void a judgment of support, and other collateral matters. This brings up an interesting question. What acts legally constitute reconciliation?

Ralph and Connie were separated while waiting their 180 day period to finalize their divorce and Ralph moved to an apartment in a nearby city. After a few months of not seeing each other, Connie called Ralph and was invited to visit him in his apartment and spend the weekend. Thereafter, on several occasions, Connie would spend the weekend with Ralph, or he would spend the weekend with her at her apartment. Ralph and Connie always had sexual intercourse when they spent weekends with each other. When Connie sued Ralph for overdue child support, Ralph answered by saying that they had reconciled and that the order for child support was therefore null.

It was once the law in Louisiana that even a single act of intercourse constituted a reconciliation and voided the divorce action. The court in Ralph and Connie's case applied the test of whether there was a clear intent on the part of both parties to reconcile and to resume living together as man and wife. An act of intercourse, or even frequent acts of intercourse, does not necessarily prove that the parties have reconciled. The court therefore found that the order for support was still valid since there was no reconciliation.

In cases where the husband and wife move back in with each other and show an intent to reconcile, the courts have held that the parties have reconciled and that the divorce action together with all orders for support and other ancillary relief are void. The parties do not need to take any legal action to void the petition for divorce since the divorce can only be made final after a hearing or other pleading are filed establishing that no reconciliation has taken place.

Support

Alimony has been defined to be what a woman who loved a man for all he is worth gets. It has also been defined to be the high cost of leaving. Alimony is actually nothing more than an obligation to provide support. Spousal support is now the accepted term rather than alimony when you are talking about support due from one spouse to another and is the term we will be using. Although this section will discuss the support that may be owed by one spouse to another, you first need to be aware that there are other kinds of support obligations.

Children have an obligation to support their parents and grandparents, while parents and grandparents have a duty to support their children and grandchildren. This obligation has nothing to do with the age of either the ascendant or the descendant. A parent has a duty to provide support to a forty year old child under certain circumstances just as a parent owes a duty to support a minor child. This duty to provide support is considered by the law as a reciprocal obligation:

"Children are bound to maintain their father and mother and other ascendants, who are in need, and the relatives in the direct ascending line are likewise bound to maintain their needy descendants, this obligation being reciprocal."

This reciprocal obligation that exists between close family members is limited to life's basic necessities of food, clothing, shelter, and health care, and arises only upon proof of inability to obtain these necessities by other means or from other sources.

There are two main differences between the child support obligation and the obligation to provide support to a family member in the ascending or descending line. The family member must be in necessitous circumstances and the obligation is limited to providing only the basic necessities of food, clothing, shelter, and health care. In addition, the obligation only exists if it is proven that the party seeking support cannot get these necessities from some other source. Several courts have decided that any person who is capable of working cannot claim that they are in necessitous circumstances. In contrast to the ascendant-descendant support obligation, the obligation to provide support to a minor child extends beyond the basics allowed for ascendant and descendant support.

There is also an obligation between spouses to provide support to each other. When the spouses are physically separated from each other after filing for a divorce, or when a demand for final spousal support is pending, this type of support is called interim spousal support (formerly known as "alimony pendente lite"). The award of interim spousal support terminates upon the rendition of the judgment of divorce.

Nonetheless, if a claim for final spousal support is pending at that time, the interim spousal support award terminates thereafter upon rendition of a judgment awarding/denying final spousal support or one hundred eighty days from the rendition of the divorce judgment, which ever occurs first. However, for good cause shown, the obligation to pay interim spousal support may extend beyond one hundred eighty days from the divorce judgment. Interim spousal support is simply spousal support "pending the litigation". It is support that is temporary in nature and automatically ceases when either party obtains a judicial divorce. Permanent spousal support is an obligation to pay support after the marriage is terminated and until a further court ruling raises, lowers, or terminates the obligation.

With both interim periodic spousal support and final spousal support, the court may award the support based on the needs of the claimant spouse and the ability of the other party to pay. Under Civil Code Article 113, regarding interim spousal support, the court may also consider the standard of living of the parties during their marriage. Like the former statutes governing alimony pendente lite, present law concerning interim spousal support is designed to preserve and continue the status quo insofar as maintenance and support are concerned, using facts as of the time litigation began, not future possibilities. The income of the claimant spouse is used primarily to determine whether that spouse has sufficient income to maintain the standard of living prior to the filing of divorce. Yet the income, resources and entire financial condition of the spouse who may owe support is examined. If the spouse from whom support is sought lacks the ability to pay, the claimant spouse is not entitled to an award of interim spousal support.

The trial court has wide discretion in awarding interim periodic spousal support. Since the object is to maintain the style of living, if there is income and resources with which to pay these expenses, the award can be quite high. The statutes do not specifically list relevant factors for the determination of interim periodic spousal support, but they do for final periodic support.

If a spouse is free from fault and seeks final support, how does the court decide how much support to award? Well, first of all, the support cannot exceed one-third of the obligor spouse's net income. Secondly, the court is required to consider:

- The needs of the parties.

- The income and means of the parties, including the liquidity of such means.

- The financial obligations of the parties.

- The earning capacity of the parties.

- The effect of custody of children upon a party's earning capacity.

- The time necessary for the claimant to acquire appropriate education, training, or employment.

- The health and age of the parties.

- The duration of the marriage.

- The tax consequences to either or both parties.

This listing is not intended to continue to maintain the claimant spouse in the style available during the marriage. All relevant factors are to be considered by the court for the setting of final periodic spousal support, not only those specifically listed in the governing statute. Final spousal support can also be established for a fixed duration for rehabilitative purposes which could later be continued if necessary.

A spouse who receives interim spousal support may or may not be entitled to final support. A spouse who requests an award of final support must be found free from fault prior to the time of the action to terminate the marriage. As noted earlier, this is the only way that the issue of fault of a spouse is required to be considered. The issue of fault is not applicable to the setting of interim spousal support, but is necessary for the setting final spousal support. Therefore, the spouse who would be paying interim spousal support may also wish to schedule the fault issue for hearing even before the judgment of divorce. This is often done to be able to forgo the possibility that the other spouse will at some point claim final spousal support.

George was an executive with a small oil exploration company and received a salary of $5,000 each month.

George and his wife Esther had been married twenty years when they separated. Esther got a job as a real estate agent and was averaging $600 per month in commissions. Esther took George to court for interim spousal support and was awarded $1,500 per month for her support. At a later hearing, Esther was found free from fault in the parties' marriage. Esther also received the house, worth $140,000, a new Cadillac, a fur coat, a Rolex watch, a grand piano, and all the household furnishings.

She also asked that the interim spousal support of $1,500 per month be made permanent as final spousal support. Esther proved to the court her monthly expenses, her husband's monthly expenses, and both their net incomes. Based on this information and the fact that she was free from fault in the dissolution of the marriage, the court made the interim support she was currently getting final spousal support.

Because of the oil recession, George's salary was later cut to $3,000 per month and he sued Esther to have the amount of his support reduced. The court reduced the support to $1,000 per month and George appealed because he did not feel that the reduction was enough. He argued that Esther was capable of earning her own living and that she had received assets in the settlement that she could sell for living expenses. George pointed out to the appeals court that he had been forced to sell his own stocks and use up his savings accounts in order to pay Esther's support. Esther argued that she had no job skills since she had spent most of her life raising their children. She also claimed that she should not have to sell assets before she could get support and that the original award should not have been reduced in the first place.

Do you think George's support should have been reduced further? First of all, a valid support judgment cannot be reduced or increased without a showing that there has been a material change in the circumstances of one of the parties. In other words, once support has been set, it cannot be changed simply because one of the parties wants it increased or reduced. There must be a showing that the person who wants a reduction is materially worse off then he was when the support was first set or that the other person is materially better off.

The court noted first of all that there had indeed been a material change that reduced George's net income by a considerable amount. In addition, if the support had been left at $1,500 per month, it would have been more than the maximum one-third of his income that could have been awarded as spousal support. The court next decided what to do about the assets Esther had available to her. The assets of a party should certainly be considered when setting support. However, the court decided that these assets were not liquid and did not want to force Esther to sell everything before she could get support, especially not her house. Since a trial judge has a good deal of discretion in deciding support awards, the appeals court found nothing wrong with the award of $1,000 per month and refused to reduce it further.

An award of periodic support may be modified if there is a material change in the circumstances of either party and shall be terminated if no longer necessary. The remarriage of the obligor spouse is not considered a change of circumstances.

The obligation of spousal support is extinguished upon the remarriage of the claimant spouse (obligee), the death of either party, or judicial determination that the obligee has cohabited with another person of either sex in the manner of married persons.

Spousal support is usually paid on a monthly basis until terminated by court order or remarriage. However, it is possible to have spousal support paid on a lump sum basis if done by authentic act or act under private signature acknowledged by the obligee or by a stipulated judgment. In other words, the spouses can agree that the spouse seeking alimony shall receive cash and/or property in one or several payments as his or her total support. If the spouses agree to a lump sum payment, the court can include the award in a court order. What is the advantage of lump sum spousal support? The award vests a current right to the lump sum, even if the lump sum is payable in installments over a period of years. The spouse who receives lump sum support has an absolute right to receive the payment or payments even in the event of remarriage or death. Also, the order cannot be modified. If the spouses agree to a lump sum payment payable in installments and the spouse making the payments loses his or her job, he or she will still have to pay the support regardless of any change in circumstances. Lump sum spousal support agreements should only be undertaken with the advice of an attorney and a tax advisor since there can be important tax implications for both parties.

At the time a petition for divorce is filed, or after, either spouse can ask for the exclusive use of the family home and certain other items of community property. This award can even be for the use of a family home that the separate property of the other spouse if the requesting spouse has physical custody of the children. The award is a type of spousal support and is taken into consideration when spousal or child support is given. The use and occupancy of the family home is usually only until there is a community property partition. This can mean that the spouse with custody of the children will get the exclusive use of the house or it can mean that the spouse who can afford to make the payments will get the house. The judge will have a good deal of discretion in deciding who gets the use of the house and other items pending a final division between the parties.

The spouse who gets the house is not obligated to the other spouse for rental unless they agree or unless it is ordered by the court at that time. Any claim for reimbursement for rental value of the home or, alternatively for use and occupancy, must be asserted at the time that use and occupancy of the home is granted. However, the parties may agree to defer the rental issue for decision in their partition proceedings and, if agreed by the parties, the record should clearly reflect their agreement.

Either spouse is also entitled to retrieve personal property that is in the possession of the other spouse. Personal property is clothing, eating utensils, and any other property the court considers necessary for the safety and well-being of the spouse or any children in the spouse's custody. The spouse can ask that the court order the sheriff or local police to accompany him or her to retrieve the property from the possession of the other spouse.

Further, either party may file a summary proceeding (rule to show cause) within sixty days of filing, allocating the use of community property even including bank accounts pending the partition of the community. The court shall make its decision as to this allocation considering custody, use of the home, the total community assets, the need for funds to maintain a household pending partition, and the need of the spouse to receive legal services during the divorce. The spouse who receives the allocation is required to provide a complete accounting of those assets.

A spouse can also ask for compensation for any financial contributions made to the other spouse's education. Compensation can be requested as part of the divorce proceeding, or within three years of the divorce judgment. The contributions to education must have increased the spouse's earning power and must have been made during marriage. The compensation can be reduced by the amount the contributing spouse benefited during the marriage from the increased earning power. If the award is for a sum certain payable in installments it does not terminate upon the remarriage or death of either party.

All awards of spousal and Child support are retroactive to the date the petition asking for support was filed. If you file the petition in June, but your case isn't heard until December, don't worry. It may be hard to get along for those months, but if you receive an award, it will take into account the several months you had to wait for your court appearance. In certain circumstances, if the judge considers it necessary, he or she can decide to not make the award retroactive and start the support effective some other date.

What do you do when you finally get an award of spousal or child support but your spouse won't pay? You file a petition asking that your spouse be held in contempt and that the amount of support that is past due be determined by the court. It used to be necessary to have the amount that was past due for child support made executory. Having the support made executory meant that a judgment was entered recognizing the amount that was overdue. This meant that you would have to go back to court every time another payment was behind. Beginning in 1987, each overdue payment of child support is automatically considered executory and a judgment by operation of law. To make this "judgment" a judicial mortgage, you must have the judge determine the amount owed in a summary hearing and you must record the judgment in the mortgage records of the parish where your spouse resides or owns property.

If the spouse still fails to pay, the judge has the option of finding him or her in contempt and in sentencing him or her to jail. Usually, a judge will suspend the sentence if the spouse agrees to pay. Otherwise, the spouse can expect to spend some time in jail.

If you file to get past due support and the judge finds in your favor, you are also entitled to an award of attorney's fees. This award is intended to make it easier for you to bring a suit for past due support. Often, however, the award of attorney's fees will not be enough to cover the actual amount that it may cost you to bring your spouse into court.

Names After Divorce

Many people have questions about the status of their names after a divorce. If a wife wants to go back to her maiden name does she have to petition to have her name changed? What if she wants to go back to a prior married name or to her children's name?

It has always been the law in Louisiana that a woman retains her maiden name even after marriage. She was free to use her married name, her maiden name, or a combination. Therefore, when she divorced, she could go back to using her maiden name if she wished since it was always her right to use her maiden name. If she wished to go back to a prior married name, however, she would have to petition for a formal change of name through a court proceeding. The law was changed in 1987, 2003 and 2004 in order to make things easier after a divorce. The changes also enable married couples to use a combination of their names, even though this could result in some peculiar blends.

The law now specifically states that marriage does not change the name of either spouse. The spouses are free to use the surnames of each other in any combination. If John Jones marries Susan Smith, he can legally call himself John Jones, or John Smith, or John Smith Jones, or John Jones Smith. Susan can also call herself any combination of these names.

Susan may use her maiden name of Smith, her former married name of Jones, any new married name, or any combination. At the time of divorce, the court may enter an order confirming Susan's name, but limited to the name she was using at the time of marriage, the name of any minor children she may have, or she can always use her maiden name without having to obtain a court order.

Being A Parent

We mentioned earlier that filing a suit for divorce was sometimes necessary to establish certain legal rights between the parties and to determine the rights and responsibilities of the parents to the children born of the marriage. While a couple is married, the parental authority over their children is shared by husband and wife equally. Either parent has the right to determine what is best for the children. But what happens when the parents separate? Who decides what is best and makes the day-to-day decisions that are necessary in raising children?

Custody

In the past, it was assumed to be an obvious fact that if the parents were not going to continue their marriage, it would be necessary to give custody of the children to one parent. The other parent had the right to visit the children at scheduled times. It was also assumed to be an obvious fact that the mother, by nature, was the preferred choice to have custody of the children. Taking note of a national trend away from the idea that one parent should have sole custody, and after studying similar legislation in other states, our Legislature beginning in 1979 passed the joint custody law and has added important changes in nearly every legislative session since that time. The theory of joint custody is that both parents should share more equally in the physical custody of the children. Joint custody is the law in Louisiana, but let's take a closer look at what joint custody actually means and how it is implemented by the courts.

In a divorce action or thereafter, the court shall award custody of a child in accordance with the best interest of the child. The "best interest" test is used by the courts for all custody determinations as the overriding test to be applied. The best interest principal has been recognized in Louisiana jurisprudence and legislation for nearly one hundred years. The best interest standard is used for all decisions regarding custody as the paramount consideration, whether for the initial award, modifications to the award of custody, and custodial/visitation privileges of the parents or other individuals in the life of the child.

In Louisiana at the present time, the parents of the child stand on an equal footing. The old "maternal preference" rule is no longer to be considered by the court; however, many judges consider the mother as preferable to serve as the domiciliary parent of an infant or young toddler as being "in the child's best interest". Race is also not an allowable consideration for determining which parent will be the domiciliary parent. If the parties have not reached an agreement that is in the best interest of the child, the court shall award custody to the parents jointly unless custody in one parent is shown by clear and convincing evidence to serve the best interest of the child. In that case, the court would award sole custody to that parent.

The Louisiana Civil Code specifically enumerates the relevant factors to be used in determining the best interest of the child. This non-exclusive list from Civil Code Article 134 includes:

- The love, affection, and other emotional ties between each party and the child.

- The capacity and disposition of each party to give the child love, affection, and spiritual guidance and to continue the education and rearing of the child.

- The capacity and disposition of each party to provide the child with food, clothing, medical care, and other material needs.

- The length of time the child has lived in a stable, adequate environment, and the desirability of maintaining continuity of that environment.

- The permanence, as a family unit, of the existing or proposed custodial home or homes.

- The moral fitness of each party, insofar as it affects the welfare of the child.

- The mental and physical health of each party.

- The home, school, and community history of the child.

- The reasonable preference of the child, if the court deems the child to be of sufficient age to express a preference.

- The willingness and ability of each party to facilitate and encourage a close and continuing relationship between the child and the other party.

- The distance between the respective residences of the parties.

- The responsibility for the care and rearing of the child previously exercised by each party.

The fact that this is an illustrative listing of factors provides the courts the opportunity to consider additional factors. In custody cases, the court must weigh and balance all factors related to the best interest of the child in view of the evidence presented, and is not bound to give more weight to one factor than another. The decision of how much weight to be given each factor is left to the discretion of the trial judge. Every child custody case must be decided based only on its particular facts and circumstances and the judge must consider all relevant evidence.

At the present time, the more common custody awards include:

- Joint custody to the parents, usually with one parent being designated as the domiciliary parent and custodial rights for frequent and continuing contact with the child granted to the non-domiciliary parent.

- Sole custody to one of the parents if custody to that one parent is shown by clear and convincing evidence to serve the best interest of the child.

- "Shared custody" to the parents which is a joint custody plan where each parent has physical custody of the child for an approximately equal amount of time and no domiciliary parent is named.

- "Split custody" in which sole custody or domiciliary status is granted to one parent of at least one child to whom support is due with visitation rights to the non-custodial parent .

- Custody to another person with whom the child has been living, or could provide a wholesome and stable environment, other than the parents of the child if an award of joint custody or sole custody to either parent would result in substantial harm to the child

The type of custody award for the child has profound implications regarding the physical custody and domicile of the child, the time spent with the child by each parent, and the financial responsibilities and rights concerning the child, including the child support payable by each parent for the child and possible tax benefits. Let's look at each of these types of child custody.

Joint Custody. If the parents have agreed on custody of their child, as long as it is in the best interest of the child, the court shall award custody accordingly. However, in the absence of an agreement, the court shall award custody to the parents jointly. If the award is of joint custody, a plan must be devised setting forth the details of how the joint custody is going to be implemented. The parents, either jointly or individually, can submit a plan, or the court can order the parents to submit a plan. At a minimum, the plan must include the time periods that each parent has physical custody of the children and the legal authority, privileges and responsibilities of the parents. The plan can also include a designation of the child's legal domicile, how the parents will communicate with the children and each other, the amount of child support, and any other matter the parents deem important. It is important for joint custody that the parents are willing and able to facilitate and encourage a close and continuing parent-child relationship with the other parent.

An award of joint custody, incidentally, does not relieve the obligation of paying child support. Support will still be awarded based on the needs of the children and the resources of the parents.

Devising a plan for joint custody of the child can be an extremely difficult task for the parents. If the parents could always agree on a plan, things would be much easier. But as a practical matter, if the parents were not able to get along with each other and separated because of marital problems, there is usually little chance that they can easily agree on a plan for custody. If they cannot agree, each side must submit a plan and the judge must decide which plan best serves the needs of the child. Or, the judge may order a plan of his or her own. A plan, once implemented, can be modified at any time by petitioning the court, or the court can modify a plan on its own motion.

If the earlier court decree regarding custody was a "considered decree" in which evidence was given and received by the trial court as to parental fitness, the petitioning party bears a difficult burden of proof. This burden requires proving that the continuation of the present custody situation is so deleterious to the child that it justifies a modification of the current custody arrangement, or of proving by clear and convincing evidence that any harm likely to be caused by the change of environment of the child is substantially outweighed by the advantages to the child.

If the earlier court decree was not a "considered decree" the burden of proof is less stringent. This usually happens when the parties have stipulated to an agreement without the court hearing evidence and rendering a decision. A party who seeks a change in a custody judgment is required to prove 1) that a material change in circumstances has occurred which affects the child, and 2) that the new custody arrangement would be in the best interest of the child.

Note that the best interest standard is paramount with all decisions related to the welfare of the child and certainly those regarding the custody of the child.

In a proceeding in which joint custody is decreed, except for good cause, the court shall render an implementation order which shall allocate the time periods during which each parent shall have physical custody of the child so that the child is assured of frequent and continuing contact with both parents. To the extent it is feasible and in the best interest of the child, physical custody of the child shall be shared equally.

A domiciliary parent is usually named when the parents are awarded joint custody under a joint custody decree as being the parent with whom the child shall primarily reside. The other parent shall have physical custody during time periods that assure the child with frequent and continuing contact with both parents. The domiciliary parent shall have the authority to make all decisions affecting the child unless an implementation order provides otherwise. All major decisions made by the domiciliary parent shall be subject to review by the court upon motion by the other parent, but it shall be presumed that all major decisions so made are in the best interest of the child. If the parents agree who is to have custody, the court shall award custody as they request unless the best interest of the child requires a different award.

The problem with trying to implement joint custody that would truly be joint is the problem of feasibility. Also, an equal sharing of the child's time might not be in the child's best interest. Joint custody does not necessarily mean that the child spends six months with one parent and six month with the other. A judge will probably not approve a plan that takes the child out of one household after six months and back again in another six months.

There is also the problem of school. If the parents live in different school districts, it would be too disruptive to change schools every six months, or even every year if the parents are considering having physical custody during alternate years. Therefore, a joint custody plan will often award physical custody to one parent, the "custodial parent," for the school year. The non-custodial parent might then be entitled to share weekends and holidays with the child and have physical custody for most of the summer.

Although there are many practical limitations in the joint custody law, especially in trying to apportion the child's time fairly between two parents, other parts of the law have cured certain aspects of the old custody laws that were basically unfair or not addressed at all. For example, under the old law the parent who was not awarded custody was often left out in the cold when it came time to make basic decisions vital to the child's welfare. In many cases in the past, schools and doctors would not even release information about the child to a parent unless that parent had custody. Current custody laws specifically forbids this and states that all information concerning the child, including medical, dental and school records, shall not be denied to a parent because he or she is not the custodial parent. The present custody law also requires that the parents share any information concerning the health, education, and welfare of the child with each other. The court can also require that any differences between the parties be mediated.

The concept of mediation which can be ordered by the court in any custody/visitation matter or can be agreed to by the parties to settle disputes between them is a valuable idea. The adversary proceeding which is a necessary result of court action, often has the undesirable effect of increasing the acrimony between the parents. The mediator who is agreed upon by the parties, or selected by the court if they fail to agree, is to assist the parties in formulating a completed agreement to mediate which shall identify the controversies between the parties, affirm their intent to resolve the controversies through mediation and specify when the mediation may terminate. The parties may have any such agreement reviewed by their attorneys prior to signing.

If agreement is reached, a consent judgment incorporating the agreement shall be submitted to the court for its approval. The recommendation of the mediator is non-binding and a judgment of the court is still required. However, the services of the impartial mediator can be extremely useful in obtaining an agreement by the parties on custody/visitation issues.

Since a contested custody case can easily take one or more full days of a court's time, mediation will probably become routinely ordered in many cases in order to save the time and expense involved in a lengthy trial. Court ordered mediation is becoming a trend in many other types of litigation as well which is line with a national trend for alternative dispute resolution.

Bob and Rhonda were divorced and both wanted to be named domiciliary parent of their three children. They finally stipulated that they would have joint custody, but could not agree on a plan to implement the joint custody. Judge Wyse ordered that Bob and Rhonda seek counseling from a licensed counselor and mediate their differences. They could still not agree on a plan, and each submitted his own plan to Judge Wyse for his decision. Rhonda's plan provided that the children spend six months with her and six months with their father. Bob's plan provided that they spend the school year with him and the summers with their mother. At the trial, the counselor testified that Rhonda had not shown a willingness to negotiate an agreement as Bob had. There was also testimony from a neighbor that Rhonda had once threatened to take the children to another state so that Bob would never see them again. Judge Wyse ordered that Bob's plan be implemented and further ordered that Rhonda post a $5,000 bond to insure that she complied with the joint custody order. Rhonda appealed Judge Wyse's decision to a higher court.

The court of appeal decided that Judge Wyse was within the guidelines of the statute, especially since he apparently felt that Rhonda was not showing a willingness to encourage the children to maintain a close relationship with their father. The Court of Appeal did decide, however, that Judge Wyse had no authority to require that Rhonda post a bond to insure that she complied with the order. Perhaps in response to this decision, the Legislature approved a bill which now gives the court the right to require that a party post a bond to insure compliance with a child visitation order.

Sole Custody. Civil Code Article 132 provides that if custody in one parent is shown by clear and convincing evidence to serve the best interest of the child, the court shall award custody to that parent. As there is a presumption in favor of joint custody in that same statute, an award of sole custody to one parent is relatively rare. The fact that the child was born out of wedlock alone was not sufficient to show that sole custody to the mother was warranted as being in the child's best interest. Neither was homosexuality of a parent not residing with his or her partner a sufficient reason to deprive that parent of joint custody and to grant sole custody to the other parent. Clear and convincing evidence must be provided to the court that the award of sole custody to one of the parents would be in the child's best interest, which is a difficult burden.

Interference with custody. Until fairly recently, there was no specific statute that would punish the parent without custody from taking the child away from the parent with custody. There is now a criminal statute entitled "Interference with the Custody of a Child" which is an addition to the kidnapping laws and carries a maximum punishment of six months in jail and/or a fine of $500. Interference with the custody of a child is defined to be "the intentional taking, enticing, or decoying away of a minor child by a parent not having a right of custody, with the intent to detain or conceal such child from a parent having a right of custody pursuant to court order or from a person entrusted with the care of the child by a parent having custody pursuant to a court order." The parent who does not have custody and takes the child may be able to offer a successful defense if it can be proven that he or she had reason to believe that the taking was in the best interest of the child.

Shared Custody. "Shared custody" means a joint custody order in which each parent has physical custody of the child for an approximately equal amount of time. In cases where the parties have agreed to shared custody, there may be no domiciliary parent named in the court order regarding custody. A designation of domiciliary parent is considered unnecessary where both parents have equal rights and obligations. Thus, when the parents have agreed on a shared custody arrangement that the court finds is in the best interest of the child, the decree need not designate a domiciliary parent.

As noted earlier regarding joint custody, to the extent it is feasible and in the best interest of the child, physical custody of the child shall be shared equally. It should be noted that only if both of the prior conditions are met should the court consider awarding equal physical time, but equal sharing is not mandatory. In *Stephens v. Stephens*, a case decided in 2002, the appellate court reversed the findings of the trial court which awarded both parents alternating weeks of physical custody stating that equal physical custody was not required and should only be ordered if 50/50 shared physical custody is both feasible and in the best interest of the child. If both tests are not met, then the court shall order a custody arrangement that proportions time spent by the child with each parent to ensure frequent and continuing contact. In *Stephens*, the appellate court felt that mere feasibility was not sufficient as the best interest of the child had not been adequately proven.

With shared custody arrangements, each parent would owe a proportionate share of a child support obligation to the other parent for the time the child spends with the other party. The parent owing the greater amount of child support would owe the other parent the difference between the two amounts as a child support obligation. Worksheet B is the form to be used by each parent to determine child support for use in the shared custodial arrangement.

Split Custody. "Split custody" is a split arrangement between parents in which each party is the sole custodial parent of at least one child of the parties to whom support is due. With split custodial arrangements, there would still be custodial/visitation arrangements for the non-custodial parent. Under a split custody arrangement, to ensure that the minor child maintains contact with his/her siblings who live with the other parent, the custodial/visitation arrangements should be drafted to allow for the continuing sibling relationships.

With split custody arrangements, each parent would owe a theoretical child support obligation to the other parent for the child or children in the custody of that other parent. The parent owing the greater amount of child support would owe the other parent the difference between the two amounts as a child support obligation. Worksheet A is the form to be used by each parent to determine child support for use in the split custodial arrangement.

The actual formula for the calculation of child support if the custody of the child is under a split custody arrangement, requires that each parent having custody or domiciliary status of at least one child of the parties shall calculate the total child support obligation owed to the other parent. The information from the parents worksheets would be compared and the parent owing the greater amount as reflected in the two worksheets owes the difference to the other parent as a child support obligation. This calculation reflects the child support obligations for the parents due to the split custody of their children.

Custody to Non-parent. Parental right to custody of the minor children has always been afforded primacy under Louisiana law. However, Louisiana law provides that if an award of joint custody or sole custody to either parent would result in substantial harm to the child, the court shall award custody to another person with whom the child has been living in a wholesome and stable environment, or any other person able to provide an adequate and stable environment.

The award of custody to a non-parent seeking custody places the burden of proof upon the non-parent to show that granting custody to a parent would result in substantial harm to the child, thus necessitating the award of custody to a non-parent.

Often it is the grandparent who is seeking custody. Even though the financial abilities of the non-parent to care for the child may be much greater than those of the parent, that reason standing alone is insufficient to deprive the natural parent of the right to have custody and other more substantial proof of neglect or abuse is usually required.

Visitation

Reasonable visitation rights to a child shall be granted to a parent not awarded custody or joint custody unless after a contradictory hearing the court determines that visitation would not be in the best interest of the child. In extraordinary circumstances, relatives by blood or affinity or former step-parent or step-grandparent not granted custody may be awarded reasonable visitation rights if it is in the best interest of the child. Factors are established for the court's consideration in setting such visitation. Additionally, certain visitation rights may possibly be obtained by a grandparent or sibling of a child in cases of death, interdiction, incarceration, or separation of the parents if the court finds that such visitation rights would be in the best interest of the child.

The United States Supreme Court case of *Troxel v. Granville* has raised some doubts as to whether a non-parent ever has the "right" of visitation over the objection of a parent. In the *Troxel* case, a grandparent was denied visitation with a grandchild even though the child's father (the son of the grandparent) had died and even though the grandparent had helped raise the grandchild. Louisiana law specifically allows a grandparent the right to at least seek a court determination as to whether visitation is in the child's best interest where the child's parent is deceased. We discuss the issue of grandparent visitation in much more detail at La-Legal.com.

Relocation

What happens when a parent with custody wants to move with the child? What if there is no custody order yet? It is clear that either party may move his or her own residence without approval by the court. However, the parent may not usually move the residence of the minor child without legal action. Louisiana law contains various provisions regarding the proposed relocation by one parent of the legal residence of a child. This proposed relocation may be from a location in Louisiana to another location in Louisiana more than one hundred fifty miles away from the other parent or from the domicile of the primary custodian at the time the custody decree was rendered. This proposed relocation may also be outside the state of Louisiana entirely. The procedures involved in a proposed relocation vary depending on many factors including the type of custodial arrangement regarding the child and the express provisions of any court order concerning the custody and principal residence of the child.

The relocation statutes were designed to give advance notice, usually sixty days, to the remaining parent when the moving parent desires to relocate the principal residence of the minor child. The notice must provide certain factual information about the proposed relocation. The required information to be provided by the relocating parent shall include the intended new residence, address, phone number, and date of the proposed relocation. It shall also include a statement of the specific reasons for the proposed relocation, a proposal for a revised schedule of visitation, and that an objection to the proposed relocation shall be filed within thirty days of receipt of the notice of the relocation.

The parent who wishes to relocate the minor child has the burden of proof that the proposed relocation is made in good faith and is in the best interest of the child. The best interest of the child is still the primary consideration to be used by the court when it considers a proposed relocation. In determining the child's best interest, the court shall consider the benefits which the child will derive either directly or indirectly from an enhancement in the relocating parent's quality of life. In reaching its decision in regarding the proposed relocation, the court is provided a list of factors to be considered most of which are similar to the factors considered in the granting of joint custody, but with other factors considered that are more specific as to possible changes caused by relocation. If relocation is permitted after a contradictory hearing, the court may require that security be put up by the relocating parent to ensure uninterrupted visitation with the other parent and the court may retain jurisdiction as long as the non-relocating parent remains in Louisiana.

Child Support

Both parents owe support to their children. Regardless of the custodial arrangement which governs the parents' rights to custody of the minor child, the court can order support based on the resources of both parents and the needs of the child. The amount of support awarded in a particular case used to vary greatly from one judge to another and from one area to another. Because child support was so inconsistent, and under pressure from the federal government to remedy the situation, legislation was passed to establish child support guidelines.

To understand how this works, let's say that there are three children, that the mother makes $1,000 per month, and the father makes $2,500 per month. The combined gross income is $3,500.00 and is the starting point for calculating child support.

Sample Child Support Guidelines

Joint Adjusted Monthly Income	One Child	Two Children (total)	Three Children (total)	Four Children (total)
$0-600	100	100	100	100
$650	102	103	104	106
$700	136	138	139	141
...				
$3,450	614	909	1066	1169
$3,500	622	919	**1079**	1185
$3,550	629	930	1092	1200
...				
$29,950	2649	3737	4296	4798
$30,000	2653	3742	4302	4805

To find the basic support obligation, our hypothetical couple finds the column with the number of children and the row closest to their combined income. Where the row and column intersect is the basic child support obligation.

Our table is just a sample of what the guidelines look like. The actual guidelines cover up to six children and extend over many pages of small print. They extend from $600 of joint income up to $30,000 of joint income in $50 increments. These guidelines establish an amount of support that is due from the parents based on their income and the number of children in need of support. It is now a relatively simple matter to calculate the child support obligation of the parents by finding the point on the table where gross income intersects the number of children.

Just the starting point. Finding the basic child support obligation, however, is just the first step for calculating the support actually owed. The next step is to figure the non-custodial spouse's percentage of the total obligation. To continue our example, let's also say that the mother was made custodial parent. The father makes more money and therefore owes a larger percentage of the combined income in child support. Since he makes $2,500 per month, his obligation is for about 72% of the total child support obligation. The mother, since she is the custodial parent and bears the daily expenses of the child, is not responsible for any support. In other words, the father will owe the mother $777 per month ($1,079 x 72%) in child support.

There are many other factors that can vary the amount of support due. For example, the court can consider any income the child receives, special medical needs, medical insurance paid by the non-custodial parent, child care expenses, special education expenses, and transportation expenses from one parent to the other. A recent change in the law requires that the Legislature review the table amounts at least every four years, starting with 2012.

Certain of these other expenses shall be added to the basic child support obligation shown on the guidelines as additional expenses including the net child care costs and health insurance premiums. Other expenses incurred on behalf of a child which are considered as extraordinary expenses may also be added to the basic child support obligation shown on the child support guidelines. These extraordinary expenses would be added by agreement of the parties or order of the court and include the expenses for attendance at a special or private elementary or secondary school to meet the needs of the child and any expenses for transportation of the child from one party to the other.

The court can also decide whether one parent is voluntarily unemployed or under employed. In other words, a parent can't avoid child support by not working or by working at a low paying job.

When Jerry and Helen were divorced, Helen was made custodial parent of their son and Jerry was ordered to pay $600 per month in child support. The next year, Jerry asked the court to reduce his child support since he was making less money then in prior years. Jerry was a stock broker and his income depended completely on the amount of work he did. At the trial, he proved that his income for the current year was less than his income for the year that support was first set.

The court refused to reduce the support. It was proven that Jerry's income was lower because Jerry worked fewer hours. The court decided since Jerry's income was dependent on how much Jerry wanted to work, support would not be reduced simply because he chose not to work as much as he had in the past.

In situations where someone quits a job to avoid support, the court will set support based on what the former job was paying. Support will be ordered even if there is no present income to enable payment.

The court can also consider other sources of income and can consider the benefit a parent receives from expense sharing. For example, a re-married parent who benefits from the income of the new spouse can have the value of that benefit added to gross income. The new spouse's income can be considered only to the extent it directly reduces the expenses of the parent who owes child support.

The child support guidelines have taken most of the guess work out of calculating child support. The judges are required to use the guidelines unless following the tables would "not be in the best interest of the child or would be inequitable to the parties." If the judge does not follow the table, he or she must state specific reasons for the deviation. Use of the information in the child support guidelines, as adjusted by additional or extraordinary expenses, will determine the amount of child support that will be owed by the non-custodial parent.

We had a case where the father had been laid off from his job as a salesman and was receiving about $700 per month in unemployment compensation. He asked the court to set support at the amount indicated by the tables: about $138 per month. Our client, the mother, was a nursing student and could not possibly raise two children with that kind of help. At trial, the father admitted that he had not put much effort into finding a job because his new wife had inherited some money. It was also shown that he had a considerable amount of savings in the bank. The judge set his support obligation at $600 per month. This was an example of having to deviate from the tables in order to meet the best interest of the children.

Child support past majority. The obligation to provide child support can extend past the age of majority as long as the child is a full time student in a secondary school, has not reached the age of nineteen, and is dependent on either parent. Once support has been ordered, it extends automatically while the child is in school. If the parent who owes support stops paying, either the major child or the primary domiciliary parent may sue to enforce this continued support. Many people make the mistake of thinking this extra year of support obligation applies to college. It only applies to dependent children who are under the age of 19 but still attending secondary school.

As a form of support, either party can petition the court for an award of the exclusive use of the family home. The court must consider the relative economic status of the spouses, including community and separate property, and the needs of the children, if any. The court must award the family home in accordance with the best interest of the family. See the section on spousal support for more details on this topic.

The above information as to the establishment of child support obligations of the parents and use of the child support guidelines applies to all child custody arrangements. However, the specific child custody arrangement can vary the child support obligation owed by each parent to the other. For example, the amount of child support owed by a non-domiciliary parent under a joint custody plan can be adjusted if that parent has physical custody of the child for more than seventy-three days in the year.

There are also modifications if the child resides with each parent for approximately one-half the year or if the child custody is pursuant to a split custody arrangement. These types of custody arrangements are discussed earlier.

Rights and Duties

Someone once said that children are a great comfort for your old age, but that they help you reach it faster. Being a parent involves hard work and many responsibilities. What many people do not realize is that there are many legal obligations imposed on parents. Some of these obligations can bring about liabilities that were never contemplated by the parents.

Leroy was seventeen years old and did not have an ideal childhood. He seemed to always be getting in trouble and had the well deserved nickname "Bad" Leroy. Bad Leroy's parents, Ray and Adele, couldn't seem to keep their son under control. Ray and Adele were divorced when Bad Leroy was fifteen, and Adele was awarded custody of her son by the court.

Adele found that trying to raise Bad Leroy by herself was no easy task. He dropped out of school and refused to work, yet he always seemed to have plenty of spending money. After nearly a year, Bad Leroy decided to move out. In rapid succession he lived with his sister, his father, and a friend named Buster. Finally, he found a room of his own for $50 a week in a boarding house.

It was while living in the boarding house that Bad Leroy met Terry who was also seventeen. Twenty minutes later, Terry was in the hospital with a broken jaw and a skull fracture. Terry and his father sued Bad Leroy, Ray, Adele, and State Farm Insurance Company which had a liability policy on Ray's house. State Farm was included in the suit because a homeowner's policy can cover acts of negligence of family members even if they occur someplace other than the home. Terry's father claimed that Bad Leroy's unprovoked attack had caused his son to suffer permanent injuries and asked the court to award over $300,000 for medical expenses, disability, pain and suffering. It was now

*up to the court to decide who would be responsible for Bad
Leroy's actions.*

If you were the judge, how would you arrive at a fair
decision as to who has to bear the burden for Bad Leroy's
actions? You would first have to look at the law to see what
provisions, if any, have been made for this type of situation.
The attorneys for Terry's father direct your attention to the
applicable article in the Civil Code: "The father, or after his
decease, the mother, are responsible for the damage
occasioned by their minor or unemancipated children, residing
with them, or placed by them under the care of other
persons,..."

It is clearly the law that parents are responsible for the
negligent or deliberate acts of their children. Ray's attorney
points out the fact that Adele had legal custody of Bad Leroy.
Adele's attorney reminds you that Bad Leroy was living in a
boarding house at the time Terry was injured and had not lived
with his mother in nearly a year. State Farm's attorney directs
your attention to the fine print in its policy which states that
it is not responsible for any deliberate or criminal acts
committed by the insured or his family. The various attorneys
step back from the bench and the courtroom is quiet while
you decide what to do.

If you decided in favor of Bad Leroy's parents, you would
be in agreement with the trial court that heard this 1981 case.
However, Terry's father decided to appeal the trial court's
decision and the higher court had a different opinion. The
Court of Appeal ruled that Ray's liability for the acts of his
son were suspended by the divorce decree that awarded
custody to Adele and therefore dismissed Ray from the
lawsuit. State Farm's policy did exclude deliberate acts from
its policy. In any event, reasoned the Court, it would be against
public policy to allow people to deliberately harm others with
the knowledge that any damages would be taken care of by

an insurance company. State Farm was dismissed from the suit, and that left Adele as the only defendant.

Adele argued that she should be dismissed as well, since the statute clearly states that the child must reside with the parent and Bad Leroy had moved out. The Court interpreted "residence" not to mean the place where someone resides, which is the common meaning, but to mean legal residence which is another thing entirely. Bad Leroy's legal residence was found to be that of Adele's. The case was sent back to the trial court for a determination of how much Adele would have to pay Terry and his father.

This case points out two things: a parent is legally responsible for the damages his child causes and the courts do not necessarily render decisions that seem fair. There have been other decisions in the Louisiana courts which did not extend parental responsibility this far. However, you should never assume that your responsibilities for your minor children end just because they move out of the house.

Parents, while they are married, have a usufruct over property that belongs to their minor children. This simply means that parents have the right to use their children's property. This right cannot be transferred to others and it cannot be seized by creditors of the parents. The right ends when the children reach eighteen or are emancipated. When the usufruct ends, the parents have the obligation to restore the property, or property of equal value, to the children.

The parental right to a usufruct over the minor children's property carries with it an obligation to support, maintain and educate the children according to their situation in life. You cannot use your children's money strictly as you see fit. There is a duty to make use of enough of the property to see that they are maintained according to the standards to which they are accustomed.

The parental usufruct does not apply to all property belonging to the minor children. Property earned by the children and property given to the children by donation are exceptions. However, a written act of donation can provide for a usufruct in favor of the parents if the donor wishes. Property inherited by the children is treated conversely. If the parents are not supposed to have a usufruct, there must be an express provision in the instrument stating that there is no usufruct. In other words, If you want to leave your property to a grandchild but not have it subject to the parental usufruct, you must make that a clear provision in your will.

The parental usufruct continues in favor of the parents while they are married and until the child reaches eighteen, marries, or is emancipated. If the parents are divorced, what happens to the usufruct over the minor children's property? The law specifies that the parent who obtains the divorce keeps the usufruct. This has the effect of giving control of the minor's property to the parent who gets the divorce regardless of which parent is awarded custody.

Adoption

The act of adopting someone has more of an impact in Louisiana than in other states. This is because of our unique forced heirship laws which require that a portion of your estate be inherited by your children who are forced heirs (see the section on estate planning). The person whom you adopt not only may become your forced heir, he may also remain the forced heir of the natural parents. In other words, the adopted child may inherit from two sets of parents. This causes a conflict between the statutes that require secrecy as to the identity of the natural parents, and the forced heirship statutes which require that a portion of the natural parent's estate be given to the adopted child.

At the time a child is given up for adoption, the record of the proceeding and the birth certificate are sealed and cannot be re-opened except by court order and only for compelling reasons. The main purpose of sealing the record is to protect the privacy of the persons giving the child up for adoption. What compelling reasons are there for invading this privacy? Adopted children have sued to open their adoption records based on the desire to know their family background, to find out if they have any inheritance rights, to find out if their natural parents need their help, and to get medical information.

The various lower courts in the state were divided as to the circumstances under which a person could have access to the adoption proceedings. In 1979 the Louisiana Supreme Court decided the issue in favor of privacy, although at least one of the judges would have allowed any adopted person access because "The compelling need of the child to know his own parents will always outweigh the interests of the blood parents in hiding their parentage from the child." It was decided that in cases where an adopted person petitioned for information from a sealed record, the court would appoint an attorney to review the adoption record to see if there are any inheritance rights or medical information. Since an adopted child owes no duty of support to a blood parent, it was decided that an inquiry to see if the blood parents were in need of help was not compelling. The privacy rights of the blood parents are therefore protected while at the same time it can be determined whether the adopted child has any inheritance rights from the blood parents.

There are basically two types of adoptions: adoptions of children and adoptions of those who are seventeen years or older. Anyone eighteen or older can adopt anyone seventeen or older without going to court. All it takes is a written declaration before a notary public signed by the adoptive party or parties and the person to be adopted. If the person to be adopted is still a minor who has not reached eighteen or been emancipated, the parents of the person to be adopted need to sign the notarial act. The name of the adopted person can be changed in the notarial act if the parties wish and the act must be filed in the parish where it is executed.

The adoption of someone seventeen or older by someone eighteen or over can lead to problems. What if someone who is twenty adopts someone who is ninety? Doesn't this make the twenty year old "parent" an heir if the ninety year old has no children? The 1988 Legislature amended the procedure for adopting someone who is seventeen years or older if the person being adopted is older than the person who is adopting. This change applies only to adoptions on or after January 1, 1989. If the person being adopted is older, the adoption must be by petition to the court. The court must decide whether the adoption is in the best interest of the person to be adopted and can even require that an investigation be made into the motives for the adoption. An adoption by notarial act, therefore, can only be done by someone eighteen or older of someone seventeen or older when the person or persons adopting are older than the person being adopted. This requirement does not apply if the older person to be adopted has been interdicted, that is, legally declared incompetent.

Adoptions of children under the age of seventeen are, of course, more common and require a petition to the court and a judgment. A single person or a married couple can adopt, but spouses must both join in the petition.

Adoptions of children are controlled by the Children's Code which became law in 1992. The Children's Code controls all juvenile court proceedings, voluntary and involuntary surrender of parental rights, delinquency, mental health, and state services to children and families. If a child is involved, the Code will control everything from traffic violations to the adoption process.

The adoption of children under seventeen years can be done as a private adoption, an agency adoption, or an intrafamily adoption. The procedures for each type of adoption will vary. If you are considering adoption, you need to know which type of adoption will work best for you.

Private Adoption. Before a child can be placed in the home of prospective parents who are seeking a private adoption, they must obtain a certification for adoption. This is a major change in the law and is to insure the safety of the child. The certification makes the prospective parents eligible to have a child placed with them in the future.

Certification for adoption is obtained by consenting first to a pre-placement home study. The exact rules for conducting the home study are formulated by the Department of Social Services. The study can be conducted by a licensed agency, board certified social worker, licensed counselor, psychologist, or psychiatrist. A criminal background check is made for federal and state arrests, convictions, and validated complaints of child abuse or neglect.

If the pre-placement study is favorable, the person who conducted the study issues a certification for adoption to the prospective parents. The certification is valid for two years and allows the placement of the child in the prospective parents' home pending the adoption process.

Instead of obtaining a certification for adoption, the prospective parents can go through the courts to get approval for placing a child in their home. The judge has a confidential hearing in chambers within 48 hours of filing the petition. At the hearing, the judge must inquire about the moral fitness and criminal records of the prospective parents, their mental and physical health, their financial capabilities, their home, and the names and ages of other family members and their attitude about the proposed adoption.

After the hearing, the court must approve or disapprove placement of the child. If placement is approved, the child can live with the prospective parents pending the adoption process. Why would someone elect to use a court hearing rather than a pre-placement home study? Because it would normally be faster and probably less expensive.

Private adoption is made by petition to the court. The petition must state the age, occupation, and marital status of each petitioner; the name by which the child is known as well as the name of the child on the birth certificate; the place and date of birth of the child; the name of every parent whose consent to the adoption is required, or the reason their consent is not required; the date and circumstances under which the child entered the petitioners' home; whether there is any relationship between petitioners and the child; and, there must be a certified copy of any order terminating the natural parents rights to the child. The petitioners must also submit an affidavit giving an accounting of any fees or charges paid by them in connection with the adoption.

A copy of the petition must be served on the Department of Social Services and on any natural parent whose rights have not been terminated by a previous court order. The Department has the obligation of contacting any parent whose consent is required to determine their attitude about the adoption. The Department is also required to investigate the petitioners' home, condition of the child, and any other factors regarding the suitability of the adoption.

A hearing on the adoption is supposed to be set within thirty to sixty days after completion of the service. At the hearing, the court must consider the confidential report of the

Department, the testimony of the parties, and the wishes of the child if twelve years of age or older. If the court considers the adoption in the best interest of the child, the court grants an interlocutory decree of adoption. An interlocutory decree is temporary pending the final adoption hearing. The court can make the decree final at the first hearing if all rights of the natural parents were terminated by a prior judgment, or if a parent is adopting his child born out of wedlock, or if a married couple is adopting the child born out of wedlock to one of the petitioners.

Once the child has lived with the petitioners for at least one year, and six months have gone by since the interlocutory decree, the adoptive parents can apply for a final decree of adoption. During the period of time between the interlocutory and final decrees, the Department of Social Services is supposed to make at least two visits to the home and is required to prepare a second confidential report. The interlocutory decree can be revoked at any time if a judge feels that a revocation is in the child's best interest.

Once a final decree is rendered, the child is considered for all legal purposes as though naturally born to the adoptive parents. The final decree can change the last name of the child to that of the adoptive parents.

Agency Adoption. The court procedure for obtaining an agency adoption is basically the same as for a private adoption. The Department of Social Services must make an investigation, there is a hearing, an interlocutory decree, and a final decree. The agency adoption, however, has one major advantage over the private adoption: a final decree can be obtained in a shorter time.

In an agency adoption, there is no pre-placement home study and no certification for adoption. An agency can place a child directly in the home after conducting its own investigation. Once the child is placed, a final decree can be granted at the first hearing if the child has lived in the home for at least six months and was placed in the home by the agency. In other words, the adoption can be finalized after six months of living with the adoptive parents rather than after one year. If the adoptive parents are not entitled to a final decree at the first hearing, then they must get an interlocutory decree. To get a final decree, the child must have resided with them for at least one year and six months must have elapsed since the interlocutory decree. In either an agency or private adoption, the petition for a final decree must be filed within two years of the granting of an interlocutory decree. If the petition is not filed within two years, the interlocutory decree may become void.

Intrafamily Adoption. The adoption of a family member requires the same basic court procedures as a private adoption, with some differences. Intrafamily adoption covers two situations: a stepparent married to the parent of a legitimate child, or a single or married grandparents of a legitimate child when the child has lived in the grandparent's home for at least six months prior to applying for the adoption. The consent of a parent may not be required if a grandparent has been granted custody and the parent has refused to comply with a court order for support of one year, or if the parent has refused or failed to visit or communicate with the child for at least two years.

A stepparent can adopt in an intrafamily proceeding if the spouse is the parent of the child and has been granted sole or joint custody and: 1) the non custodial parent lives out of state and has not provided any support for at least one year after the custody award; or 2) the non custodial parent has failed to provide court ordered support for at least one year; or 3) the non custodial parent has failed or refused to visit or communicate with the child for at least two years.

Intrafamily adoptions do not require an investigation by the Department of Social Services, although the court can order an investigation. The Department is required to contact the natural parent to discover his or her feeling about the proposed adoption. A hearing is set after service on the natural parent and a final decree can be made without further delay, if the court finds the adoption to be in the child's best interest.

Rights of the Natural Parent. Before any adoption, there has to be either a termination of parental rights, or a surrender of parental rights. The parental rights of the natural parent or parents is terminated when the State of Louisiana takes legal steps to end a person's privilege to be a parent. This can happen is cases of neglect or abuse. When the state terminates the rights of a natural parent, the child is often placed in a foster home or agency. When the rights of a parent end because of a surrender, it is a voluntary procedure and the child may be place directly with the prospective parents. This happens most frequently when a young woman is pregnant and does not plan to keep the baby. Remember, the child can not be placed directly with the adoptive parents without a certification for adoption or court order.

The procedure for surrendering a child voluntarily is spelled out in detail in the Children's Code and must be followed carefully. If a mistake is made in the surrender process, the natural mother or father may have the right to take the child back during the adoption process. A great deal of care is taken to locate the natural father, even if he is not listed on the birth certificate. If he is located, he may have a right to take the child if he agrees to admit paternity. Before accepting a baby through a private or agency adoption, make very sure that the surrender was done properly.

Where do prospective parents find children available for adoption? The old idea of going to an orphanage and picking out a likely child is more common in old movies than in

Louisiana today. Most children are voluntarily surrendered for adoption or the state declares a child abandoned and, therefore, available for adoption.

There are many more prospective parents who wish to adopt than there are babies available for adoption. Adoptions through an agency will involve being placed on a waiting list and being subject to certain restrictions, such as the age of the adoptive parents. A private adoption may not have these restrictions, but will probably take longer.

In many cases, a couple who wish to adopt may not have any alternative other than through a private surrender. We have done several adoptions this way for people who have given up waiting for an agency adoption or may be not be eligible through an agency. The difficult part is in finding someone who plans to give up their child. This will frequently be a young, unmarried girl who does not want an abortion, yet realizes that she is too young or financially unable to raise a child properly.

One way to become aware of a potential surrender is to contact obstetricians, hospital staff, and clergymen in your area, and let them know that you wish to adopt. One of them may know of a girl who is considering giving her child up for adoption. If the people you contact do not know of anybody at the time you talk to them, don't be afraid to talk to them again in a few months. Make them aware that this is really important to you so that they keep you in mind when an opportunity does arise. Although you should not pay the natural mother, it is sometimes customary to pay for her hospital and legal expenses.

Because of the tremendous importance of handling a private adoption correctly, it is advisable that you use an attorney to insure that mistakes are not made. Another advantage in using an attorney is that you are insulated from the natural mother, since the actual surrender of the baby must be made directly to you or to your attorney. The attorney, rather than you, can be named in the act of surrender so that your anonymity is protected. The act of surrender can also be made to an agency instead of directly to the adoptive parents.

The act of surrender cannot be signed until at least five days, not counting the day of birth, have passed since the child was born. The surrendering parent or parents must be represented by an attorney at the execution of the act of surrender to insure that she or they are aware of what they are doing. The natural parents or parent are also required to execute a separate statement disclosing their ages and which provides an extensive medical genetic history of themselves and their immediate families.

> *Jenny, a college student, found herself pregnant and unmarried. Her father told her that she was an embarrassment to her family, that she had caused her mother's ulcers, and that she would not be allowed back home unless she gave the child up for adoption. Jenny's grandmother said that Jenny should keep the baby and come to live with her. Jenny's father threatened to force the sale of her grandmother's farm if Jenny kept the child. Jenny sought counseling from the Volunteers of America, a licensed adoption agency. During the period of her counseling, she vacillated between keeping the child and giving it up for adoption. Finally, she signed a voluntary act of surrender to the agency and the child was placed with an adoptive family who had been waiting for the opportunity to adopt a baby.*

Shortly after surrendering the child for adoption, Jenny changed her mind and decided that she should have kept the baby and gone to live with her grandmother. She sued to have the act of surrender declared invalid based on the coercion of her father and based on the agency's awareness of her vacillation in deciding the best thing to do.

The court decided that Jenny had freely given her consent and that vacillation and torment over deciding the best thing to do was a normal part of giving up a child for adoption. In general, the courts do not want to allow people to agree to a surrender and then to change their minds.

Obtaining a child through a surrogate mother has received publicity in recent years. In these cases there is usually a contract in which the mother agrees to carry the father's baby for a fee and turn over custody to the father and his wife when the child is born. In response to the lawsuits and uncertainty that these cases tend to bring, many states have passed laws against surrogate mother contracts. Louisiana is no exception and surrogate mother contracts are null as of September 1, 1987. This does not mean that the contract is illegal, it means that there is no obligation under the contract to turn over the child or to pay any fee. In other words, you can enter into a surrogate contract, but you cannot use the courts to enforce it.

Sharon was married at age fifteen and shortly afterwards gave birth to a baby daughter. Six months later, she learned that she was pregnant again and decided to leave the baby with her older sister to raise, partly at the insistence of her husband. For the next two years, neither Sharon nor her husband contributed to the baby's financial needs or welfare. Sharon and her husband separated when their daughter was two years old. Sharon demanded that her sister give the child back to her since she no longer lived with her husband. Sharon's sister refused and petitioned the court to have the child declared abandoned and to have the child placed in her custody.

The court decided to declare the child abandoned since her natural parents had shown no interest in her for two years and had led Sharon's sister to believe that she would be raising the girl as her own.

It must be emphasized that gaining legal custody of a child, either through private placement or through an agency, is not the final step. It is still necessary to complete the adoption by going through the proper court proceedings. These procedures should only be undertaken with the advice of an attorney.

Voluntary Registration. The Children's Code also includes a procedure for adopted children to participate in a central registry. Some adopted children have a strong urge to locate their natural parents. Likewise, some natural parents have a desire to find out more about the child they gave up for adoption. The Department of Social Services has a central registry for those natural parents and adopted children who wish to make contact with each other. Registration is purely voluntary and is not permitted until the adopted child reaches the age of twenty five. The registration is good for five years and may be renewed. The state is required to monitor registrations to see if there are any matches. If a match occurs, a social worker is supposed to contact the parties.

Emancipation

Any person under the age of eighteen years is a minor and therefore subject to parental authority. A minor is not able to contract or carry on a business as an adult. Emancipation relieves a minor of some or all of these disabilities and allows the minor limited or unlimited freedom from parental control, depending on the type of emancipation. Emancipation also means that the parents may no longer be responsible for their children's acts, again, depending on the type of emancipation. Emancipation can be judicial, by marriage, or by notarial act.

A person who is at least sixteen years old can petition to be judicially emancipated which makes him an adult with full power to perform all acts as if he had reached the age of eighteen. He can contract, run a business, bring or defend a lawsuit, and is no longer under the authority of his parents. The parents are also no longer responsible for the damages inflicted by their emancipated child. Bad Leroy's parents, for example, could have avoided all of their problems if they had joined in a petition to emancipate Bad Leroy. The parents must consent to the emancipation unless it is being brought on the grounds of ill treatment or refusal to support. Judicial emancipation is granted after a court hearing if the judge agrees that emancipation is in the minor's best interest.

A minor is also emancipated by marriage. Emancipation by marriage carries with it almost all the rights of an adult, including the right to appear in court and conduct a business. However, a married minor under the age of sixteen cannot sell or mortgage any of his immovable property (real estate) without court authorization. Once a minor is emancipated by marriage, the emancipation continues even if the minor is later divorced.

> *Harriet married at the age of fifteen. Her husband became disabled, and she called upon her father, Jake, to help them out financially. Jake refused, stating that once Harriet married and moved out of the house, she became an adult. Jake argued that Harriet became her husband's responsibility, for better or worse. Harriet sued her father for support.*

The court had to decide whether she was entitled to support and, if so, under what theory of law. Parents are obligated to support their children according to Article 227 of the Civil Code which says that the act of marriage is a contract and obligation to support, maintain, and educate the children of the marriage. The court decided that this article and other articles which discuss the obligation to support children refer only to minor children and not to children that are emancipated by marriage.

The court then considered Article 229 which creates the obligation of children to support their parents who are in need and the reciprocal obligation of a parent to support any descendants who are in need. This obligation, the court concluded, has nothing to do with whether the party in need is a minor, an emancipated minor, or an adult. The court ordered Jake to pay his daughter a monthly allowance during the disability.

Emancipation by authentic act. A minor of sixteen years or older can be emancipated by an authentic act executed by his parents This type of emancipation is generally limited to the actions specified in the document and is usually done for a specific purpose, like enabling the minor to contract so he can run his own business.

The emancipation by authentic act does not relieve the parents from any legal responsibility (or liability) for their child.

Part 2

Your Property

Buying Your Home

Buying a house is usually the biggest investment a person makes and is very often the first time a person has need of a lawyer. Despite the importance of this investment, it is surprising how many people handle this transaction in a careless manner that is sure to result in problems.

Louisiana has very precise laws covering the transfer of real estate. If these laws are not followed, the buyer of a house may find himself with a defective title that may make it impossible to resell the house. The seller of a house may find himself forced to take the house back and refund the purchase price plus pay damages. Let's look at the steps necessary to insure that the sale is successful for both the buyer and the seller.

The Purchase Agreement

In many situations oral agreements can be binding, but lead to disputes as to the terms of the agreement and even to claims of fraud. Because the law considers the transfer of real estate so important, transfers of real estate, or even agreements to transfer real estate, must be in writing. Once you have found your dream house, the first step to make sure that the sale takes place is to execute a purchase agreement with the seller.

The purchase agreement affords protection to both the seller and the buyer. The seller, in return for taking his house off the market, is certain as to the price he will receive, the expenses that will be his responsibility, and the time the closing will take place. The buyer, who may have to go to some expense to find a loan, is certain as to the price he will pay, the expenses that will be his responsibility, and the time he will be able to move in.

All of the terms of the proposed sale should be included in the purchase agreement so that both sides know what to expect. If a real estate agent is involved, a standard form purchase agreement will probably be prepared by the agent for the buyer and seller to sign. Keep in mind that even though it is a pre-printed form, you are still free to alter or even cross out any terms that are not to your liking. Also keep in mind that the pre-printed forms used by real estate agents are designed to make sure that the sale goes through and to protect the real estate agent's commission. There is usually a provision in these agreements that the defaulting party, whether buyer or seller, and whether the sale actually goes through or not, is still liable for the real estate commission.

Whether you use a standard form or write your own, the purchase agreement must:

- Be in writing.
- Accurately describe the property.
- Set forth the purchase price.
- Set a time limit within which the sale must take place.

If you do not set a time limit, it will be assumed that a "reasonable time" within which to execute the sale was intended. Arguments over what constitutes reasonable time have led to many law suits. These are the minimum requirements for a valid purchase agreement.

In addition to the minimum requirements, the purchase agreement also should state:

- The other items in or around the house which are included in the sale, such as drapes or appliances.
- The exact terms of the sale, such as assumption terms, the responsibility for the payment of fees, and time

> limits for arranging financing if the sale is contingent on finding financing.

- Whether a termite certificate is required from the seller.

- How taxes for the current year are going to be paid and by whom.

- Who will pay closing costs, or how they will be divided.

- When the sale must take place, and how soon after the buyer will be entitled to occupancy.

- Whether a deposit is to be given, and whether it should be considered earnest money.

- What extensions are to be automatically given if problems arise, such as title objections.

- Any other terms and conditions.

As you can see, the purchase agreement should be a comprehensive document so that both sides understand exactly what is expected. To be valid in Louisiana, any sale must have a clear meeting of the minds as to the price and the thing sold, and there must be a clear consent to the sale. The other conditions that can be specified in the purchase agreement simply insure there are no misunderstandings or surprises. Remember, if a substantial misunderstanding does occur, it might give either party grounds to withdraw from the agreement. It is to your advantage to make sure the purchase agreement is clear and comprehensive.

Whether or not a deposit is considered earnest money is extremely important. If the deposit is earnest money, which the law presumes is not the case unless the purchase agreement states otherwise, either party is free to withdraw from the agreement without cause or explanation. The only obligation is for the buyer to forfeit his deposit or for the seller to return twice the deposit to the buyer. If the purchase agreement is silent or states "this deposit is not to be considered earnest money," either party can sue the other to force them to go through with the sale. Purchase agreements provided by real estate agents always state that the deposit is not earnest money. If you are interested in buying a house but feel that you might want to change your mind, call the deposit earnest money and make it as small as you can.

Roger and Aubrey signed a purchase agreement in which Roger agreed to buy Aubrey's house for $490,000. Roger gave his real estate agent $5,000, which the standard form purchase agreement stated was "not to be considered earnest money" and that the parties can demand specific performance in the event of a default. Aubrey made a counter offer the same day for $530,000 and added a handwritten provision that occupancy would be granted 7 days after closing. A few days later Roger countered for $528,000 and added a handwritten provision that should the sale falls through, the deposit is to be given to Aubrey. A few weeks later, Roger lost his job and notified Aubrey that he would not be buying the house after all. Aubrey sued for specific performance relying on the terms of the purchase agreement. Roger counter sued asking that his deposit be returned.

The trial court awarded Aubrey $72,000 in damages saying that the handwritten language did not "do away with" what was written before it and that the $5,000 was not earnest money. Roger appealed on several grounds, but when the case was heard in 2009, the higher court determined that the Civil Code states that if a deposit is to be earnest money, the agreement must clearly say so. Roger lost on appeal as well.

There is a general rule that any material fact about the property that is kept from the buyer can justify canceling the purchase agreement. Withholding a material fact can even allow the buyer to rescind after the sale takes place, as we shall see later. In 1991, the Legislature passed a new law that the seller does not have to inform the buyer that the property is "stigmatized" or psychologically impacted. If a buyer finds out after the sale that a prior occupant had AIDS or that a homicide or suicide occurred on the property, this would not be legal grounds to cancel the sale. A seller *does* have to disclose if the property was used as a meth lab. Why the Legislature thought it was important to add this is unclear.

Title Insurance

We are often asked whether it is necessary to get a title opinion before buying a piece of real estate. Sometimes the person is buying the property from a friend and "knows everything must be all right." We answer this question by pointing out that banks and mortgage companies always require that the chain of ownership be examined to insure there are no problems with the title to the property. Whether the friend from whom you are buying the property is reliable is not the question. There are many types of title problems that even the friend may not be aware of. It is even possible for a lien to be placed on the property without the friend's knowledge.

Other title problems can result from divorce, inheritance and our forced heirship laws, judgments, federal tax liens, a mistake in a prior sale, and many other problems too numerous to list. The point is, when you buy property, you become liable for any charges or debts recorded not only against the property, but against the person from whom you are buying (but not for more than the value of the property). This is the case because a judgment against an individual operates as a judicial mortgage against all of his real estate. Even if there is a judgment against another individual with a similar name, it can involve time and expense in tracking down the person who obtained the judgment and getting him to file a document making it clear that the judgment is not against the same person who is selling you the property. If this problem is caught before the sale, you can require that the seller straighten it out at his expense. After the sale, it becomes your problem because the person who buys from you will probably have the foresight to insist on a title examination.

The title opinion is a written statement from an attorney, either on letterhead stationery or a special form, in which the attorney states his opinion as to the merchantability of the title in question. The opinion will briefly describe the property, give the full names of the owners, and list any exceptions that the attorney has discovered to the title. Some exceptions are always listed and are acceptable because they do not really interfere with the merchantability of the title. These types of exceptions include recorded building restrictions, servitudes, and building set-back lines. The attorney might also state that the opinion is based only on what he has found in the public records of the parish in which the property is located and that he is not responsible for surveys, zoning restrictions, inheritance rights of illegitimate children, and unrecorded liens.

What is the purpose of a title opinion opinion? If the attorney's title opinion says that there are no mortgages or liens and it turns out that there are, he is personally responsible for either fixing the problem at his expense or even for paying the mortgage or judgment. The attorney's malpractice insurance stands behind him to insure that enough funds are available to correct any problem that may occur, even if the problem doesn't arise immediately. The title opinion is, in effect, a low-cost insurance policy that lasts as long as the attorney is legally obligated to fix any problem he overlooked. This obligation is limited to the period of time that an attorney can be sued for malpractice. Since recent changes in the law probably set a maximum three year limit on malpractice, other types of protection are advisable.

Title insurance is also available and will probably be required if you get a first mortgage to buy a house. The title insurance that a bank or mortgage company will require protects only the money lender in the event a title problem occurs, even though you will be required to pay for the premium. Title insurance is usually required in addition to the title opinion because the mortgage may be sold to an investor in some other state who wants to be able to recover against a national insurance company rather than an attorney. Also, title insurance may cover the mortgage holder against title defects that the attorney will not be responsible for, such as unrecorded liens, survey problems, and certain other defects.

Title insurance for the home owner is also available and can be quite inexpensive if purchased at the same time the mortgage policy is issued. The home owner is given some credit for the money that he has paid for the mortgage holder's policy and basically pays for coverage that he may want above the mortgage amount, plus a small additional premium. Since mortgages are always less that the purchase price, the premium would be for coverage up to the full amount paid for the house. An owner's policy of title insurance can always be purchased at a later date, but the premium will be more expensive and you will probably be required to have the title examined again.

Title insurance premiums are set on a sliding scale. The larger the premium, the smaller the charge per thousand dollars of coverage. As a very rough estimate, you can figure around three dollars per thousand dollars of coverage for the average home for the policy you will be required to purchase. If you want coverage for yourself, it might cost an additional dollar or so for each thousand dollars of coverage. Why would you want title insurance for yourself? For the same reasons the mortgage holder does. If there is a serious title problem, it might not be something that the attorney is responsible for. Or, the attorney may not be available or legally liable since these problems usually do not show up until you go to sell the house years later. When you apply for a loan, you can ask for an estimate of how much extra an owner's policy will cost.

The Closing

The closing generally refers to the formal execution of the transfer of the property, whether a mortgage loan is involved or not. The sale, in order to be valid, must be by authentic act. That is, the buyer and the seller must both sign the sale in front of two witnesses and a notary public. The mortgage, if one is involved, must also be by authentic act. A sale or mortgage can be authenticated after the closing if one of the witnesses goes before a notary public and two witnesses and swears that he was one of the original witnesses to the sale or mortgage.

The typical closing in Louisiana is held at the office of the notary public who has prepared the closing documents. The notary public is usually an attorney who has some experience in examining titles. By custom, and usually by the terms of the purchase agreement, the buyer chooses the notary and is responsible for his fees. However, the lending institution has the last word in approving the notary because it wants an attorney who is familiar with its procedures and will render a title opinion that it can rely on. Most lending institutions have a list of approved attorneys that you can choose from. Some lending institutions, particularly savings and loan associations, require that you use its attorney at your expense. The fees charged by the closing attorney vary, but might typically start at $120 for the document preparation and as low as $350 for a title opinion.

Unless the purchase agreement states otherwise, the buyer is usually responsible for closing costs such as origination fees, discount points, credit report, appraisal, survey, attorneys fees, and recording costs. Veteran's Administration loans, however, will restrict the charges paid by the veteran buyer.

The seller is usually responsible for the real estate commission, termite and any other type of certificate, and any costs involved in satisfying mortgages that he has on the property. If there is a first mortgage to be placed on the property, the seller and buyer must be provided with a settlement statement before the sale and mortgage are signed. Copies of the settlement statement statement, if you make a request, must be provided to you as much as two days before the closing.

The closing attorney usually collects the deposit, if one was made, and a check from the buyer. The attorney then makes all of the disbursement checks from his trust or escrow account. Some attorneys will accept your personal check, but most attorneys and title companies will require that you bring certified funds to the closing.

The transfer of the property and the mortgage are complete as of the moment the documents are signed, witnessed, and notarized. The notary public then has the responsibility for recording the sale and mortgage and for making sure that he has retained enough of the proceeds of the sale to pay off any of the seller's mortgages. The sale and mortgage are not effective as to third parties until they are recorded. This means that the public can rely on the mortgage and conveyance records of the clerk of court in the parish in which the property is located for information on ownership and mortgages. Theoretically, if the seller went immediately from your closing and sold the same property to someone else, the second buyer would own the property if he recorded his sale before you recorded yours. Your only recourse would be to sue the seller for fraud and try to recover the sales price.

Liability After the Sale

A great deal of any real estate attorney's business involves suits that arise after the sale of a house, even many years after. A seller can be liable for defects in the house he sells, even defects of which he was unaware. The defects, depending on how severe they are, can lead to the seller having to return a portion of the sales price or even to refunding the whole sales price and taking the house back. If the defects were known to the seller but kept hidden from the buyer, he may also have to pay the buyer's attorney's fees and damages.

Professor Jones, a research chemist newly employed by Tulane University, found exactly the house he was looking for. It was located close to the university and had a den that he could convert into a study. A floor plan diagram prepared by the seller's real estate agent showed that the den was 13 feet by 24 feet. Professor Jones knew that this was just the right size to build bookshelves along one wall to store his extensive research library. After purchasing the house, Professor Jones discovered that the den was actually 13 feet by 20 feet. Professor Jones sued to have the sale rescinded since the size of the den was a major factor in his decision to buy the house. The sellers refused to take the house back and claimed that since Professor Jones had inspected the house, the burden was on him to discover any defects. Besides, the sellers argued, it was an innocent mistake made by the real estate agent and didn't really alter the house that the Professor had seen and liked.

The court held that Professor Jones was entitled to rescind the sale. It is true, the court reasoned, that a buyer must make a reasonable inspection to discover any obvious defects. However, this defect was not obvious and the professor should be able to rely on what the seller claims are exact measurements. The court ordered that Professor Jones get back the purchase price, together with his reasonable costs connected with the sale. Because the court found that the misrepresentation was innocent, no other damages were awarded. The suit took three years to get resolved in the courts, during which time Professor Jones lived in the house. Because of this, the court reduced the award to the Professor by the fair rental value of the house for the months that he had a place to live.

The action to rescind a sale because of defects is called redhibition. In this type of suit, the unhappy buyer must prove that the defect is so serious that the thing bought is useless or so inconvenient that it must be concluded that he would not have bought it had he known of the defect. He must also show that the defect existed before he bought and that he could not have discovered the defect by a reasonable inspection of the property. If the seller tells the buyer of any defects before the sale, the buyer cannot sue for redhibition after the sale because of those defects. If the seller makes a declaration in good faith that the property has some quality and it turns out after the sale that it does not, the buyer has an action in redhibition. That is why Professor Jones won his case.

In all suits for redhibition where the buyer is seeking to rescind the sale, the judge has the option to reduce the price rather than order that the property be returned to the seller. This will frequently happen when there is a defect that can be repaired. In that type of case, the judge will most likely order a reduction in the purchase price to equal the cost of making the repairs. In cases where repair is not an option, like with Professor Jones, a rescission is the only remedy that will put the buyer back in the position he was in prior to the sale. In one case, a buyer sued for rescission because he found that his back yard flooded every time there was a heavy rain. The court felt that the defect was not serious enough for a rescission and ordered that the purchase price be reduced by $20,000. The defect of flooding could not be repaired, but the court felt that this award would make up for the inconvenience to the buyer.

In cases where a seller knows of a defect but does not make it known to the buyer, the seller may also be liable for damages beyond returning the purchase price and selling costs. This happens frequently with termite damage cases. The seller has the infestation treated and then covers over the damage with paint or other materials so that it is not discoverable by a reasonable inspection.

Bill and Martha were looking for a house that they could move to their property and fix up. Martin had exactly what they were looking for and even agreed to reduce the price on the condition that Martin first would sell the house to a mover who would in turn sell it to Bill and Martha. This was necessary, Martin explained, because he would have to pay a realtor's commission if he sold it directly to them. The sale was done to the mover and then to Bill and Martha. The same mover was hired to take the house apart and transport it to the new site. When the mover started to dismantle the house, he discovered severe termite infestation in the walls. The damage was so severe that the mover refused to try to move the house until extensive repairs were made. Bill and Martha sued the mover to rescind the sale. The mover defended himself by saying he was an innocent third party to the sale and that he couldn't possibly have known of the termite damage. The mover also sued Martin saying that Martin should be liable for any money that was awarded to Bill and Martha. Because Bill and Martha alleged that the termite damage was known to the sellers, they sued for additional damages for all their expenses, and for mental anguish. Martin claimed that he couldn't be sued since he was not the seller.

Bill and Martha were successful in their suit and Martin was made to pay the judgment since the mover was held to have been a part of the transaction only for the convenience of the parties. The court found that Martin was well aware of the termite damage and that he had deliberately sought to insulate himself from any liability by selling to the mover. The court found that Martin was guilty of fraud and ordered him to pay the cost of the house, all expenses, and Bill and Martha's attorney's fees. The court, however, did not allow damages for mental anguish since that was not allowed in a redhibition suit at the time this case was heard.

A suit for redhibition must be brought within one year of the purchase. However, if the buyer alleges fraud, the suit may be brought within one year of the time the defect is discovered by the buyer. Liability after the sale, therefore, can extend for a considerable amount of time. If the home is purchased from the original builder, however, a new set of laws may apply.

New Home Warranty Act

The New Home Warranty Act made some significant modifications to existing law. This act became effective in 1986 and applies to any structure which is designed and used as a residence. Certain warranties are made by the builder to the original purchaser of a new home and to subsequent owners who purchase the home during the warranty period. This act seems to provide new remedies for the consumer, but let's take a closer look at exactly what the act means.

All new homes are automatically covered by a warranty starting from the time the first purchaser obtains title to the house or occupies the house, whichever occurs first. There are three different warranty periods. The first period is for one year and warrants that the house is free from any defects due to noncompliance with the building standards. The building standards are defined to be those standards adopted by any city, parish or other political subdivision in the building, electrical and mechanical codes. If the house is not located in an area that has any of these standards, then the Code applies.

The Standard Building Code is a national guideline for local codes that may or may not be as comprehensive as local codes.

In 1991, the Standard Building Code of the Southern Building Code International, Inc., and the National Electrical Code published by the National Fire Protection Association were adopted by Louisiana as our State Uniform Construction Code. It is likely that this code would be applied in determining whether a warranty is breached.

The next warranty period covers all electrical, heating, cooling, ventilating and plumbing systems for a period of two years. This warranty does not include appliances or fixtures and only comes into effect if a defect is the result of a failure to comply with the building standards.

The final warranty period is for a period of five years and warrants that the house will be free of major structural defects due to non-compliance with the building standards. Major structural defects are defined to be actual physical damage to certain load-bearing parts of a house if the damage is extensive enough to make the house unsafe, unsanitary, or unlivable. Load-bearing parts would be foundations, walls, beams, roof-framing systems, columns, girders and lintels.

Sounds like a good warranty doesn't it? Let's analyze it for a minute and see. Building codes are set for the primary purpose of public safety. Codes are usually minimal and cover such things as minimum framing requirements to insure the building doesn't collapse and minimum electrical requirements to insure that two toasters on the same circuit don't cause a fire. The New Home Warranty Act does nothing more than make the builder liable for a limited amount of time if he does not adhere to these minimal types of standards.

The Act also provides several exceptions to the builder's minimal liability. For example, the home owner is required to notify the builder of any defects by certified or registered mail. If this isn't done within one year after knowledge of the defect, the builder may no longer be responsible. Also, the home owner must give the builder a chance to repair the defect before the home owner can attempt his own repair. The home owner, after giving the builder a chance to repair, has only thirty days after the expiration of the warranty period in which to file suit. In other words, if suit is not filed within two years and thirty days because of a defect in the plumbing, the right to recover terminates. Remember also that the defect in the plumbing must have resulted from the builder's failure to comply with the building standards. There are also many specific exclusions, mold and mold damage, for example.

We have saved the best part of the New Home Warranty Act until last. This act is the exclusive remedy for the home owner against the builder. In other words, the owner of a new home does not have the right to sue the builder for redhibition or for any other reason resulting from defects in the home. The home owner can only sue if the builder fails to comply with the building codes. Subsequent buyers of a home, as long as the original warranty period is still applicable, are also faced with this limitation. So, if your builder completes your home but it is nineteen inches out of square (which happened in a case we handled), the New Home Warranty Act seems to say this is fine as long as the local building code is not violated. Also, if the home owner discovers some horrible defect one day after the warranty period, he can no longer recover from the builder even if the defect was caused by the builder's failure to comply with the building code.

The New Home Warranty Act was last updated in 2004 and there have been several cases seeking to interpret whether certain defects are building standard related. For example, let's say the builder finishes the house nineteen inches out of square. Let's also assume that the local building code says nothing about this type of defect and that the structure of the building is not weakened. In the construction contract between the builder and home owner, let's assume that there is the standard clause that the house will be finished in a "workmanlike manner."

Can the home owner still sue the builder under the contract because it was not finished in a workmanlike manner? This certainly would have been the case before the New Home Warranty Act was passed. Since the act states that it is the exclusive remedy against the builder, there may be some doubt as to whether the act or the terms of the contract would control.

Landlord And Tenants

As the cost of new housing and mortgages increases, more people are renting houses and apartments then ever before. This gives rise to an ever increasing number of suits against tenants by landlords and against landlords by tenants. A clear understanding of what is legally expected from the landlord, or "lessor," and the tenant, or "lessee," could easily preclude the majority of these suits.

The Lease

Unlike the purchase of a house, which must be in writing, the rental agreement for a house or apartment can be an oral agreement. Whether in writing or not, this agreement is called a lease, and the law is going to make certain assumptions about the agreement unless the parties specifically agree otherwise. The law only requires that the price be a specific amount, the premises be described, and that the consent of both the lessor and lessee to the lease be certain.

A lease can be for any length of time. If the lease agreement does not specify a term, the law assumes that the lease is on a month to month basis. When a lease is month to month, either party can terminate the lease by giving notice at least ten days before the end of the current month. Most leases, however deficient they are in other respects, will state the term of the lease and provide for a way to renew before the term of the lease expires. If the lease provides that the lessee agrees to stay for three years, then that is the agreement between the parties and the lessee may be liable for the whole three years of rent if he defaults on the lease prior to its expiration.

An oral lease is a dangerous thing. Whatever the agreement is, or was, between the lessor and the lessee, time has a way of changing each party's recollection of exactly what the understanding was. An oral lease can be just as binding as a written lease, but the burden is going to be on one party to prove what the lessor and the lessee had agreed to. If there is a dispute, the judge will be in the position of trying to decide who is telling the truth or who has a better recollection of what was said. It is obviously better to have a written lease in which all of the terms are definite and the chances of a misunderstanding are decreased.

> *Johnnie decided to get into the convenience store business. He leased an old grocery store from Ed, a local developer, and remodeled the store into "Johnnie's Buy and Bag." But first, Johnnie had his lawyer prepare a comprehensive lease which spelled out all the terms and conditions of the agreement. One important provision of the lease allowed Johnnie to renew each year for seven consecutive years as long as he gave Ed written notice at least sixty days before the end of the year.*

> *It was a lot of work, but at the end of the first year Johnnie was doing very well with his store and was considering opening others. On the day before the end of the first year of the lease, Johnnie remembered that he was required to give sixty days notice if he wished to renew for another year. Johnnie called Ed and told him that he had forgotten*

to give written notice. Ed told Johnnie that he would renew without written notice. Later that day Ed called Johnnie back and told him that he had changed his mind and that Johnnie would have ten days to vacate the property. Johnnie refused to move and Ed filed suit to have him evicted. In court, Johnnie claimed that Ed's oral agreement to let him stay had renewed the lease for another year. Ed claimed that it was too late to renew since sixty days had long passed. In any event, Ed argued, an oral agreement to modify a written lease is invalid and should not be allowed to change the terms of the lease.

The court decided that the lease had been renewed. Although it is generally true that you can't change the provisions of a written agreement with subsequent oral modifications, the court decided that since a lease does not have to be in writing in the first place, any modifications may be oral. Johnnie won this case because the court believed his testimony as to the telephone conversation with Ed. If Ed had denied that Johnnie had called, the case might have been decided the other way.

Let's take a look at just one section of a typical lease which was prepared for an apartment owner's association and is used extensively in Louisiana. The lease is 160 lines of small print and considering the source of the lease, it is obvious why the lessor is favored in most of the terms. As we shall see, even those terms that seem to favor the lessee are probably only there because state law requires them. Here is the section on liability. Believe it or not, we have paraphrased it in an attempt to make it easier to understand:

Lessee agrees that lessor will not be liable for injury or damage to person or property of lessee, his family, friends or guests whether in the leased apartment or anywhere on the grounds. Lessor shall not be liable regardless of who is hurt and regardless of how the injury happened or whose fault caused the injury. Lessee agrees that if lessor is found at fault in a court of law, lessee will reimburse lessor for the amount of any judgment against lessor, unless the lessor is proved to be directly negligent.

> Lessor will not be responsible for any repairs except to the roof. If the building falls down, lessor will not be responsible for repairs nor will lessor be responsible for the injuries suffered by any persons who are hurt as the result of defects in the structure. Lessee agrees to make all repairs to the structure at his own expense and to pay all damages to other parties who may suffer injury. The only exception is if lessee notifies lessor in writing of a defect and lessor does not make repairs in a reasonable time. If lessee does not notify lessor in writing promptly of defects, lessee shall be responsible for all damages regardless.

This lease makes the renter responsible for nearly everything under the sun. It makes you wonder why they bothered to relieve the lessee for liability if he promptly notifies the lessor of a defect. Well, the reason for this is clear. Louisiana law allows the lessor to relieve himself from liability for injuries that result from the condition of his building if the lessee signs a lease agreeing to this. However, the law will not allow the lessor to relieve himself of liability for defects that he was aware of or if he was notified of a defect and failed to repair within a reasonable time. This lease, therefore, merely states the minimum requirements of the law and adds that the notice must be in writing and must be made promptly.

Leases will frequently contain provisions that are illegal or unenforceable. These provisions are made even when the party writing the lease knows that they can't be enforced in a court of law. Why is it done anyway? Because the party knows from experience that a legal appearing document will probably not be questioned and that it would not occur to many people that a document signed by them has illegal provisions. The lease quoted above is a good example. It has probably been signed by tens of thousands of renters without a complaint. Yet in that lease, the renter makes himself liable if the mailman who is delivering a package to him falls over a rotten balcony. To make things worse, that particular provision of the lease is enforceable and could probably be used against the tenant successfully in a court of law. We have only one recommendation for someone who voluntarily signs this sort of lease: have plenty of tenant's liability insurance.

A lease is an agreement, written or oral, between the landlord and the tenant. Do not assume that a type-set lease cannot be altered if you find some of the terms objectionable. You may not be in a position to negotiate different terms with a landlord who has hundreds of apartments, but it would certainly be worth a try to have some terms altered to be more in line with what you consider fair. This may especially be true for a pre-packaged lease that the landlord has probably never read. Make your concerns known and if you don't seem to be able to get anywhere with the apartment manager, don't be afraid to go directly to the owner.

Being a Landlord

The landlord is probably viewed in the public mind as someone who is several notches below the used car salesman when it comes to ethics and social responsibility. However, the landlord provides an invaluable public service in making dwelling space available. The landlord must also put up with the dishonest renter who cheats him out of the last month's rent and leaves the house or apartment in need of a new carpet, paint and, perhaps, a new stove. Besides having to put up with dishonest tenants, the landlord also has to put up with property taxes, insurance, and assessments as well as federal, state and local laws, rules and regulations. These are the sort of things that tenants do not have to worry about and are probably completely unaware of.

As we have seen, the lease can itemize all of the rights and responsibilities of the landlord and the tenant. Nearly anything that the parties agree to can be made binding on them. The only exception would be an agreement that is against the law or public policy, such as a lease for a business that is prohibited by a zoning code. If there is no specific lease agreement, or if the lease does not cover everything, the law contains certain provisions as to the rights and responsibilities of the landlord. Some of these provisions are basic to the concept of a lease and without them a court could find that there is no lease agreement at all.

The law provides that the landlord must, at a minimum, deliver possession of the leased property to the tenant, maintain the property in a condition that makes it usable for the purpose intended, and keep the tenant in peaceable possession during the term of the lease. If there is no specific agreement as to which repairs to the property are the responsibility of the landlord, the law provides that the landlord shall repair everything but broken windows, unless broken in a hail storm; hearth and chimney casings; plaster of interior walls; the pavement of rooms; shutters, locks, and hinges. If the items that must be repaired by the tenant sound strange, that is because this particular law was last revised in 1869. The courts have yet to agree on what modern building components fall under these old classifications.

The presumption is that the landlord is responsible for all repairs that are not specifically mentioned as an exception. That is why nearly all leases shift the burden to the tenant when it comes to this responsibility. In one case, the lease simply said that the lessee must maintain the premises in good condition at his expense. The court held that this was sufficient to place the burden on the tenant to make all repairs.

The landlord has the obligation to pay all taxes, assessments, and other charges against the property. Again, this can be changed in the lease to make the tenant responsible for taxes or even for a pro-rata share in any increase in taxes during the term of the lease.

In return for providing the tenant with a place to live, the landlord is entitled to rent. If the tenant fails to pay his rent, he is in default, and there are very specific provisions in the law to protect the landlord.

The landlord has a legal right to seize and sell property belonging to the tenant in order to see that the rent is paid. This right is called a lessor's privilege, or lien, and if handled properly, is a very effective way to protect the landlord's rights. If handled improperly, the landlord could be faced with a suit for damages by the tenant. The lessor's privilege automatically attaches to all property belonging to the tenant that is on the leased premises. This right results from the legal conclusion that the tenant, when he rents, pledges his property to the landlord as a guarantee that the provisions of the lease will be honored. Specifically excluded from this privilege are the tenant's clothing and linen and those of his family; his bed and each family member's bed; his arms and the necessary tools of his trade or profession, and those of his family; one cooking stove and utensils and all pots, pans, dishes, knives, spoons and forks; and one dining room table and dining chair for each family member.

The landlord also has the same privilege on any property that belongs to a sub-lessee. If the tenant sub-leases the property, or part of the property, to another person and then fails to pay the rent, the innocent sub-tenant may find most of his assets seized by the sheriff. Even property belonging to an innocent third party that just happens to be on the premises is subject to seizure, although there is a procedure that the third party can go through to regain the property prior to being disposed of by the landlord.

The lessor's privilege even follows the tenant's property after he moves from the leased premises. The landlord can seize property belonging to the tenant, except exempt property discussed above, at any time while the property is on the premises or, for a period of fifteen days after the tenant moves, at any place the property can be found. The landlord only has to show that the property still belongs to the tenant and that it is the same property that was at the leased premises.

Farmer Fred decided to increase the size of his crops and leased three thousand acres from Bill. Fred did not do well, and after his first year stopped paying rent to Bill. Bill sued to have all of Fred's farming machinery seized to satisfy the back due rent and proceeded to have the sheriff sell the equipment at auction. Before Fred could sell the equipment, Fearsome Finance Company joined the suit and asked that they be given the proceeds of the sale since Fred had mortgaged all of his equipment to them before leasing from Bill. Fearsome Finance argued that their mortgage, which had been legally recorded prior to the lease, had to be paid before any other claims which arose after the date of the mortgage.

The lower court agreed with Fearsome Finance and ordered that the proceeds of the sale be applied first to the amount owed on the mortgage before Bill got anything on his lease. Since that would leave nothing for Bill, he appealed. The appeals court reversed on a technicality. Fearsome Finance failed to add the serial numbers of the machinery on the mortgage. Since mortgages have to describe the property mortgaged carefully so there is no doubt about exactly what is mortgaged, and since there was a great deal of equipment involved, Bill's lessor's privilege came ahead of Fearsome Finance's mortgage. A landlord has the right to exercise his lessor's privilege, but there may be another privilege that must be satisfied before the landlord sees his rent.

The law gives the landlord a privilege on his tenant's property, but the landlord must be careful that he follows the legal procedures exactly if he wants to successfully exercise the privilege. Before seizing any property belonging to the tenant, the landlord must obtain a court order authorizing a seizure and directing the sheriff or constable to hold the property until a sale or until the tenant pays the rent. Any attempt by the landlord to seize property without court authority can lead to a lawsuit and even to criminal charges. To make the seizure properly, the landlord must petition the court for a writ of sequestration and must sign an affidavit stating that he is entitled to the relief he requests. This writ is directed to the sheriff of the parish or the constable in some cities and is full authority to take the property described in the writ.

Eviction

Sooner or later, all landlords are faced with the problem of having to evict a tenant who has not paid the rent or has defaulted on the lease agreement in some other way. Unless the tenant has abandoned the premises, the landlord has no right to remove the tenant without a judicial determination that the tenant has no right to be on the premises. Remember, one of the obligations of the landlord is to give the tenant peaceable possession of the property he is leasing. Failure to follow the eviction procedure exactly can also lead to a lawsuit for damages for wrongfully depriving the tenant of the peaceable possession of the premises.

An eviction is a very fast procedure and can usually be combined with a petition to seize the tenant's property. The landlord is very often in the position of wanting to get rid of a tenant who is in default, and the landlord will also want to insure that the tenant's property is under seizure before the tenant is evicted. If the tenant is in default, whether for not paying the rent or for breaking some other condition of the lease, the landlord has the right to have the tenant forcibly removed from the premises. The landlord must first give the tenant notice that he is in default. If the term of the lease is expired, or if the tenant has defaulted, the landlord must deliver to the tenant written notice to vacate and must allow a minimum of five days to leave. If the tenant has not left the premises, the landlord may file suit for a judicial eviction, and the tenant must go to court to show by what authority he is still on the premises. At the hearing, the tenant must offer some positive defense to the eviction, or he will be ordered to vacate immediately. If the tenant is still on the premises twenty-four hours after the hearing, the court must issue a warrant ordering the sheriff or constable to remove the tenant forcibly from the property. The tenant can appeal from the eviction, but the procedure has been made difficult and expensive.

The tenant can waive the requirement that he be given notice five days before an eviction can be started. The waiver must be in writing and must be contained in the lease. The prudent landlord would add the following paragraph to his lease to avoid the problem of notice and delay: "Pursuant to Code of Civil Procedure Article 4701, lessee hereby waives the requirements of law that lessee receive at least five days notice before he may be judicially evicted from the premises. Lessee hereby waives such notice and agrees that in the event of his default, lessor may immediately, and without notice, bring suit to evict lessee from the premises."

Tenants' Rights

Very few tenants are aware of the laws we have for their protection. It would probably be a good idea if landlords were required to disclose in the lease a summary of the rights available to tenants. The procedures dictated by the law to enforce these rights must be followed exactly, or the right is lost.

Defending against eviction. To defend yourself against an eviction, you must set forth an affirmative defense. Examples of affirmative defenses would be that the rent was paid, that you are not in default, or that the term of the lease is not up. To preserve your right to appeal an eviction, should you lose at the first hearing, you must have filed an answer setting forth your affirmative defense, and your answer must have been made under oath. In other words, you must include a statement swearing that your allegations in the answer are true, and you must sign the statement in front of a notary.

If you lose the eviction, you only have twenty-four hours after the judgment of eviction is signed to file an appeal that will suspend the eviction. We have never seen anyone successfully represent himself in an eviction. That is because the landlord generally is familiar with the procedures, and the tenant is not. Many tenants would have liked to appeal a decision to evict, but by the time they find out that they were required to file an answer under oath, it is too late. In the typical case, the disgruntled tenant goes to see a lawyer a few days after the eviction hearing and is informed that his right to appeal has passed. The tenant may still have the right to appeal the correctness of the decision, but it is too late to keep from being thrown off the premises.

The most frequent complaint tenants have against landlords is the loss of their deposit. Many landlords found from experience that they could keep the tenant's deposit and that there wasn't much that the tenant could do about it. It simply wasn't worthwhile trying to sue to recover a few hundred dollars. The legal expenses alone generally exceeded the amount of the deposit. In 1972, the Legislature recognized this problem and passed several laws controlling the return of tenant deposits. But, the tenant needs to be familiar with these laws and the procedures that they require.

A lessor who holds a deposit from a tenant for the faithful performance of the lease is required to return the deposit within one month after the termination of the lease. However, the lessor can retain all or any part of the deposit that is necessary to remedy a default by the tenant or to repair unreasonable wear to the leased premises. As long as the tenant has not abandoned the premises prior to the termination of the lease, the landlord is required to give the tenant an itemized statement showing why the deposit or any part of it was withheld. If the deposit is not returned and no written statement is given to the tenant, the tenant can demand the return of his deposit in writing. If the lessor still does not make a refund or accounting within thirty days from the written demand, the lessor's failure to refund will be considered willful, and the tenant will be entitled to the greater of his actual damages or two hundred dollars. The court can also order the landlord to pay the tenant for his attorney's fees and court costs. An award of attorney's fees can often be more than the deposit and damages combined and can be the real incentive for the landlord to make a prompt refund once the tenant makes it clear that he is aware of the deposit laws.

If you find it necessary to make a written demand for your deposit back, make sure you can prove that you gave the notice and when the notice was given. Bring a witness with you if you hand-deliver the notice, or send the notice by certified mail. Your notice only has to say that you gave a deposit and expect a refund within thirty days, or you will take further legal action. If the lessor makes a reasonable accounting of why your deposit was withheld, you would not be entitled to damages and attorney's fees. You could still recover the portion of the deposit that you can prove was unreasonably withheld. See the Do It Yourself Guide for the proper forms to recover your deposit.

Estate Planning

Estate planning is generally a systematic attempt to control the eventual distribution of your assets. Estate planning is not limited to planning for events after your death. A comprehensive plan takes into account various methods of conserving and managing your estate before death through proper investment and tax planning.

Making Your Will

Louisiana is the only state out of fifty that requires that a portion of your estate be left to your forced heirs. In all of the other United States, you can pretty much leave your property to anyone you want. You could even leave your estate to a cat or dog, something that has been done on more than one occasion.

In Louisiana we have a doctrine called "forced heirship." We have inherited this concept of law from the French Revolution and the Code Napoleon. It was felt at the time that forcing parents to distribute their estates among the children would prevent family fortunes from accumulating. Before the forced heirship laws, the oldest son would usually inherit the family fortune, and a ruling class would be maintained by keeping wealth concentrated. By dividing inheritances, no single family would be able to amass a fortune and, it was thought, the excesses that led to the French Revolution would be avoided.

In the United States there is certainly little chance of this happening because of estate taxes. Nevertheless, Louisiana has kept the tradition of forced heirship despite frequent attempts to get the Legislature to abolish the forced heirship laws. There is a feeling among advocates of the law that it is more fair to insure that each child receives an inheritance. Opponents of the law argue that it interferes with what should be a basic freedom to dispose of your property the way you want.

In what might be called a compromise between these two positions, the Legislature has amended the forced heirship laws to apply only to children under the age of 24 years. In other words, once you reach 24 you are no longer a forced heir. Forced heirship is discussed more fully later in this chapter.

We are frequently asked the question "Who should have a will?" The answer is: anyone who 1) has assets and cares who gets them; or, 2) has children under the age of eighteen and cares about who is appointed as tutor (guardian) of the children; or, 3) cares who is appointed to administer the estate; or, 4) will leave anyone behind that he cares enough about to insure that everything will be handled in an orderly way according to the best interests of the survivors. In other words, nearly everyone needs a will unless he absolutely does not care what happens after he dies.

There is an important exception to the general rule that nearly everyone needs a will. If someone dies with a gross estate of $75,000 or less, the heirs can simply sign an affidavit and avoid court proceedings entirely. However, this procedure cannot be used unless the deceased died without a will. In this sort of case, your heirs are actually better off if you do not have a will. See the section on small successions for the details on how to settle an estate without court proceedings.

Without a will, you are considered to have died intestate and the State of Louisiana will make all the provisions as to the division of your property. The division may or may not be close to what you actually wanted, but since you left no binding instructions as to your wishes, a certain amount of guesswork will be made.

The first thing the law will do is make a presumption as to who should be the person responsible for handling the estate. If you appoint someone in a will for this job, he or she is called the executor or executrix. Since you did not have a will, the court will make the appointment and he or she will be called the administrator or administratrix. Anyone who applies to the court can have this job, although there is an order of preference in case more than one person wishes to be responsible for handling your affairs. Preference is given first to the best qualified among the surviving spouse and the adult heirs; then, to the best qualified of the nominees of the surviving spouse and the adult heirs; next, to the best qualified of the creditors of the deceased; and finally, to any other qualified person. As you can see, there can be very bitter court battles between various parties who consider themselves more qualified and even among family members.

Why would anyone want to be the administrator in the first place? Because that person has a great deal of control over the estate and because that person is entitled to a fee for serving as administrator. The person appointed, with the exception of the surviving spouse, has to put up a bond to insure the faithful performance of their duties. This can be an extreme hardship on a family member. If you have a will, you can stipulate that the executor does not have to put up a bond.

Independent Executors. A new provision in Louisiana law allows a testator to designate the executor an "independent" executor. What does this mean? In short, it allows the executor to handle most estate business without having to seek the approval of the judge handling the probate case. This makes the independent executor somewhat more like the trustee of a trust. Although the independent executor is still subject to court supervision and must make a final accounting, the day-to-day workings of the estate can be done faster and with less expense. To make an executor "independent" the testator merely needs to say so in the will. For example, "I hereby name Jane Doe as independent executrix of my estate" would be sufficient.

An executor or an administrator can also be made independent after a death if all the legatees under the will or all the heirs if there is no will consent to the appointment. Again, this can often be desirable since the process of estate administration will usually move faster and with less expense.

Tutorship. The next presumption the law will make, in the absence of your instructions, is who will care for your children. The surviving spouse by right has the job of guardian, or "tutor" as it is called in Louisiana. In the situation where your spouse dies before you do, or where you both die together in an automobile accident, the court will decide who is most fit to raise your children. This can also lead to bitter court battles among family members since the law requires that the judge appoint a tutor or tutrix from among the qualified of the grandparents, great-grandparents, aunts, uncles, great-aunts, great-uncles, brothers, sisters, step-fathers and step-mothers. If you have a good friend who would raise your child the way you think a child should be raised, you had better have a will appointing this person. Otherwise, your maiden great-aunt in Minnesota has a legal preference over the person you would have chosen. Or if you have one brother who would be a disaster as a parent and another brother who you think would do a good job, you had better appoint your choice in a will because the court will not be able to see that there is a difference between your two brothers.

Louisiana used to have some colorful types of wills that were abolished in recent years. Some types were arcane and seldom used because they were complicated or left over from older times. One such type was the "mystic will" in which you handwrote your wishes and sealed them in an envelope. A notary and three witnesses must see you seal the envelope, and all of you must then sign and date the outside of the envelope.

Today there are only two types of wills that are recognized in Louisiana, the "olographic" will and the "notarial" will. Both of these wills have one thing in common: they must be done exactly as the law prescribes, otherwise they are worthless when it is time to go to court.

Olographic Wills

The olographic will (also called a holographic will in some states) is simply a will that is handwritten by you. You state your wishes, date, sign and leave the will for your survivors to find. It is extremely simple but can lead to problems if not properly thought out and executed.

Mrs. Jones, a retired school teacher, entered the hospital for tests and was informed that she would need immediate heart surgery the next morning. That night, she decided to write a will just in case things did not go well the next day. Since she did not have any children, she left most of her belongings to a friend, and the remainder to her sister. She mentioned the fact that she was worried about the next day's surgery and dated the will 2/3/69. The surgery was successful, but Mrs. Jones died six months later of other causes. After the succession was opened, the sister asked that the court give her all of Mrs. Jones' assets since she was the nearest relative and since there was no will. As for the will written in the hospital, the sister said it was invalid since the law requires an exact date, and the date 2/3/69 could be read as February 3, 1969 or the second day of March, 1969. The friend of Mrs. Jones intervened in the case and pointed out to the judge that the date could be proven since Mrs. Jones referred to her surgery in the will. Hospital records introduced by the friend showed that Mrs. Jones was only in the hospital on one occasion in 1969 and that was in the month of February.

The court decided in favor of the sister and said that the exact requirements of the law must be met and that extrinsic evidence to prove the date of the will could not be allowed. In other words, the judge could only consider what was in the will itself, not testimony and hospital records that would remove any ambiguities. In subsequent cases, the courts have decided that other evidence can be used if the date is not clear. Mrs. Jones' friend would probably have won her case if it had been decided today. But in any case where the date is ambiguous, the proof must be certain. Just the year alone, for example, should make the will invalid, although in one case the court allowed outside proof to establish that a will was executed in 1977 when the will itself was dated simply "November 11." Whether a court will eventually allow the will or not, a misdated will leads to suits by potential heirs who would prefer an intestate succession.

The olographic will must be entirely handwritten by the maker, or "testator," and must clearly be intended as a last will. The type of language used by the testator does not necessarily have to be "legal" as long as it is clear that the maker wants to make provisions for how things will be done after his death. A document that was handwritten, dated, and signed, but simply stated "all to my sister" with a list of belongings, was held by the court not to be a valid will since it was not clear that a last will was intended.

> Mr. Burns saw an advertisement for pre-printed wills on television and decided that it was time he made his will and that this would be the easiest and least expensive way to do it. The wills were guaranteed to be valid in all fifty states; all he had to do was fill in the blanks. Mr. Burns filled in the date, his name and the names of the people he wanted to inherit his property together with what each person was to get. After his death, some family members sued to have the will declared invalid because it wasn't entirely handwritten and because it did not fit under the description of any other type of will recognized by Louisiana law.

The court decided that the will was valid to the extent that the portions that were handwritten qualified as an olographic will will. In other words, all the pre-printed parts would be ignored, and if there was enough left to accomplish the intent of the deceased, it was a valid will. Mr. Burns did not have any children, so there were no problems with the forced heirship laws. It was also lucky that he put enough detail in the blanks provided to qualify as a will. But the point is, any time someone claims that a legal document or advice is "valid in all fifty states," you can almost assume that it is not, especially not in Louisiana. We have not yet seen a book produced for nation-wide use that states Louisiana law completely or accurately.

> *Mrs. Kling died at the age of 83 without any close relatives. A spiral notebook was found in her home in which she had written "Will of Elaine Kling." Directly underneath she had written her signature and the date. There were several numbered paragraphs following with words like "house to Caddo Children's Home" and "City Bank savings account to cousin Joe." One of the paragraphs leaving property had been crossed out and some paragraphs had question marks next to them. Mrs. Kling also had written notes in the margins of the notebook about the requirements for executors and some comments unrelated to her will. Mrs. Kling talked to an attorney on the telephone about preparing a will but had not kept her appointment. She did mention to a neighbor that her will was prepared.*

> *When Mrs. Kling died, her closest relatives opposed admitting the notebook to probate by claiming it was not a will but merely a collection of notes needed to prepare a will. The legatees named in the notebook claimed that it was a will since all of the requirements of an olographic will were met: it was hand written, signed, dated, and clearly was intended to dispose of her property. Was Mrs. Kling's notebook a will or notes to prepare a will?*

The court decided that it was not a will since it was not signed at the end. Although the statute authorizing olographic wills does not require that the signature be in any particular place in the will, Louisiana courts have added this requirement through a long line of decisions. If Mrs. Kling had wanted her notebook to be a will, her efforts were wasted because she failed to keep her appointment with her attorney.

After death, the olographic will has to be "probated" or proven. This is done by the testimony of two witnesses who swear that the handwriting on the will is that of the deceased. This testimony is usually done by people who knew the deceased. Even a grocer who had seen the deceased's handwriting on grocery lists has been used as a witness. Sometimes it is necessary to use a handwriting expert when there is a claim that the will is a forgery. The main problem with an olographic will is that there is too much room for claims by disgruntled relatives as to whether the will is genuine. That is one reason the notarial will is a better choice.

Notarial Wills

The notarial will (formerly known as a "statutory will") is a relatively new creation by the Legislature that is probably the best type of will to make, as long as all the requirements are strictly complied with. The will must be dated and must be signed on each page by the testator. This must be done before a notary public and two witnesses and all must sign an attestation clause. The notarial will, if properly done, is self-proving after death. In other words, it is taken on it's face as authentic and no further proof is required. There is very little chance of anyone claiming that the will was forged, that there was any undue influence, or that the deceased was incompetent at the time the will was signed. The notarial will lessens the chances that any of your survivors will try to go against your wishes or start a family squabble.

To probate the statutory testament, on the other hand, the law required that the notary and one witness file affidavits after death confirming that the deceased had indeed executed the will. This was obviously difficult to carry out in most circumstances since the notary and/or witnesses might be dead themselves by the time the testator dies. The notarial testament did away with this requirement.

Although you can prepare the notarial will yourself, it is usually prepared by the same notary who signs the will. As a matter of fact, there is probably a legal presumption that the notary prepared the will, and most notaries would therefore hesitate to sign a will prepared by someone else. The notary may also have to testify one day swearing that he notarized the will. At the very least, you should state in the will that it was not prepared by the signing notary, and you should ask the notary what his or her policy is before coming to the office.

The person executing the will, the witnesses, and the notary must all sign in each other's presence. Even if a witness turns away to answer the telephone during the signing of the will, it can invalidate the whole will. The notarial will must have a concluding paragraph in which it is stated that the will was executed in the presence of the testator, the notary, and the two witnesses. Witnesses must be at least sixteen years old, mentally competent, and may not be heirs or legatees of the testator.

Adam went to a notary to have a notarial will prepared. Since he did not have any children, Adam left property to several nieces and nephews including John, who went with Adam to the notary's office. The notary prepared a statutory will based on Adam's wishes and used his secretary and John as witnesses. After Adam's death, John tried to sell a house he had inherited from Adam, but the attorney examining the title for the buyer refused to render a title opinion. It was the attorney's belief that John's title was not good since there was doubt about the validity of the will that gave John the house. Since John was a witness to the will, and since a legatee cannot qualify as a witness, the attorney felt that the will was invalid. John's attorney filed suit to determine whether his title was good and also sued the notary and his malpractice insurer for damages in case it was decided that the will was invalid.

The court decided that the will was indeed invalid since a will must comply in form to the requirements of law. Since a notarial will must have two witnesses, and since John could not legally qualify as a witness, the document that Adam signed could not be used as a will, and John did not inherit the house Adam had wished him to have. John recovered his losses from the notary since it is assumed that the notary should know what the law provides before attempting to prepare a will.

Whenever possible, the court will try to qualify a will as valid under some other definition of a will, even though the type of will intended may be invalid. For example, if Adam's notarial will had been handwritten by him, it might have qualified as an olographic will and been probated to allow John to inherit the house. Since it was typewritten and there was only one other witness, it could not qualify as either of the types of wills recognized in this state.

The law was amended after John's case to provide that a will is not made invalid just because an heir or legatee signs as a witness. However, the heir or legatee who signs as a witness cannot receive his inheritance. If the case were heard today, the will would be declared valid but the result would be the same. John would not receive the house since he signed as a witness and the notary would still be sued for malpractice.

Recent provisions have also been made by the Legislature to allow people who cannot read to make notarial wills. The requirements for a notarial will under these circumstances are slightly different, but must be followed exactly.

If a person's sight is impaired to the extent that he cannot read, or if he does not know how to read, the notarial will is done in the same manner as described above except the witnesses must be given copies of the will. The will is then read aloud in front of the testator, and the witnesses must follow the reading with their copies. After the reading, the testator must acknowledge that the will is indeed his last will and testament, that he heard the entire reading, and the closing paragraph of the will must state that this procedure was followed and must state the reason that the testator could not sign. A notarial will can also be done in braille if the testator is deaf and able to read and write in braille.

Remember, the olographic will does not have to be witnessed, but at a minimum it must be handwritten, properly dated, clearly be a will, and must be signed by the testator. The notarial will must be dated, must be signed by the testator on each page, and must have a closing paragraph in which a notary and two witnesses together with the testator all acknowledge that this is the testator's will and that they have all signed in each other's presence. An example of an olographic will can be found in the Do It Yourself Guide.

Designating Bank Accounts

A simple sort of estate planning can be done by taking care of how your bank accounts are set up. A bank, credit union or savings association can designate an account as "in trust for", "as trustee for", or "payable on death to" a spouse and/or children or grandchildren. If this is done properly, some of the time delays of the probate system can be avoided. Only close relatives can be named as beneficiaries of this sort of account. You could not name, for example, a charity, or friend. When you set up the account, you must supply the bank an affidavit swearing that the beneficiaries you name on the account are related to you in the degree required. If you do not designate otherwise, the beneficiaries will receive equal shares in the account. If you do not want the shares to be equal, you can designate the percentage interest each person has in the account. The funds in these types of accounts can be paid immediately after death without waiting for probate.

As an example, you could open an account with XYZ Bank & Trust entitled "Joe Blow payable on death to Jane

Blow, Edward Blow, and Ellen Smith." In this case, let's say that Jane is Joe's wife, Edward is his son, and Ellen is his granddaughter. If Joe did not stipulate otherwise when he set up the account, the money in the account would be divided equally among Jane, Edward and Ellen after Joe's death. Or, Joe could have stated on the bank's account records that he wanted one-half of the account to go to Jane and the rest to Edward and Ellen equally.

If you set up this type of account, you have to be careful that there is not a conflict with your will. The statute authorizing these types of accounts states that naming a beneficiary on the account out-weighs any statement in your will. In other words, if your will says that you give all your money in bank accounts to your wife, but one of the accounts names a child as beneficiary, the named bank account will go to the child.

Although money in this type of account can be paid directly to an heir without the delay of probate, it does not eliminate either probate or estate taxes. It merely allows you to see that money can be paid to heirs immediately and without any court proceeding. The money in the account will still be considered part of your estate and will still be subject to death taxes. Also, this law is new and there is some resistance on the part of many banks, credit unions, and saving associations who will not offer these accounts. Some feel there might be liability to other heirs if they pay out these accounts to a named beneficiary. Since the law specifically relieves the bank of any liability to other heirs or for the payment of taxes, it is hard to see why this resistance still exists.

Trusts

A trust is created when the title to property is transferred to a person to be administered by him as a fiduciary for the benefit of another party. A trust can be created while the settlor (the person who creates a trust) is alive, or it can come into effect after the settlor's death. Louisiana has enacted a trust code (*LSA R.S. 1721)* that controls the manner in which trusts may be created. Trusts are usually created for one or both of two reasons: to manage trust assets and distribution to beneficiaries, and to take advantage of possible tax benefits. Anyone considering a trust for the tax benefits needs specific and comprehensive advice because of the complexity of the tax laws and because these laws change so frequently.

The typical trust may be created because a person does not like the idea of his children inheriting his property and receiving his life insurance benefits at the age of eighteen. Let's say that Joe has two children, ages twelve and fifteen. Joe has property worth $120,000 after debts are paid off, and Joe has a term insurance policy that will pay $200,000 at his death. Joe has made his wife beneficiary on his insurance policies with his children as alternate beneficiaries. He has also left his wife all he could under his will and made his children alternate legatees should his wife die before him. At his death, Joe's wife would suddenly be in complete control of $320,000 in assets. If Joe's wife dies before he does, some other person may have control of the money, and when the children turn eighteen, they will each have $160,000 to spend as they please. Joe remembers when he was eighteen and does not want his children to be suddenly, and probably temporarily, wealthy. Joe also feels that there are other family members who would convince his wife to make poor investments.

The solution is for Joe to create a trust. Joe would then leave all or part of his property to the trust in his will, and Joe would make the trust the beneficiary under his life insurance policies. Joe could decide in advance how long the trust would last after the children are eighteen, how the money will be invested and spent, and who will make investment decisions. Joe could provide for a living allowance for his family from the trust income and could stipulate that the trust principal be used for emergencies and for his children's college education. Joe could make a bank or other party the trustee and give the trustee detailed instructions as to how the trust is to be operated.

A trust set up like Joe's would not have any assets until after the settlor dies. A trustee is appointed in the trust instrument, and the trustee's duties are spelled out. The trustee's first duty is to collect all of the assets that have been left in trust and to invest the assets in a prudent and responsible manner. The trustee who fails in his obligations can be held personally responsible for any unwise investments. For this reason, it is usually advisable to make a bank or other stable investment professional the trustee rather than an individual. It is more likely that the individual would not have the training to make investment decisions, and it is more likely that an individual would not have the assets to reimburse the trust if an improper investment decision were made.

A bank will typically charge around one per cent of the trust assets per year with a minimum of $800 to act as trustee, although a higher fee is permissible under the Trust Code. The fee is not charged until the trust comes into effect, which would be at death in Joe's case. Although banks do not normally require that a minimum amount be left in trust, most banks will tell you that a trust below around $100,000 in value is not worth the cost of administration. It is usually a good idea to provide that the trustee can terminate the trust should assets fall below an amount that the trustee feels is worth the expense of keeping assets in trust. If you want to create a trust for a specific purpose, such as making sure there are some assets for a college education, then the cost of running the trust would be secondary, and you would not want to enable the trustee to terminate the trust before your goals were accomplished.

Trust assets can be invested in any reasonably prudent manner unless the settlor puts some restrictions on the manner of the investment. A bank may not accept a trust that unduly restricts how investments will be made since banks will normally pool the assets of many trusts in several types of investments to lessen risk and maximize return. A bank will also require that you dispense with the necessity of the trustee posting a bond to insure the trustee's performance, since this creates an expense for the trustee. Any trust instrument in which you intend to appoint a bank or investment professional as trustee should be approved and accepted at the time the trust is written. This is to insure that all of the bank's requirements are met. If the trust is not accepted prior to death, the proposed trustee can always refuse to accept the trust, leaving the way open for some other party to become trustee, someone that perhaps you would not have chosen.

Joe wants a trust to be sure that no one takes advantage of his wife and to be sure that his children do not squander his money should his wife not survive him. Joe also wants his money to be wisely invested by a professional, and he wants to make sure that a college education is available to his children. Joe has decided that the trust will stay in effect until his last child is twenty-five years old, or until his last child finishes college, whichever comes first. However, Joe is free to change any of the provisions of his trust should circumstances change. Joe is even free to revoke the trust entirely since the type of trust Joe has chosen does not really come into effect until after Joe's death.

We have had clients change their trust many times as their children get older, and they are better able to judge how mature and capable their children are becoming. We have even had a client change the age at which the trust terminates in steps from twenty-one to forty over the years, as he saw his son growing in age, but not in judgment.

Mike has three children from a prior marriage and is also an example of someone who needs a trust. Mike knows that he has to leave a portion of his estate to his children who are under the age of twenty four. But he also knows that as long as his children are under eighteen, their mother may have control of the money that he leaves to them. Of course she is under an obligation to use the money for the benefit of the children, but as a practical matter there is no one to make sure that she does. And if she does not, she may not be financially able to make restitution to the children when they turn eighteen and find that they have no money. Mike can create a trust and make a bank, or even his current wife, the trustee. The trustee can make sure that all expenditures are necessary and for the actual benefit of the children and no one else. Although the prior wife is still the tutor of the children, Mike has made sure that she will have no control over any of his assets that he wants used only for his children. Mike can also stipulate that the trust continue until the children are old enough to use the money wisely, should he feel that eighteen is too young for his children to receive the amount of money that will be in his estate. Mike can even make his trust extend for the lifetime of his children and stipulate that the principal of the trust go to his grandchildren after the deaths of his own children. Mike also knows that the legitime, the portion of his estate that he must give his children, can be tied up in a trust as long as the income from this portion is distributed at least annually. A trust can be an excellent way to get around the forced heirship laws, at least to some extent.

Martha's will established a trust in which she directed that her husband receive as much as possible, including all of the income of the trust for his lifetime; that after his death, her son Johnnie receive the income for his life; that none of her real property be sold after her death; and that the trustee act only after consent from advisors appointed by her in the trust. When Martha died, Johnnie realized that he would receive nothing during his father's lifetime and only income from the trust after his father's death. Johnnie therefore filed suit to have the trust dissolved or, in the alternative, to have it modified to give him income from the portion that was his legitime. Johnnie argued in his suit that since the trustee was responsible and liable for trust decisions, making him depend on trust advisors was against the provisions of the Trust Code. Also, Johnnie argued, the trustee shouldn't be allowed to keep all of the immovable property tied up in land which did not produce income since this also interfered with his forced heirship rights to receive a share during his lifetime.

The court would not dissolve the trust even though there were problems with the trust instrument. Since the Trust Code states that a trust can be interpreted or even modified to comply with the law, the court decided to make modifications that would save the trust.

The trustee must act as a reasonably prudent investor, much the same as he would looking after his own affairs. Since a prudent investor might have expert advisors, there was nothing wrong with a trustee also having advisors. The court did feel that Johnnie's legitime had been impinged. The Trust Code in allowing the legitime to be tied up in trust as long as the forced heir got the income attributable to his forced portion, contemplated that there would at least be some income. Because the property of the trust was mostly in land that produced no income, the court ordered that the trustee sell sufficient land to be able to re-invest in something that produced some income that could be distributed to Johnnie after his father's death.

Federal Estate Tax Exemptions

Every individual is entitled to an estate tax exemption. This basically means that if an estate falls below the exempt amount, no taxes will be due and there will be no requirement to file a federal estate tax return. For married couples, the actual exemption can be doubled —if there is some estate planning in place.

The exempt amount was $600,000 for many years, which meant that with some good planning a couple could exempt $1.2 million from federal estate taxes. The whole area of estate taxes has been changing drastically in recent years which has lead to confusion and a big headache for estate planners.

President Bush signed the Economic Growth and Tax Relief Reconciliation Act of 2001 which was intended to phase out the estate tax over a period of ten years. The intent was to permanently eliminate the estate tax in the final year. Unfortunately, Congress has seen fit to make something relatively simple into a complicated affair. Someone dying in the year 2009 would only pay federal estate taxes if his estate totaled more than $3.5 million and someone dying in 2010 would pay no taxes at all, or would pay taxes on estates worth more than $1 million –depending on the whims of Congress.

So, as it turned out, Congress waited until the final hours of 2009 –and did nothing. That is why Joe Stein-brenner, the owner of the new York Yankees, had the ideal estate plan. His family paid zero estate taxes on an estate worth over a billion dollars because he chose to die in 2010 when there was no estate tax at all.

Here is the multi-million dollar question: if the estate tax was to be phased out, why did it come back again in the year 2011? It is back again because Congress failed to carry though (at this point) with a complete estate tax repeal? The idea of a full repeal of the estate tax was probably doomed from the beginning. At this point Congress passed yet another temporary fix buried in other legislation that created a flawed and temporary $5 million exemption. That exemption is scheduled to end soon after this book goes to press –unless Congress takes some action, or not.

Estate planners at this point just have to plan around the reality of the situation.

Living Trusts

Are living trusts the best estate plan to ever hit Louisiana or are they just a gimmick that do not deliver as promised? Arguments are made on both sides by estate planners who are educated and experienced in this area. The fact that there is controversy makes it hard to decide who to believe and whether a living trust is a good choice for your estate plan. The only way to resolve this question is to first explain what a living trust is, and then go through the good and bad points. You can then decide for yourself.

What is a living trust? The concept of a living trust is not new to Louisiana. Only the name "living trust" and the idea of using this type of trust as part of an estate plan are new. The living trust phenomenon started in California as a method to avoid the probate procedure. The living trust is simply a revocable inter-vivos trust which has been authorized in Louisiana for as long as we have had a Trust Code. A revocable trust can be amended or revoked at any time by the person who creates the trust (the "settlor"). Typically, you would name yourself (and your spouse if you are married) as trustee (or trustees). Upon death or incapacity, you name a successor trustee. In the meanwhile, you receive the income from the trust and can amend or revoke at any time. You can sell assets, borrow money, and, in general, treat the assets in the trust pretty much the same way you did before the assets were in your trust.

Living trusts are said to avoid probate, save taxes, prepare for disability, avoid multiple probates for people with property in more than one state, afford privacy, and allow you to test the ability of a trustee while you are still alive.

Avoiding probate. Does a living trust avoid probate? The basic idea behind any type of trust is that the trust owns assets for the benefit of a person or group of persons. Since the trust, not you, owns the assets, your death is not relevant to how those assets are handled. If you sell your house to a stranger, your house is not part of your estate and is not subject to probate. The same is true if you transfer your house to a trust. You do not own it at the time of your death and probate (but not estate tax) is avoided. As simple as this basic concept sounds, the biggest problem with living trusts is making sure that all assets are properly transferred to the trust. Any asset that is overlooked may make probate necessary.

What exactly are you avoiding if you avoid probate? Louisiana does not impose a probate fee like California and some other states. In Louisiana, the cost of probate is court costs and attorney fees. Court costs will typically be around $500 unless something is contested or if there are minor heirs. In any event, court costs never amount to any significant amount. The attorney fees are another matter. Since attorneys can charge any "reasonable" amount to handle the succession, we have seen fees range from very reasonable to very unreasonable. You might expect the average fee to be about 2% of the gross estate, although we have seen a fee of $25,000 charged for a $85,000 estate. The probate process also involves time delays. It can sometimes takes years to finish a succession and distribute the funds to heirs. More often than not, however, the time to finish a probate is measured in months rather than years.

Tax issues. Do living trusts avoid taxes? A living trust is neutral for federal and state income taxes . Since these types of trusts can be revoked, they are considered an uncompleted gift. It is not complete until you die and can no longer change your mind. You report any income you receive from trust property on your annual 1040 just as you do now. There is no less tax, but there is no additional work. Federal estate taxes, however, are a different matter. A living trust can save a great deal of estate taxes for married couples with an estate that exceeds the federal estate tax exemption. In calculating the size of the combined estate of a married couple, do not overlook the value of death benefits from life insurance.

A living trust created for a married couple can insure that two federal estate tax exemptions are used. This variation of the living trust is sometimes called an A-B living trust and makes provision for the automatic split of the living trust into two trusts when the first spouse dies. The maximum exempt amount for the deceased spouse goes into the "B" trust which is not revocable. The remainder goes into the "A" trust which is still revocable. The surviving spouse is still income beneficiary of both trusts. In the typical situation in which the spouses do not have a will, or in which they have wills that leave everything to each other, only one exemption is available. This happens because one spouse inherits everything from the deceased spouse and does not pay death taxes because of the unlimited marital deduction.

When the surviving spouse dies, however, only one exemption is available for an estate that is made up of all the property owned by the two spouses. The heirs pay federal estate taxes on all amounts over the exempt amount they have received. The tax starts at 37% and rises rapidly to 55% –although this is a moving target since Congress cannot seem to get a handle on what the rates should be.

Although very few people these days are lucky enough to have assets that would benefit from split trusts, the concept is still sound since it is still unclear what will happen in the future. Congress has left this uncertainty an estate planners nightmare. A living trust will save estate taxes when compared to a simple will or no will at all when the property of

134/ Louisiana Legal Advisor

the spouses (including life insurance) exceeds the exempt amount –whatever that may turn out to be.

Detractors of the living trust will quickly point out that both exemptions can be used by leaving the exempt amount to the children by will and giving the spouse the usufruct of the children's inheritance or by setting up a testamentary trust. This is certainly true, but very few people seem to elect these methods of making sure both exemptions are used.

Property in other states. Does owning property in more than one state matter? If you have real estate in two states, lets say a home in Louisiana and a condominium in Mississippi, your heirs will be subject to multiple probate proceedings. Although the law of Louisiana will determine probate procedure, costs and the distribution of your home and movable assets, the laws of Mississippi will control the distribution of your condominium. That is because real estate is subject to the laws of the state where the real estate is located. Your heirs will have to open a succession in Louisiana and they will have to open an ancillary probate proceeding in Mississippi. If you owned real estate in other states, probates would have to opened in each of those states as well.

This problem can be avoided with a living trust. Title to all real estate, regardless of location, is transferred to the trust while you are alive. The trust, through you as trustee or through a successor trustee, can sell the property or distribute the property to your heirs at any time. Since you do not own the property at the time of your death, there is no necessity for any succession or probate. Not in Louisiana, not in Mississippi, and not in any other state.

Disability. How does a living trust handle disability? One of the greatest problems facing our aging population is incapacity. Unfortunately, Louisiana law only provides one procedure for taking over the affairs of someone who is incapacitated. It is called an interdiction and involves the filing of a suit against the person incapacitated. It does not matter whether the incapacity is physical or mental, the incapacitated person must be served by the sheriff with a copy of the suit and must file an answer. If the person cannot respond to the suit (which is usually the case) an attorney is appointed to represent him. The court costs and fees for both sides come out of the incapacitated person's estate if the court agrees that the person cannot handle his affairs. This is an extremely disagreeable and nasty procedure that is costly in terms of money and in terms of damage to family relationships. With a living trust, you appoint a successor trustee who automatically takes over in the event of incapacity. There is no court proceeding, no expense, and you choose the person who handles your affairs and estate rather than the court.

Interdiction proceedings can also be avoided by the use of a power of attorney giving someone that you designate the authority to handle your affairs.

Privacy. Does a living trust give you more privacy? Probate records are public and open to anyone who wants to go to the court house and look at the succession proceeding. The record will show the original of your will (if you had a will), an inventory of all property with values, a list of creditors and how much they are owed, and a list of heirs together with how much each received and how much tax each owed. In other words, the probate process affords no privacy. A living trust, detractors will tell you, also affords no privacy since the trust has to be recorded. The truth is probably somewhere in between.

A trust that owns real estate is supposed to be recorded where the real estate is located. This means that a copy of your trust would be available to anyone who wanted to inspect the conveyance records. A trust, however, does not usually contain the detailed information that a succession proceeding contains. You can create a trust and make transfers of assets to the trust at any time. These assets, other than real estate, would not necessarily be revealed in the trust document. The trust would reveal, in a general sense, who your heirs are. A trust will typically set up classes of beneficiaries. For example, the trust may state that one-half of the assets will eventually go to a class made up of children and one-half to a class made up of grandchildren. Unlike a probate proceeding, there would be no listing of names, addresses, social security numbers, and values of the property received. A trust, generally, contains many pages of legal structure but very little personal information.

There is also the alternative of filing an extract of the trust rather than the trust itself. If a trust owns real estate, the trustee or settlor can elect to file a short summary of the trust instead of the trust itself. This is certainly more private and less expensive to file. However, at some point a title examiner may still require that the trust be filed if there is a sale of real estate by the trust.

When does a successor trustee take over? Most living trusts include detailed provisions for transferring the office of trustee to a successor. The person or spouses who start the living trust are usually trustee until: 1) the last settlor dies, or 2) the last settlor becomes incapacitated, or 3) the last settlor resigns as trustee.

In the typical living trust, a husband and wife are the settlors and the first trustees. If one dies or becomes incapacitated, the other becomes sole trustee. When the last settlor dies or becomes incapacitated, one or more children take over as trustees. The original settlors of the trust, since the trust can be amended or revoked by them, can resign some or all of their powers as trustee in favor of a successor trustee. This gives the settlor the opportunity to turn over some power to a son, for example, and see how he does in taking care of the trust. If the son does not do well, the settlor can replace him. The living trust, unlike most irrevocable trusts, allows you to test your successor trustees before turning over complete control.

Disadvantages. What are the disadvantages of a living trust? The opponents of living trusts insist that other methods of estate planning can accomplish the same goals by using more traditional and tested methods. Those who support living trusts point out that many of the opponents make a comfortable living by writing a will and eventually doing the probate work, thereby having a vested interest in the status quo. The supposed disadvantage that much of what can be accomplished with a living trust can also be accomplished by using a combination of other methods just does not seem like much of a disadvantage. The living trust, if properly done, can be a rather elegant way of accomplishing everything in one document.

Although we do not consider the standard arguments against living trusts to be persuasive, there are a few points you should consider before deciding that a living trust is for you.

1) Living trusts aren't for everybody. Although we generally favor living trusts, they tend to be sold as the answer to everyone's estate planning needs. You should have the right combination of estate planning needs to truly benefit from a living trust. How do you know? You read all you can about the subject and then you talk to an estate planning professional who handles both traditional estate planning methods and living trusts.

2) A living trust costs more than a will. Although the expense of creating a living trust should certainly be far less than the expense of probate, the expense comes now rather than after your death. It is your heirs who benefit in the savings.

3) A living trust usually involves more work. Since the settlor, beneficiary and trustee are initially the same person,

it is advisable to keep complete records of financial transactions. There is also the initial work of transferring assets to the trust and in making sure that records are changed at banks and brokerages showing the change in ownership. On the other hand, your heirs are relieved of a lot of the work involved in settling an estate.

4) A living trust must be prepared by someone who truly is experienced in this area. Having a living trust that is not properly drafted will cause you many more problems than it will solve. Do not attempt to use any mail order or pre-printed form. We have seen many of these types of living trusts—not one was valid in Louisiana. There is one living trust kit that is sold for $12.95 in many Louisiana office supply stores. The cover states that it is "valid in all fifty states." It is not valid in Louisiana because the Louisiana Trust Code requires that all trusts be in authentic act form. In other words, it must have a notary and two witnesses. Another living trust that we have seen was prepared by a Missouri corporation and was certified as valid in Louisiana by someone claiming to be a lawyer. This trust was brought to us after one spouse died and it was immediately obvious that the trust was worthless since it was not an authentic act. This invalid trust cost $1,500, so price alone does not guarantee a good trust.

A living trust must also address forced heirship and other matters peculiar to Louisiana. For example, almost every living trust prepared in the other 49 states will have a power of appointment (the power to authorize someone else to direct where assets go). This type of authority can be illegal in Louisiana. If you are not willing to pay a professional to create a living trust that is drafted for your exact needs and takes into account Louisiana law, you should not be considering living trusts.

5) A living trust does not avoid all probate type expenses. When the first spouse dies there will have to be docu-

ments prepared and valuations made if the trust is going to be divided into A and B trusts. Annual tax returns will have to be filed for the B trust. When the last spouse dies, there may still have to be federal death tax forms to be prepared and filed. The fees involved should be considerably less than would be involved in a probate.

A living trust, if properly done, can be an excellent estate planning tool. But like any tool, it has to be suited to the person using it.

Irrevocable Trusts

The living trust is an example of a revocable trust. That is, it can be changed, amended or revoked at any time. An irrevocable trust, on the other hand, can not be changed once it is created. Why would anyone want an irrevocable instead of a revocable trust? Quite simply because a revocable trust is generally tax neutral while an irrevocable trust may have tax advantages.

Since the federal government taxes estates that exceed the exempt amount and since the tax starts at 37% and goes up, people with taxable estates are interested in ways to pass more of their estates to their children rather than to the government. If an estate is kept below the exempt amount, there is no federal estate tax. One way to keep an estate small is to spend enough money to insure that it never becomes large, something that all of us do well. Assuming you want to pass assets to family members and still not pay as much estate taxes, an irrevocable trust may be the answer.

The concept is simple. You create a trust, which is a separate legal entity from yourself, and you transfer some of your assets to the trust. Since you do not own the assets when you die, your estate is not taxed for those assets. Unfortunately, there are many laws, rules and regulations that make this simple concept difficult and that keep armies of accountants and tax attorneys busy.

The federal government is not going to just let you give property to a trust to avoid estate taxes. Any gift over $13,000 is subject to gift tax at the same rate as estate taxes. In addition, a gift must be something with a present value to the person who receives the gift. Since the beneficiaries of a trust have no immediate right to the use of the gift, a trust would not be entitled to any of the $13,000 exclusion. To avoid the problem of present value, a trust can be structured so that each beneficiary has the right to take out his share of a gift made to the trust within a reasonable time after the gift is made. These types of trusts are called "Crummey Trusts" and would allow, for example, a married couple with three children to get as much as $78,000 per year out of their estates. Assuming the beneficiary does not exercise his right to take out his share of the gift (which is the whole point of the Crummey Trust), the trust could become quite large and save a considerable amount of estate taxes. Gifting to a trust is also subject to special rules that can somewhat reduce the $13,000 exclusion depending on the size of the trust and other factors.

Insurance trusts also are a method of reducing the size of an estate and the resulting taxes. The proceeds of life insurance are counted as part of your estate for federal estate tax purposes if you own or have any powers over the policy. In other words, if you have a life insurance policy with a cash value of $10,000 that will pay $500,000 when you die, the $500,000 (not the $10,000) will be added to your estate and will be subject to federal estate taxes. If you transfer owner-ship of the policy to someone else, the policy will not be part of your estate when you die. However, there are rules that complicate how this must be done. If you transfer ownership of a policy to a trust, for example, you must survive for a period of at least five years (three years if the transfer is to a person). If you die within the five year period, the amount paid by the policy will be counted in your estate. The cash value of the policy, if any, would be subject to a gift tax.

If you want to get the value of life insurance out of your estate and set up a method that controls how the proceeds of your life insurance will be used, it is best to create a trust and have the trust purchase a policy on your life. This avoids the five year wait problem. You could then make annual gifts to the trust that would enable it to pay the premiums on the insurance.

Charitable Trusts

If you are at all interested in leaving some of your estate to a charity when you die, a charitable trust can be an excellent way to accomplish this goal while giving you immediate tax advantages. There are several variations on the charitable trust. For example, you could transfer $100,000 to a trust and stipulate that you will receive 8% income from the trust for your life. You would receive 8% of the value of the trust even if the income actually realized by the trust is lower. The percentage stipulated in the trust instrument is guaranteed regardless of what else happens in the economy. Upon your death, the remainder of the trust assets would be distributed to the charity. You would receive a tax deduction on your income tax return for the present value of the contribution. This deduction could be carried forward an additional four years, if necessary. Stocks or other assets that would ordinarily be subject to capital gains taxes when sold would not incur a capital gains tax if transferred to a charitable trust and then were sold by the trustee.

A charitable trust can also be set up to pay someone else income after you are gone. For example, the trust could pay you and your spouse income and then pay the surviving spouse for his or her life. The number of people you want to receive income and the amount of the income influences how much of a charitable deduction you may have. The deduction can be taken on your income tax return for the year that you set up the trust. If the deduction is more than you can take in one year, you can carry the deduction over for additional years. You can also make additional contributions to the trust in the future for some types of charitable trusts.

A charitable trust can be used with an insurance trust to produce an interesting combination. The charitable trust is set up to produce enough extra income to pay you and to pay the premiums on a life insurance policy that is owned by a separate trust. The beneficiaries of your policies are the heirs that would have received the funds that are now in the charitable trust. If done properly, you receive the same income you had before, your heirs receive their inheritance through life insurance instead of from your estate, the charity receives your donation, estate taxes are reduced because your estate is smaller, and you receive a large income tax deduction.

There are many types of irrevocable trusts that can be created to handle a particular estate planning need. They share one thing in common, however. They can be extremely complicated and must be handled by a professional who knows every aspect of the tax laws involved. We have discussed a few types of trusts on a very basic level just to give you some idea of how trusts work. The details of how these trusts must be set up would require a separate book.

Gifts

A gift is a transfer of property from one person to another, usually without receiving anything in return. The more proper legal term for this transfer under Louisiana law is "donation." Like everything else, a donation is subject to limitations and restrictions. Failure to follow the proper form can result in consequences that may not have been intended by the donor, the person making the gift, or the donee, the person receiving the gift.

As a general rule, everyone is free to give whatever he wants to whomever he wants. As you may have guessed, the law sets forth specific requirements as to how the donation is to be accomplished. The donation of real estate must be by an authentic act, that is, it must be done in writing and signed before a notary and two witnesses. Even a donation of movable property, such as furniture or automobiles, must be done by an authentic act unless the donation is accompanied by actual delivery and acceptance by the donee. In other words, if you wanted to donate a bank account to your nephew, you could do it by authentic act or by delivery. You would do it by authentic act when you describe the account, make it clear that you intend a donation, and both of you sign the act in front of a notary and two witnesses. You could do the same thing by delivery if you go to the bank and your nephew accepts a transfer of the account to him. A donation of movable property by actual delivery and acceptance is called a "manual gift."

There are also restrictions on who can be a donor and who can be a donee. A minor cannot make a donation except through a will if he or she is sixteen or older. A minor, however, can be a donee. Even an unborn child can receive the benefit of a donation as long as the child has been conceived at the time of the gift and is subsequently born alive. A donation cannot be made to a physician or minister who has professionally attended the donor during an illness that led to the donor's death. This is to avoid donations, directly or by will, to a person who is in a position to unduly influence the deceased. This prohibition would not be against a doctor or minister who is related by blood to the deceased, and it would not prevent a donation to compensate the donee for actual services rendered. Also, the prohibition is against a donation to an individual. The donee could still make the donation to the minister's church.

Prior to 1987, persons living together in "open concubinage" could not donate real estate to each other, and they could not donate property other than real estate if the donation exceeded 10% of the donor's property. Open concubinage is the situation in which a man and woman live together as husband and wife when the parties are not actually married and when they make no attempts to hide the illicit nature of their relationship. If the couple subsequently marries, any donation made before the marriage is good.

Times change and the 1987 Legislature repealed the law against donating to a concubine. This type of donation had been prohibited since the Civil Code of 1808 and before. It is unclear, however, whether wills and donations in favor of a concubine made before the law was repealed are invalid. Many people live together these days and would probably be dismayed to know that a donation, whether directly or by will, might be invalid.

William and Effie were in their fifties and had been carrying on an affair for many years. William left everything to Effie in his will except the forced portion which he left to his son Junior. After William's death, Junior sued to have the donation to Effie declared null since the two, Junior claimed, had lived in open concubinage. If the donation was indeed null, Junior would inherit everything. Junior had Effie's house watched by two detectives prior to William's death so he could break up the relationship. At the trial, the detectives testified that William spent about 85% of his time at Effie's house, usually overnight. Effie did not deny that William spent most of his time at her house and further confirmed that they usually had sexual relations. It was also proven at the trial that William did not keep his clothes at Effie's house, and that he usually only brought his shaving kit.

The court, no doubt uncomfortable with the idea of undoing a will because of open concubinage, found that they were not really living with each other. William and Effie both kept separate houses even though William spent most of his time at Effie's house. Since William did not even keep his clothes at Effie's house, the court reasoned, they were not really living together as man and wife.

Bob and Roger lived together as lovers for many years. Before Bob met Roger, Bob adopted Stan, an adult, in a notarial act of adoption. Bob also left all of his $700,000 estate to Stan in a typewritten will. Bob was never married and had no children or other living relatives except for two cousins. When Bob found out that he was dying, he wrote out a hasty will by hand that left everything to Roger. After the death, Roger filed to probate the will. Stan objected and claimed that even if the will could be proved to be valid, Bob and Roger were living together in open concubinage and that Roger therefore could only get 10% of the estate.

When this case was heard on appeal in 1987, the court was presented with a novel issue: could homosexuals live together in open concubinage? If they could, Roger's $700,000 inheritance would have to be cut to at least $70,000. The court decided that it was actually an easy case. Open concubinage is the living together as man and wife when there is really no marriage. Since two men cannot get married, they cannot possibly hold themselves out to the public as a married couple.

The court also decided that the will Bob had scribbled shortly before his death was valid and that the prior typewritten will was therefore void. But Roger still did not inherit the entire estate. Why didn't Roger get the whole $700,000? Because the notarial adoption was held to be valid, which made Stan a forced heir. Even though Stan wasn't mentioned in the will, he inherited 25% of the estate as a forced heir and Roger inherited 75% of the estate under the terms of the will.

This idea of not being able to donate to someone with whom you are living without benefit of matrimony is a good example of how people can be really hurt by obscure laws. To be safe, anyone who made a will or donated property to a concubine prior to September 1, 1987, should prepare a new will or donation to be certain that the old prohibition does not apply.

There are still other limitations on donating property. The law prohibits someone from giving away everything that he owns. This may sound strange, but Louisiana law requires that a person keep at least enough for his own subsistence. Any donation that violates this law is subject to nullification. The courts have lessened the harshness of this rule by deciding that someone with a steady income always has enough for subsistence and can therefore give away everything else.

You can't avoid the forced heirship laws by donating property before your death and, for the same sort of reasons, you can't avoid inheritance taxes by giving things away while you are alive. The federal government now has a unified gift and estate tax that, in effect, taxes gifts you make during your lifetime as a deduction against your estate tax credit. Any person can make gifts of $13,000 or less free of federal gift taxes to as many individuals as he or she wants each year. Any gift above that amount is subject to a gift tax (which can be applied to your unified credit), and a gift tax return must be filed by the donor with the Internal Revenue Service.

The $13,000 gift exclusion is not available unless the recipient of the gift has the immediate right to use the gift. For that reason, the gift tax exclusion usually does not apply to a gift made to a trust. In other words, you cannot set up a trust and then donate money to the trust each year to take advantage of the annual exclusion. A type of trust commonly known as the Crummey trust, if properly drafted, can qualify for the annual $13,000 gift tax exclusion. The trust must allow each beneficiary the right to withdraw his or her portion of the gift within a reasonable time after the gift is made. Gifts to a Crummey trust also must comply with IRS regulations that can become complicated. For example, it is expected that the beneficiary will decline to remove his portion of the gift from the trust. When he declines and leaves his gift in the trust, he is making a partial gift to the other beneficiaries. At least that is the way the IRS views it. For that reason, rules have been established that can limit the effective exclusion to as low as $5,000, depending on the total value of the trust. As you can see, this is an area that requires expert advice and careful preparation.

Louisiana repealed it's own flavor of the gift tax soon after the inheritance tax was repealed. At least that is one estate planning headache that no longer exists.

The law makes an interesting distinction between donating so much property that it interferes with the forced heirship laws and donating so much property that it interferes with keeping enough for subsistence. A donation that interferes with forced heirship rights is subject to reduction. In other words, if you have three forced heirs and give away $60,000 of your $100,000 estate to a third person, your forced heirs have the right to have your donation reduced to $50,000 so that their forced portion is left intact. If you donate your property, let's say to a church, but do not leave enough for your subsistence, any interested party can have the entire donation nullified, not just reduced.

Collation

Payments made by a parent or other ascendant during his lifetime to a forced heir can also cause problems. Louisiana law presumes that any transfer of property made by an ascendant to a forced heir is intended to be an advance payment of a part of that heir's forced portion. The other forced heirs have the right to demand that lifetime payments to co-heirs be returned to the succession for equal distribution to all the forced heirs. This is called "collation" and can cause many problems unforeseen by the parent, including suits between brothers and sisters.

Margaret was a wealthy widow with four children and several grandchildren. Over a period of several years, Margaret gave to her children gifts of about $2 million. She took care to see that the gifts were equal in value so that each child would be treated the same. However, two of Margaret's children requested that their gifts be made instead to a trust for their children, Margaret's grandchildren. Margaret prepared a hand written will which gave the remainder of her estate to all the children equally. The will also stated that all gifts made by Margaret to her children during her life were to be considered an extra portion and should not be collated. After Margaret died, the two children who asked that their gifts be given instead to the grandchildren sued the other heirs and demanded collation. They claimed that they had not received all that they should because the grandchildren received the trust payments.

There are exceptions to the presumption that all transfers to forced heirs are subject to collation. The person making the transfer can state in the instrument making the transfer, or in a document that is executed before a notary and two witnesses after the transfer, that the transfer shall not be collated. Also, a gift that is hand delivered by the parent to the child for that child's personal pleasure or use is not subject to collation. Margaret stated in her will that she did not want the gifts collated. However, her will was hand written. The court decided that since the will was not notarized and witnessed as it would have been in a statutory will, the portion of the will dispensing with collation was invalid. The court did decide, however, that the gifts to the grandchildren should be counted towards the portion that should have been received by the two children who brought the suit. After all, they were the ones who refused the gifts so that their own children would benefit.

After this case, the law was changed to allow collation to be dispensed with in any type of valid will, including the type of will that Margaret executed. Because of forced heirship and the collation problem, you should always make it clear that any transfers to your children are intended to be an extra portion and not subject to collation. This can be done with a statement as to a particular transfer that is notarized and witnessed or it can be done with a will that covers all your lifetime transfers.

Suits among brothers and sisters are more frequent than most people would like to believe. We have found that the best way to avoid this problem is to remove the temptation for heirs to sue each other. A general statement in your will that you do not want transfers to your descendants collated will apply to all transfers made by you to your heirs. It will even apply to transfers made by you after your will is executed.

Even if you dispense with the necessity for collation, the right still exists if the value of the transfers exceed the disposable portion. In other words, you still cannot impinge on the forced portion and the part that interferes with the forced heirship laws can still be collated by the heirs.

As you can see, even something that should be simple, like giving someone a gift, can be complicated by legal presumptions, restrictions and taxes. As a general rule, you can give anyone $13,000 in a year without being concerned about the federal gift tax consequences. Also, gifts to religious or charitable institutions are not necessarily subject to gift taxes. Any gift you wish to make to an individual or a charity above $13,000 should be done with the advice of a tax expert and after a consideration of the forced heirship and collation laws.

Recently, to keep in line with the elimination of forced heirship for children 24 years of age or older who are not permanently disabled, the law of collation was also modified. Civil Code Article 1235 now says: *"The right to demand collation is confined to descendants of the first degree who qualify as forced heirs, and only applies with respect to gifts made within the three years prior to the decedent's death, and valued as of the date of the gift. Any provision of the Civil Code to the contrary is hereby repealed."* As you can see, this certainly avoids the problem of having to go back over a lifetime of gifts made to children to see what might have to be collated.

Asset Protection

What is asset protection? In short, where estate planning is geared towards making sure assets go where you want after your death with the least amount of taxes, asset protection is geared more towards making sure assets stay with you and your family during your life. An obvious result of good asset protection techniques is that there should be more available for your heirs through estate planning. That is, there should be if you do a good job with asset protection.

The Risks

If you carefully save money, have good credit, and avoid risky investments, do you really have to worry about being sued or being forced into bankruptcy?

What if you cause a traffic accident and put someone into a wheelchair for life? A recent case put the tab at $5 million *just for future medical bills*. Do you have a $5 million liability policy? Do you at least have some sort of umbrella policy? The fact is, there is almost no upside limit to potential liability. If you are at fault you will be sued and the insurance you have may not be nearly enough. All your non-exempt assets will be subject to seizure: you bank accounts, your stock and other investments, and your home. Yes, your home. Most people don't understand that a home is not exempt from seizure, only the first $35,000 in value is exempt. So, a creditor can seize your home sell it for whatever it is worth, and is only obligated to pay you $35,000.

At this point we are only talking about legitimate suits by people who may be injured or killed through your fault. What about suits by others who are just searching for deep pockets? It is estimated that 50,000 lawsuits are filed each and every day in this country. If you have worked hard to accumulate some assets, you will be more of a target than someone who has nothing. That, unfortunately, is just human nature.

So, what can you do to protect yourself, other than immediately increasing your liability insurance? You look at how much you need to live on and put enough assets into investments that creditors cannot touch to make sure you are not wiped out.

Creditor-proof Assets

Some types of assets are beyond the power of creditors to reach. For a good example, let's look at the case of the $40,000 dining room table.

In 1825, the Irish furniture company of Mack, Williams & Gibton created a beautiful dining room table. This four-pedestal, mahogany table found it's way to the United States as the result of a buying expedition undertaken by a wealthy cotton planter who was furnishing his plantation home prior to the Civil War.

A few generations later, one of the heirs of the plantation owner sold the table to an established antique dealer on Royal Street in New Orleans. The table was restored with care to it's original glory and was purchased by the president of a local savings and loan for the sum of $40,000. It decorated his house for years until the great savings and loan scandals of the middle 1980's put the savings and loan president out of business and into prison.

The savings and loan president had many, many creditors, including the United States government which had fined him close to a million dollars as part of his sentencing. Everything was lost to creditors. Everything, that is, except the Mack, Williams & Gibton table. How was the former savings and loan president able to keep a table that was easily worth more than $40,000 in the face of so many relentless creditors? Simply because of Louisiana Revised Statute 13:3881 which states that certain things are exempt from seizure. You will be happy to know that regardless of debt, suits, or even bankruptcy, nobody can take your chickens, one cow, family portraits, chinaware and *dining room table*, "used by him or a member of his family." The list of exempt assets is actually quite extensive, but the point is that nobody could touch his table because a statute specifically made the asset exempt from seizure. As a practical matter, some recent cases have indicated that an intrinsically valuable item that is more decorative than useful would not necessarily be exempt. However, it can still be argued that the type of table we are discussing would still be considered exempt:

The purpose of telling this story is not to get you excited about the idea of investing in antique furniture as a way to preserve assets, but to introduce you to the idea that the law makes some things safe. They are safe from ex-spouses, from bankruptcy filing (even your own), and from lawsuits.

Now we can get to the types of assets that are important, can make up a large portion (or even all) of a family's wealth, and are also exempt from seizure. These are investment quality assets that creditors cannot touch.

Retirement plans. Specifically on the list of "things" that creditors cannot touch are qualified retirement plans, such as IRAs (including Roths), Keoghs and 401(k) accounts. You could have $100,000 in a CD at the bank and $100,000 in an IRA and despite any bad luck you might encounter (other than bad investments), that IRA will still be there while the CD would be available for seizure by any creditor in the blink of an eye.

Life insurance. The proceeds and cash value of life insurance are not only exempt from seizure by the policy owner's creditors, the creditors cannot go after the assets upon the death of the owner —not even if the insurance is payable to the owner's estate. So, even if our owner of the $40,000 table had a million dollar policy payable to his children, none of his creditors could touch a penny of the money, not even once his children received their shares.

Annuities. Life insurance is generally payable after your death while annuities are available as an investment while you are alive. Unlike IRAs and similar retirement plans that limit the amount that you can invest in a year, you could transfer all your wealth into an annuity or group of annuities which would put those investments beyond the reach of creditors. There is one exception: transfers made within a year of a creditor getting a judgment against you would not be exempt. This exception is to keep people from defeating an existing claim by simply putting their money into annuities just before a seizure. Asset planning with any exempt class of investments takes thinking ahead and not waiting until trouble is already at the door.

An annuity is basically a contract with a life insurance company that provides a means to invest and pay out income while you are alive and then to your named beneficiaries when you are gone. Annuities can also be left in deferral and allowed to grow. There are many flavors of annuities, but most have some things in common:

- Income taxes on the growth of the annuity are deferred and are only payable on withdrawals (like an IRA).

- You can leave the annuity alone to grow, or you can "annuitize" at some point to create an income stream for yourself and your family.

- Anything left in an annuity when you die is paid to your beneficiaries.

- Annuities are very safe investments since they are backed by an insurance company and by a pool guaranteed by other insurance companies.

- Annuities pass to heirs immediately and free of probate.

- Most annuities are guaranteed against loss, the initial investment (and sometimes gains) is always protected.

There are three major types of annuities: fixed, variable and indexed. The fixed annuity pays interest at a determined rate. It can be left to grow at that rate, or the income interest can be taken out as payments, or a set amount can be taken out. Variable annuities actually involve investments in the stock market and are the only major type of annuity that can involve risk for the investor. Indexed annuities are usually indexed to the S&P 500 or some other market indicator so that there is a guarantee of no loss, yet the potential to share in the growth of the stock market.

Variable annuities lost a great deal of money for some investors in recent years and gave all annuities a bad name. The indexed annuity was the insurance industry's answer by creating an investment that was safe (none of the investment is actually in the stock market), guaranteed not to go down in value when the market does poorly, yet able to go up in value when the market does well. Many indexed annuities also guarantee that any gains will not be lost. So, if the annuity goes up in value by 15% in a year, that is the new guaranteed point and any losses in the market in following years will not reduce whatever gains have been realized.

Offshore Trusts and Banking

This "glamorous" side of asset protection brings up images of numbered Swiss bank accounts and tropical havens where your money is hidden from creditors and from Uncle Sam. There are a few fairly obvious risks with offshore asset protection techniques and some risks that are less obvious.

One obvious risk is that you are making yourself financially dependent on the political stability of the foreign country that will have your investments. It is not only the stability of the country, it is the ability of the country to withstand the pressure from Washington to divulge information or change their laws to allow the exchange of information. Switzerland is a good example of increased cooperation in tracking down money laundering that can result in the disclosure of private information.

Other countries that have (at the present time) strong secrecy laws to protect your information are the Cayman Islands, the Bahamas, and the Cook Islands. Other nations are also now competing for your investment dollars, with Belize looking like a good prospect. All these countries have in common a few things: relatively stable governments, favorable tax laws, and strong secrecy laws.

So, it is quite possible to set up a bank account in the Caymans and wire transfer your money into a secret account just days before the sheriff is scheduled to seize your assets. The down side of this strategy is that you remain a citizen of the United States. What some people fail to think through in this strategy is the subpoena power that creditors have. So, consider this: if you are asked under oath what you did with your money, are you going to lie? The creditor knows that you had $1 million in investments until last week. If you refuse to answer, the creditor will get a court order compelling your answer and now failure to disclose can mean contempt of court and jail time.

On the whole, why not just avoid these issues and gray areas? Investment in assets that the law exempts from seizure is a rock-solid way to protect yourself and your family.

IRA Planning

IRAs will probably soon surpass home ownership as the single most valuable asset a person owns. With employment benefits being rolled over to IRAs, it isn't uncommon to see an IRA worth millions. Most people are familiar with the concept of home ownership and have a pretty good grasp on how to maximize the value of their home and how to pass the home on to their heirs. IRAs are a different story. Very few people, including tax professionals and investment advisors, understand the complexity of the IRA and how valuable an estate planning tool it can be *if you know how to use it properly*.

Basic Concepts

The first concept to understand with this type of investment is that the laws surrounding IRAs preempt Louisiana inheritance law. So, if you have left your ex-spouse's name as beneficiary on your IRA but name your new spouse as receiving "all your property" in your will, federal law requires that your IRA go to your ex-spouse. What you do with a will or anything else is irrelevant in the face of how you chose to list your beneficiary on your IRA. As with many aspects of the IRA, the Internal Revenue Service is unforgiving with beneficiary designations and mistakes of this type cannot be fixed.

The next concept that needs to be appreciated more than understood is the importance of compounding in conjunction with the deferral of taxes. Inherent in the concept of the IRA, is that all the taxes you deducted and deferred (if any) when you made contributions and all the income taxes on the growth of the IRA investment over the years that have also been deferred, must be paid at some point. The longer you can defer the payment, the more money you have working for you. This will be the case in nearly every situation: you want to put off giving Uncle Sam his share as long as possible.

The reason you want to delay payment of deferred taxes until the bitter end is the miracle of compounding. We will look at an example of what this miracle can do not only for you, but also for your children and even grandchildren a bit later.

Finally, it is extremely important to understand what will happen with your IRA once you are gone. It is important because 1) nearly everyone dies without using up their IRA, and 2) how you set up your IRA will determine whether your children and grandchildren will be able to further grow the IRA you started or whether they will get slammed with all those taxes Uncle Sam has been waiting to get.

Failing to make sure your IRA can be "stretched" so that your children can continue to take advantage of deferral and compounding is probably the biggest estate planning mistake made. You want to make sure that your children have options other than the most common one: immediate liquidation and payment of all deferred taxes. This is the option taken 69% of the time and results in the loss of almost half of the value of the IRA in most cases. Not only is the IRA lost, but all the money that would have been made in the future by not paying the taxes and letting the money grow is also lost. Again, the miracle of compounding together with deferral is the goal we should be working towards.

IRAs that can be passed on to children and grandchildren because you planned things properly are called "stretch", "inherited", or even "multi-generational". "Inherited" IRA is probably the most accurate term to use, but we will be referring to IRAs that can continue for decades after your death as "stretch" IRAs since that seems to be the most common term.

The Stretch IRA

The "stretch" or "inherited" IRA is usually set up for descendants. That is, children, grandchildren, and so on. You can also set up a stretch IRA for your nephew, domestic partner or girlfriend. Basically, a stretch can be done for any individual that you can make a beneficiary of your IRA. You can create a trust that can benefit from a stretch and a charity can be a beneficiary under certain circumstances, but that is beyond the scope of this book.

The stretch IRA is not a particular product or type of IRA. This is a common misconception as is the idea that the stretch is an equivalent to an IRA rollover. Only a spouse can actually rollover a deceased spouse's IRA to their own IRA. There is a great deal of confusion on this issue as people are told one minute that their children will be able to rollover their IRA once they are gone and are told the next minute that this cannot be done. The confusion is compounded because the rules have changed drastically in recent years and many "experts" who advise investors are still giving advice that might have been accurate several years ago, but certainly isn't now.

A stretch and a rollover are not the same for several reasons, but here are the two most important, with a rollover you can:

- Add more money until you reach mandatory minimum withdrawal age (usually 70½).

- Continue to defer minimum distributions until you reach the mandatory withdrawal age.

On the contrary, with a stretch the beneficiary cannot ever add to the investments regardless of age, and the beneficiary must start taking Required Minimum Distributions almost immediately, also regardless of age.

So, if a stretch is not a particular type of IRA, how do you make sure that your children and grandchildren can continue to benefit from the deferral and compounded growth of your IRA? It is relatively simple:

- The beneficiary designations you put on your IRA must be correct and set up to allow the option of stretching.

- The custodian of your IRA must be able to handle a stretch.

Beneficiary designations. The beneficiary designations are your call. If you don't do this correctly, your children may or may not be able to fix this after your death. For example, if you name your children as beneficiaries (after your spouse) but don't name grandchildren as successor beneficiaries, then your children may have to disclaim their interest if they want to further defer taxes in favor of their children. This can get complicated and they may not even know the possibility exists unless they are getting really good tax advice. If you simply make sure you include both generations, then your children will have more options open to them.

You may also want to specifically include grandchildren first in line (after a spouse) for a portion of your IRA so that they have a lifetime of deferral and compounding working for them. For example, you could name your two children as beneficiaries of 50% of your IRA and your six grandchildren as beneficiaries of the other 50% of your IRA. Your children would start receiving distributions soon after your death based on their life expectancies. However, your grandchildren's distributions would be at their life expectancies and would extend over a much longer period of time. Now you would have deferral and compounding working perhaps fifty years after your death.

The reason we say that a spouse should normally always be the first beneficiary named is that a spouse is the only person who can do a true rollover of the deceased spouse's IRA to their own name. This has no tax consequence and is usually the best strategy. However, there can be situations where a spouse is better off as an IRA beneficiary rather rolling the IRA over.

Choosing a custodian. The custodian or administrator of your IRA is an extremely important part of the stretch strategy. It is sad but true that a fairly significant number of investment companies acting as IRA trust custodians don't know anything about stretching. In fact, if the custodian does not provide for a stretch capability within the contract they have with you as beneficiary, then a stretch may not even be possible. There can be ways around this problem, but your children would need to know how and the fix (if a fix is even possible) must be done within a relatively short time after your death. It is far better to make sure that whoever handles your IRA is knowledgeable as to stretch IRAs and is already set up to handle the account for the next generation and even beyond.

We have seen investment companies tell their clients that they can handle a stretch, but the truth is that they cannot.

They only know that a "stretch" is something the client seems to want, so they are therefore sure they have such an animal rather than see the investment moved elsewhere. The only acceptable way a stretch account can be set up after you are gone would be something like: "John Smith, deceased 9/9/05, for the benefit of Jim Smith and Jane Smith." It is probably better still to actually split the stretch into separate IRAs for each beneficiary, which is something else that can be done by a knowledgeable administrator.

Another critical point with the choice of an custodian of your stretch IRA involves the assumptions that have to be made about the very reason a stretch works: growth. If your IRA is not growing in value above inflation so that the Required Minimum Distributions that the beneficiary must take out are not keeping pace in real dollars, then the whole thing is not really going to work the way it should. So, here are a few things from the custodial side that will jeopardize that growth and the ultimate success of the stretch IRA:

- Commissions and fees.
- Risky or volatile investments.
- Investments that are traditionally low interest (CDs).

The key to IRA investments and especially stretch IRAs is safety. If you want to go with a broker's advice that Gizmo, Inc. is the latest up and coming stock, then that's fine —if the possibility of growth at the risk a high loss is acceptable to you. However, the whole concept of the stretch IRA is contrary to risk. There has to be slow and steady growth if the investments are going to fund reasonable sums for Required Minimum Distributions. Losses are not compatible with the idea of deferral and growth.

Ideally, the stretch IRA should be invested in a manner that removes the risk of loss and, better yet, with a guarantee of at least some level of gain. Further, commissions, fees, and loads are also geared more towards producing income for someone else, not for your stretch. If the custodian of your IRA is going to be doing some buying and selling over the years (and some selling will have to take place to fund distributions in a typical brokerage account), that is not conducive to steady growth. Also, if your present advisor is someone you like and trust, that person will not be around long enough to see your stretch through the next couple of generations.

There are investment vehicles that make more sense for a stretch IRA. One safe investment is a fixed or indexed annuity with a major insurance company. This will be the case for several reasons:

- There are no fees or commissions at any time.
- The amount you invest is guaranteed not to lose money.
- The gains in each year can also be guaranteed against. loss
- Insurance companies have a great deal of experience as custodians of large sums of money.
- With an annuity, there can be growth keyed to the growth of the market (without the risk) and/or there can be a guaranteed minimum amount of return that is added to the investment each year.

When you are looking at the performance and safety of your IRA investments over not just your lifetime, but the lifetimes of your beneficiaries, it is critically important that the custodian be able to offer absolute safety together with guarantees against loss. Insurance companies seem to be the only institutional custodians that can guarantee against loss. The annuity investment also insures that there will never be someone in charge of your IRA account that may make risky market decisions and charge a commission into the bargain.

Tax Deferral and Compounding

You will never make money for yourself or your beneficiaries with a certificate of deposit. Why? Because of the miracle of deferral and compounding. With a CD, you are paid a low rate of interest and the small income you do realize is subject immediately to income tax. With an IRA (and other tax-deferred investments like annuities), the income accumulates and grows *including what would have gone to pay taxes*. So, if what you would have paid Uncle Sam instead earns more income for you, not only this year but in every year it is allowed to grow, you have deferral and compounding.

As an extreme example of how much wealth can be built up by making sure taxes are not paid any sooner than required, suppose you include a one year-old grandson in your stretch IRA as a beneficiary of $100,000. Upon your death, he would inherit that IRA and would be required to take out minimum distributions starting almost immediately and continuing over his entire life —which the tables say will be about 82 years. That first year he would be required to take out about $1,200. At college age he would have to take out about $5,000, however he could take out more to fund his college education if he wanted. At age 40, and assuming he has been taking out the minimum distributions (as he should) his distributions would be around $25,000 each year. At 70, he would be up to about $250,000 per year. Can you guess how much he would actually receive over his lifetime if he lived to the year he was expected to die? Believe it or not, he would receive over $8 million in payments from that initial $100,000 you left him.

Successions

When someone dies, there must be an orderly way to determine what happens to his property and his debts. In Louisiana, this process is called the succession. The succession is the transmission of the estate of the deceased to the successors. The successors are the heirs and legatees. The estate means the rights, obligations, and property that a person leaves after his death together with whatever income, charges, property, and rights may accumulate after death but before the succession is closed. The estate is transmitted to the successors immediately upon death, but the successors do not have the right of possession until the requirements of law are met.

Successions are either testate or intestate. They are testate when the deceased left a valid will, and the people who inherit are called testate successors or legatees. They are intestate when the deceased left no valid will, and the people who inherit are called intestate successors or heirs. When a succession is intestate, the law defines who the successors will be, and to what percentage of the estate they are entitled.

Intestate Successions

Many people assume that they do not need a will because they believe their spouses will inherit everything anyway. Well, it isn't that simple. Whether a spouse or someone else will inherit depends on whether the property is community or separate, and it depends on what relationship or class the person falls in. Depending on the circumstances, it is even possible for a nephew to inherit before a spouse does.

Community property is treated differently than separate property Property accumulated during a marriage is presumed to be community property. However, property acquired before the marriage, inherited property, and gifts to one spouse are examples of separate property. Property might also be separate because of a marriage contract or by operation of law because the property was acquired after a divorce or judgment terminating the community.

Many successions are made up of both community and separate property. In general, without a will, the spouse is given certain rights as to the deceased spouse's share of the community, but has few or no rights as to any separate property. Insuring that both types of property are treated the same can only be done by a will. So, who gets what if there is no will?

To make it easier to understand what happens to your property in a succession in which there is no will, let's look at a few variations on a typical case. Ken and Marsha have been married ten years and have no children. Marsha has one brother, and her parents are living. Ken has three sisters but his parents are both dead. Ken bought his house before he married Marsha, and he recently inherited $50,000 from his mother's estate. Neither Ken nor Marsha have wills.

If Ken were to die, what would Marsha get from his estate? Marsha, because they have no children, would only get Ken's one-half of the community. Ken's sisters would inherit the house that Marsha is living in and the $50,000 that Ken inherited. Marsha received almost nothing because most of Ken's property was separate and went to his closest heirs, his sisters. If either or both of Ken's parents were alive, the sisters would still have inherited the property itself, but his parents would have received a usufruct over that separate property. A usufruct is the nearly unlimited right to use and enjoy something as long as the substance of the thing is not used up. When one parent dies, the remaining parent retains the usufruct individually.

Order of Succession

Community Property	Separate Property
❶ To children or children's descendants with usufruct to spouse.	❶ To children or children's descendants.
❷ **To spouse**, if there are no children or descendants of children.	❷ To brothers and sisters, with usufruct to any living parents.
❸ To brothers and sisters, with usufruct to any living parents	❸ To nieces and nephews, or their descendants, with usufruct to any living parents.
❹ To nieces and nephews, or their descendants, with usufruct to any living parents.	❹ To parents, if there are no brothers and sisters or their descendants.
❺ To parents, if there are no brothers and sisters or their descendants.	❺ **To spouse.**
❻ To grandparents or other ascendants.	❻ To grandparents or other ascendants.
❼ To nearest collateral relative.	❼ To nearest collateral relative.
❽ To State of Louisiana.	❽ To State of Louisiana.

If Ken and Marsha had children, Marsha would have been even worse off, in a way —the children of the marriage would inherit all of Ken's share of the community and all of the separate property. Marsha would have received the legal usufruct over the community property inherited by the children, but not over the separate property inherited by the children. Also, the usufruct that Marsha received would terminate if she remarries.

Marsha could only get separate property or the usufruct over separate property if Ken had given it to her in a will. In an intestate succession, the surviving spouse gets only community property if there are no children, or she gets the usufruct over the deceased's share of the community property if there are children. The usufruct over the children's share would end if she remarries.

As you can see, the spouse comes after the nieces, nephews, and their descendants for the deceased spouse's separate property, and after the children, grandchildren, and so on, for the deceased spouse's share of community property. This order of succession can only be changed by a valid will. We have bolded the "To spouse" in both columns so you can easily see where a spouse stands in Louisiana on intestate successions.

Testate Successions

A succession is testate if dispositions of the estate are made according to the deceased's valid last will. The main difference between a testate succession and an intestate succession concerns control over the order of succession. In a testate succession, the deceased makes the decisions as to who inherits. In an intestate succession, as we have seen, the state makes this decision.

When a testate succession is opened, one of the first steps is to file the will with the court and have it probated. Probating a will simply means proving it. The procedure for probating a will varies depending on the type of will that was made by the testator. If it is an olographic will, there may have to be a hearing and the testimony or affidavits of two witnesses must state that the will was entirely written, dated, and signed by the deceased. This involves finding witnesses that were familiar with the deceased's handwriting, or it can even involve hiring handwriting experts.

> *Aunt Verna was lucky to have her niece Rhonda live with her during the last years of her life, since Rhonda took care of Aunt Verna during the months of her final illness. After Aunt Verna's death, Rhonda petitioned to open the succession and filed an olographic will which, claimed Rhonda, Aunt Verna had given her on the way to the hospital, folded in a Bible. The probate of the will was opposed by Aunt Verna's husband and her other relatives. Since the probate of the will was opposed, a hearing had to be held to determine whether the will was genuine. Rhonda testified that she recognized her aunt's handwriting and that the will was entirely written, dated, and signed by Aunt Verna. Knowing that at least two credible witnesses must prove an olographic will, Rhonda had another aunt testify that the will appeared to be in Verna's hand. On cross-examination, the aunt admitted that only parts of the will looked as if they were written by Verna, while other parts looked as if they were written by someone else. Verna's separated husband testified that the will was not written by his wife. He also had a handwriting expert testify that comparisons of the will to the deceased's checks and correspondence showed that the will was not written by Verna.*

The court decided that the will was not properly proven and that the children should inherit everything since it was an intestate succession. The court felt that the only witness who claimed with certainty that the will was genuine was the person who would benefit and who had control of the document until it was filed in the succession proceedings. It then became a matter of who was more credible: Rhonda, who would inherit everything if the will was valid, or a handwriting expert, who had no personal interest in the outcome of the hearing.

When a notarial will is probated, no formal proof of the genuineness of the will is required. It is presumed on the face of it. If there is any question as to capacity of the deceased, the trial judge could require the actual testimony of the notary, witnesses, and anyone else with relevant information.

Forced Heirship

Although a person is free to leave his property to anyone he chooses in a will, and is free to completely change the order of succession, we come back once again to the forced heirship laws which limit this freedom. Louisiana law makes a fictitious division of your property into disposable property and the forced portion, or legitime. This simply means that if you have direct descendants who are forced heirs, the law restricts what you can do with your property in a will. Your children under the age of 24 years and your children who are permanently disabled regardless of age are your forced heirs, and you must leave them the forced portion or legitime. The remainder is called the disposable portion, and you can do what you want to with it, just like in all the other United States. If you attempt to leave all your fortune to the Fund For Cats, the court will deduct enough from the estate to make sure your forced heirs get what the law says they are entitled to.

The category of forced heir and the amount of the forced portion has changed in recent years. In the absence of children or other descendants, parents used to be forced heirs. Now only descendants who are a certain age (or disabled) can be forced heirs, and the portion to which they are entitled has been reduced. If you have one child who is a forced heir, the portion that you must leave him, or his legitime, is 25% of your estate. If you have two or more children who are forced heirs, the forced portion is 50% of your estate to be divided equally among the forced heirs. In other words, if you have four children who are forced heirs and leave an estate of

$80,000, each child who is a forced heir must receive at least $10,000. The forced portion is $40,000 and the disposable portion is $40,000.

If one of your children dies before the age of 24, his descendants are your forced heirs for the amount he would have received. If he had five children, they would each have to receive $2,000 from your estate. This is called representation and simply means that all descendants are entitled to represent their deceased ascendant so that they share the same forced portion that he would have received had he not died. Since you can do what you want with the disposable portion, you could leave one child $50,000, and the remaining three children $10,000 each. Or, since you don't know how big your estate will be, you could simply leave three children the "forced portion" and the remaining child, obviously your favorite, the "disposable portion," in addition to the forced portion.

Forced heirship out of control. The whole concept of forced heirship is a bit beyond the ability of most people to comprehend. We have said for years that forced heirship needs to be abolished in Louisiana because of the problems the outdated concept causes. For example, Louisiana is probably the only state that does not recognize the concept of joint ownership with rights of survivorship. Where other states allow a husband and wife to own their home jointly and if one dies, the survivor owns the home outright without having to take any action, Louisiana does not allow this. In our state, a surviving spouse must open a succession, with the expense and waste of time, to get title to the home –assuming there was at least a will to accomplish this. Why has Louisiana taken this backwards approach? Forced heirship is usually given by the Legislature as the reason. If a spouse (or any other party) can get title by rights of survivorship, that would interfere with the rights of forced heirs. Our response to that has always been "So what?" Better yet, why don't we just get rid of the concept in the first place?

Instead of taking that very logical step, the Legislature has made it much worse in recent years. Rather than making the transfer of property in accordance with the deceased's wishes easier, our Legislature, in their wisdom, decided to make the succession process even thornier. They decided that any child, regardless of age, who has an illness or condition that <u>may</u> make them disabled one day, is also a forced heir. A recent change to Civil Code Article 1493 added this gem to the list of those who are to be considered forced heirs:

> "...descendants who, at the time of death of the decedent, have, according to medical documentation, an inherited, incurable disease or condition that may render them incapable of caring for their persons or administering their estates in the future."

Stop and think for a minute about where that leads. Not only do we have a class of people who are forced heirs because they are under the age of 24, and a class that can become forced heirs at any age because of disability, we also have a class of forced heirs based on genetics and the future chance of illness based on guesswork. Can the argument be made that all illness has a inherited component? What about diabetes, Alzheimer's, or heart disease? Laws based on such lose concepts invariably lead to lawsuits, and guess what? That is exactly what has happened. We already have no fewer than three suits in which children with bi-polar disorder, which they admitted had not made them disabled at the time they filed suit, declared forced heirs because they might be disabled at some future time.

> *Mrs. Arbitrage left a short will leaving all of her estate to her husband, Joseph. Shortly after her death, Jane, the daughter of Mrs. Arbitrage, sued Joseph claiming that she was a forced heir since she was recently diagnosed with bipolar disorder. Dr. Landry, a psychiatrist who conducted*

*a psychiatric examination of Jane prior to trial, opined that
"Jane's disorder is likely an inherited, genetic disorder."
Another doctor testified that "Despite the appearance that
Jane can appear 'okay,' and able to care for her affairs,
the next day it may be totally different. Jane won her case
and was awarded the forced portion of her mother's estate
because Jane could likely be more disabled in the future.*

Getting around forced heirship. There are a few ways
to get around the forced heirship laws, at least to some extent.
One way is to invest in life insurance. Since life insurance
with a named beneficiary other than your estate is not considered part of your estate in Louisiana, your life insurance is
paid directly to the beneficiary completely free of the forced
heirship laws. However, if the beneficiary has died before
you, the benefits would be paid to your estate, and the heirs
might have to pay taxes. It is therefore a good idea to have
alternate beneficiaries named on your life insurance policies
to lessen the chances of this happening.

Not many people realize it, but life insurance proceeds
that are payable to a forced heir can be counted as part of that
heir's forced portion. In other words, you can pay off a forced
heir with an adequate amount of life insurance so that the rest
of your estate can be disposed of exactly the way you want.
It must be very clear, however, that you intend that the
insurance benefits be counted as part of the forced portion of
that beneficiary.

Qualified retirement plans also are free of the forced
heirship laws if there is a named beneficiary. These plans can
include employer and employee retirement contributions,
IRS approved plans such as IRAs, 401(k)s, Keogh Plans and
many other types of retirement or savings plans including
some types of thrift accounts. If a forced heir is named as
beneficiary, the amount paid can be applied to the forced
portion.

Another way to avoid the forced heirship laws is to own immovable property (real estate) in another state. Since real estate is controlled by the laws of the state in which the property is located, our forced heirship laws would not apply to the distribution of that property. Careful wording in a will can give you a good bit of control over the distribution of your property and the way in which Louisiana's forced heirship laws are implemented. The effects of the forced heirship laws can also be modified through the granting of a usufruct or the creation of a trust, as we have seen earlier.

We are frequently asked if there is any way to disinherit a child despite the forced heirship laws. You can make a provision in your will that disinherits a forced heir, but only for certain limited reasons.

Clyde had always had problems with his son George. There were seven kids and George was the only one who made no attempt to hide his dislike for his father. One day George and Clyde got into a fight, George struck his father, and then held a rifle on him while both wondered if George would fire. A police report was made of the incident, but no arrests were made. Many years later, when Clyde died of natural causes, George was upset to find that he had been cut out of Clyde's will. The will stated "I specifically disinherit my son George due to the incident in the spring of 1978 in which my son struck me three (3) times and fired at me with a .22 caliber automatic rifle." George filed suit for his share of the estate and testified that he never struck his father, never fired the rifle, and only had the rifle with him that day in self defense because he feared his father. A witness testified that he didn't see who started the fight and didn't hear a shot, but that he did see George and Clyde grappling with each other.

The court did not believe George's testimony and found that Clyde had properly disinherited his son. In order to disinherit a forced heir, you do not need to have cause as extreme as Clyde apparently had. You do need to specifically allege in your will that you are disinheriting a forced heir because the forced heir:

- Struck or attempted to strike you.

- Was guilty of cruel treatment towards you.

- Attempted to take your life.

- Refused to support you if you were in need and he had the means to give support.

- Has been convicted of a crime punishable by death or life imprisonment.

- Refused to communicate with you for a period of two years after reaching adulthood and if he knew how get in contact with you. If the forced heir is in the military, the two year period is interrupted.

Virtually all of the forced heirs that we have disinherited on behalf of clients over the years were done based on the failure to communicate for a period of two or more years.

Small Successions

A small succession is simply defined as the succession of any person who dies leaving property in Louisiana with a gross value of $75,000 or less. If the small succession qualifies, the heirs can be put into possession and the whole succession can be cleared up without having to go to court.

In order to qualify as a small succession which does not need to be judicially opened, the deceased must not have left a will and the sole heirs must be made up only of descendants, ascendants, brothers, sisters, nieces, nephews, and/or a surviving spouse. If there are qualified heirs other than these, such as a cousin, the succession must be judicially opened.

A recent revision to the small successions law for the first time would allow the small succession to have real estate. It is hard to imagine a succession that includes real estate and still totals under $75,000. The only case we have had where real estate was included in a small succession affidavit was where the house had been condemned and the property was close to worthless.

If the small succession qualifies, the procedure is extremely easy and can be handled without an attorney. An affidavit must be prepared which states: 1) the date of death and the domicile of the deceased; 2) the fact that he died without a will; 3) the marital status of the deceased and the names and addresses of the spouse, if any, and the heirs together with the relationship of the heirs to the deceased; 4) a brief description of the property belonging to the deceased with the values at the time of death and the total value.

This affidavit must be witnessed and notarized after being signed by two persons, including the spouse, if any, and one or more adult heirs. A copy of any multiple original of the affidavit is full authority for any bank, or any other party who has property belonging to the deceased, to turn over the property to the heirs. It is important to describe some types of property completely in the affidavit so that there is no doubt about what must be turned over. For example, automobiles should include the vehicle identification number so that the Department Of Motor Vehicles can change the title. Descriptions of accounts, whether checking, savings or certificates of deposit, should include the name of the institution and the account number. Safe deposit boxes should include a description of the contents, otherwise the bank may not release the box to the heirs.

It is also important to include the full legal description of any real estate and to record the affidavit along with a certified copy of the death certificate in the conveyance records to show the change of ownership. Recordation is not necessary if there is no real estate in the succession. It is also important to note that a specific provision was included so that if a person domiciled in another state had property in Louisiana, then the small succession process can be used even if the person had a will in the other state. In those cases, the foreign will would be attached to prove who the heirs are.

See the Do It Yourself Guide on settling a small estate for an example of a small succession affidavit. Or, you can go to our Web site at *La-Legal.com*.

Part 3

Your Business

Starting A Business

There is probably no area of law where more disputes arise, or more money is lost, than when people try to start a business. This is because people invariably think they can enter the business world without competent legal and tax advice. The business world is based on competition, and there seems to be no end of novices who think that they can start a business simply because someone else did it and seems to be doing well. The fact is, that person is doing well because of a lot of hard work and good advice.

It is an unfortunate fact that many of the businesses that are formed one year provide a good living for the bankruptcy attorneys the next year. Most of the failures that we see can probably be traced to a combination of three things: poor planning, poor management, and under capitalization. As part of poor planning, there are a surprising number of people who are unrealistically optimistic about the type of business they wish to start. These people either want to start something completely new without considering the demand that may or may not exist, or they want to get into an already over-crowded area.

Under capitalization is part of poor planning and results from the unrealistic hope that a business will be profitable in a short time. The fact is, many new businesses do not pass the break even point for two years or more. Of course, that is assuming that they ever break even at all. To avoid failure by under capitalizing, you must plan for enough capital investment to keep your business going through the period of time that you realistically predict your business will not be self sufficient.

If you are considering a business in which you already have some experience, your chances of success are much greater than the person who is getting into something completely new to him. We will assume that you have already done the basic research, that you have read some of the many good books available on starting a new business, and that you have some experience in the field or intend to hire someone who does.

Having to predict necessary capital and the point at which a business will break even can sometimes be avoided by buying an existing business. At least with an existing business you can inspect the books and see what the track record has been. If the business is more than two years old and still is not breaking even, that should tell you something. Buying someone else's business, however, has problems as well.

Purchasing a Business

The purchase of an existing business is full of legal pitfalls waiting for the inexperienced or unwary purchaser. However, there is some protection available for the buyer of a business if the legal requirements are met. We assume that you have already considered the reasons someone would want to sell a business and that you are satisfied with the reasons or think that you can succeed where someone else has not. We also assume that you have checked the court records for pending suits, judgments and mortgages against the seller or his business, and with the Better Business Bureau or other agencies to see if there have been any problems.

It is important to understand that the purchase of a business often involves the assumption of all the liabilities of that business. Liabilities can include taxes, mortgages, liens, judgments, and existing contracts. Personal liabilities of the business owner or partner in the business can also be transferred with the business. You need to not only check the public records as to the business, but as to the individuals who own the business.

Don't forget that this is a community property state. If Joe is married and wants to sell you Joe's Shoe Store, Joe's wife must join in the sale since she probably has a one-half interest. You can't rely on Joe's word that he is not married or is divorced. You must check the public records as to Joe's marital status. If Joe is indeed divorced, the former wife still may have an interest in the store unless there is a recorded community property settlement that transfers her interest to Joe. If there is any doubt, insist that Joe's former wife join in the sale.

This brings us back to what we originally said about getting professional advice before starting or buying a business. It just does not make any sense to invest money in a business and not spend the little extra to make sure everything is done properly. Have a tax or accounting professional and lawyer advise you on each step. It will save you money in the long run.

Whether you purchase an existing business or start a new business, the first decision you will have to make is how your business will be organized. That is, whether you will be a sole proprietorship, a partnership, a limited liability company, or a corporation. The way you decide to organize will have drastic consequences as to the way you must operate and the way your business is viewed legally and for tax purposes.

Most businesses are organized as sole proprietorships and the business is basically considered an extension of the owner. It may be to your advantage, however, to operate as a partnership or corporation. This is especially true if there are other people involved in your business, if the potential for liability is high, or if a tax consultant determines that your tax liability may be lower if you start your business in a form other than a sole proprietorship.

Partnerships

The partnership law in Louisiana used to recognize several different types of partnerships and different rules applied depending on the type of partnership the law assumed you had. These laws were extensively modified in 1981 and in 1992 so that now there are only three types of partnerships: limited partnerships, limited liability partnerships, and regular partnerships. A limited partnership has one or more general partners who run the business and one or more limited partners who invest in the partnership but have no voice in the business decisions. Limited partnerships are usually formed to raise money from investors and are often used in real estate ventures. Because limited partnerships are used rarely and for a specific purpose, we will limit our discussion to regular and limited liability partnerships.

The new law made a very basic change in the way the partnership is treated. The partnership is now considered a separate and distinct legal entity, different from the partners who make up the partnership. Therefore, when a partnership is formed it is not just a matter of entering a contract with other partners, it is also a matter of creating a separate legal entity. This fiction of viewing the partnership separately from its partners makes some substantial differences in the way the partnership is treated. For example, the partnership itself must be sued as well as the individual partners. Any judgment resulting from the suit must first be satisfied out of partnership assets before the individual partners are liable on the judgment. Unlike the former law which made each partner in a commercial partnership liable for the entire debt of the partnership, now a partner is personally liable for partnership debts only to the extent of his share in the partnership.

The new law also requires that partnership contracts be filed with the Secretary of State in certain circumstances. Basically, all partnerships formed on or after January 1, 1981, must be filed if the partnership law requires that the particular partnership agreement be in writing. Also, a partnership formed prior to 1985 must be filed if it is a limited partnership or if the partnership owns or intends to own land. If the partnership agreement is registered with the Secretary of State, it also must be filed in the mortgage records of the parish in which the partnership maintains its principal place of business.

What is a partnership? A partnership is a legal person, separate and distinct from its partners, created by a contract between two or more persons to combine their efforts or resources in determined proportions and to collaborate at their mutual risk for their common profit or commercial benefit. The proportions of investment and profit can be in any amount that the partners wish to agree. However, if the agreement says nothing about the proportions, it will be assumed that each partner shares risk, investment and profit equally. In other words, if there are three partners, each partner has one-third of the liabilities and one-third of the ownership and profits unless an agreement states otherwise.

A partnership agreement can be oral and legally binding in some situations, but it should always be in writing so there is no doubt as to exactly what the agreement is. If your partnership agreement is not in writing, the law will treat the partnership much as it does an intestate succession: it will make assumptions as to what was intended by the parties as to proportion of ownership and liability.

A partnership can only be formed if there are two or more partners and if the partners clearly indicate their consent to form a partnership.

Dr. Daniels formed a partnership with two other doctors and practiced medicine in the partnership for several years.

When Doctor Daniels and his wife Roberta divorced, Roberta demanded a one-sixth interest in the partnership as part of her community property settlement. One-sixth represented her one-half of Dr. Daniel's one-third of the partnership. Dr. Daniels was willing to pay her the value of one-sixth of the partnership assets, but he was not willing to give her the ongoing ownership of part of the partnership itself. Roberta sued to have her one-sixth ownership recognized by the court and to start payments to her of one-sixth of the doctor's profits. Roberta said that the interest in the partnership was the same as a shareholder's interest in a corporation. If the doctors' business was a corporation, she argued, she would be entitle to one-sixth of the shares in the corporation. Dr. Daniels answered the suit and said that he was only liable to her for one-sixth of the value of his interest in the partnership as of the day they separated, not to a share in the partnership itself.

The court looked at what it takes to form a partnership or to become a partner in an existing partnership. Roberta, in effect, was attempting to become a partner with the other two doctors without their consent. She was also trying to become a member of a partnership that practiced medicine as their commercial venture, without the ability to contribute to the common venture of the other doctors. The court ruled against Roberta since a partnership can only be formed through the contract and consent of all the partners. Also, each partner must "combine their common efforts for the common profit." Since Roberta was incapable of practicing medicine, she was incapable of contributing anything to the partnership and could not, therefore, be a partner.

A partnership can transact business under the names of the partners or it can assume any name it wants. If the partnership does not use the names of the partners, it must record the business name in the conveyance records with a statement as to the actual partners' names and addresses. As a matter of fact, you will not be issued any licenses to conduct your business under an assumed name unless you show a certificate from the clerk of court indicating that you have recorded the assumed name.

The partnership agreement itself can provide nearly any condition that the partners wish to agree upon. In the absence of specific provisions, all partnership decisions are made by majority vote except for a decision to amend the agreement, admit a new partner, or allow a partner to withdraw without just cause. The last three cases require a unanimous vote of the partners, absent a provision in the partnership agreement to the contrary. Each partner is entitled to full access to the partnership books and records even if the partner has no decision making power. This right is one of the few provisions that cannot be eliminated in the partnership agreement.

The most crucial thing to understand about a partnership is that all of the partners can be bound by the actions of one of the partners. For example, one partner can enter into a contract to buy supplies for the business and make all the partners liable for their share of the cost. This is true even if the other partners do not know that the contract exists. Each partner is an agent for the partnership in all ordinary business matters other than for the selling, leasing, or mortgaging of immovable property belonging to the partnership. Even if the partnership agreement says that a particular partner has no right to bind the partnership, that partner can still bind the partnership in favor of an innocent third party who is not aware of the restriction. Likewise, a provision in the agreement that one partner is not liable for losses has no effect as far as third parties are concerned. Each partner will still be liable to third persons for his share of the losses.

The partnership is considered the primary obligor for all of its debts. This simply means that a creditor of the partnership must look first to the partnership for payment before the individual partners. As a practical matter, a creditor will sue the partnership and the individual partners in one action. If the assets of the partnership do not cover the judgment, the assets of the partners are then seized. At this point, each partner is liable in proportion to his share in the partnership.

Tom was an engineer who designed a new pump that could recover crude oil that could not be pumped economically by any other method. Tom formed a partnership with his brother Harry who was good at sales and with George who wanted to invest money in the project. Harry sold one of the new pumps to a large company which installed it on one of its drilling sites. The new pump came apart soon after being installed and caused part of the drilling rig to fall on a worker, thereby causing him numerous injuries. The drilling company and the injured worker both sued Tom for designing a defective pump. Tom brought Harry and George into the suit to share any judgment that Tom might suffer. After all, Tom reasoned, it was a partnership and each partner was liable. George and Harry argued that this was a tort, not a business dealing, and they should not be liable for a design defect that they knew nothing about.

Harry and George were held to be equally liable with Tom for the damages. Partners can be liable for the torts committed by another partner even though they have nothing to do with the incident that caused the tort. It is only necessary that the tort be committed in the course of the partnership business. A tort, incidentally, is a harm caused to someone else that results in some damage or loss, usually by accident. Each partner is an agent of the partnership and can make the partnership and each individual partner liable for his actions. It is important to understand this liability before entering into a partnership and it is important to have plenty of insurance to cover against loss.

The partners also owe a fiduciary duty to the partnership. This means that all business dealing must be for the benefit of the partnership, not for individual gain. If a partner breach-es his fiduciary duty, he may be personally liable to the partnership and the other partners for his breach.

A partnership terminates with the unanimous consent of the partners, when the partnership is reduced to one person, by a court order terminating the partnership, by order of the Bankruptcy Court, by the expiration of the term if the agreement sets a date to terminate, or by the impossibility of attainment, or the attainment, of the object of the partnership. The termination of the partnership has no affect on existing debts or debts that come about as the result of the partnership. These debts are still the obligation of the partnership and the individual partners.

A partnership has the advantage of sharing the cost and the work with other parties. But, you also give up some of the decision making power and open yourself up to liability for decisions and actions made by others that you may have no control over. In some circumstances, running your business in the form of a corporation will insulate you from personal liability for debts of the corporation and for torts committed by corporation employees.

Corporations

Forming a corporation is extremely easy. Complying with the federal and state tax laws each year and even quarterly thereafter is not so easy. The tax consequences of creating the separate entity known as the corporation must be carefully considered before attempting to start a business in the corporate form. Once you elect to form a corporation, there may be severe tax consequences if you decide to convert to another form of ownership later. This is because the Internal Revenue Service creates many fine and subtle distinctions as to the property, debts and income of a corporation. With a partnership, each partner receives his partnership profits, if any, and reports these profits or losses on his personal income tax return. The corporation, on the other hand, is treated by the IRS as a separate and distinct taxpayer which is subject to different rules than an individual partner or sole proprietor.

There can be many definite tax advantages to the corporate form but these advantages and the possible disadvantages must be explored with a tax expert prior to forming the corporation. You should be aware that you can make an election with the IRS to operate as an "S" corporation. This election generally passes corporate profits and losses through to shareholders to be taxed or deducted at the shareholder's individual rate. This can be especially attractive in light of the changes in the federal tax laws that became effective in 1987. These changes generally put a heavier tax burden on corporations. Whether to incorporate or not from a tax standing is beyond the scope of this book. Expert advice from an accountant or tax expert is absolutely necessary before taking this step.

The formation of a corporation is subject to the Louisiana Business Corporations Law. Compliance with this law must be strictly adhered to or you may end up with all of the disadvantages of a corporation and none of the advantages. The corporation is formed when the articles of incorporation together with the initial report are filed with the Secretary of State. Corporate existence starts when the articles are filed, or, if the articles are executed within five days of filing, corporate existence is retroactive to the day the articles are signed.

The articles of incorporation are simply a declaration of some of the basic purposes and limits of the corporation. The articles operate much the same way as the Constitution does for the federal government. It is a framework within which the corporation must operate. Actions by the corporation that are contrary to the articles might be invalid just as actions by our government might be invalid if contrary to the Constitution. Let's look at some of the minimum requirements of law to form a corporation in Louisiana.

Contrary to popular belief, it only takes one person to form a corporation. The person who forms the corporation is called the incorporator, although there is no limit on the number of people who can be the incorporators of the corporation. The incorporator is simply the person who starts the corporate existence by executing the articles and may or may not actually have any real connection with the operation and ownership of the corporation.

The first requirement is that the articles be executed by authentic act. That is, they must be in writing and they must be signed by the incorporator or incorporators in front of a notary and two witnesses who must also sign the articles.

The articles must state, at a minimum, the name of the corporation, the purpose of the corporation, the duration of the corporation if not perpetual, the number of shares that the corporation is authorized to issue, the par value of the shares or the fact that they are without par value, the classes of stock together with the details of shares and values within each class, and the full name and address of each incorporator. The articles may also state any other provisions that are desired. As a general rule, however, you want to say as little as possible in the articles since they have to be recorded. Any changes that you want to make later require the time and expense of amending the articles and filing the amended forms with the Secretary of State and the parish where the corporation is domiciled. Because of the trouble of changing the articles, it is better to keep them as general as possible and instead make the by-laws more specific.

The by-laws are not required by law and can be changed at any time. The by-laws are the rules enacted by the shareholders for the day to day operation of the corporation. The by-laws, however, cannot conflict with the provisions of the articles of incorporation. The by-laws do not have to be filed with the Secretary of State nor with the clerk of court.

You can give your corporation nearly any name you want as long as the name is not already in use or indistinguishably similar to a name in use, and as long as it does not contain certain words which are reserved. Bank, trust, insurance, savings and several others are reserved words. Other types of names are also reserved to parties who have the right, by virtue of training or license, to use a name that implies to the public special training. Words like "engineers" and "surveyor" are examples. The Secretary of State will require proof that a party wishing to use these names has been certified by the appropriate state board before allowing the articles to be filed.

The name must contain the word "corporation," "incorporated," or "limited" or the abbreviations of any of these words. The name can instead contain the word "company" or "co." as long as it is not preceded by "and" or "&." The name cannot contain the phrase "doing business as" or "d/b/a."

When you file your articles, you can take the chance that they will not be refused because the name is already taken or you can call or write the Secretary of State, Corporations Department, to find if the name is available. Also, for a small fee, the Secretary of State will reserve the name for you if you are not ready to file but do not want to lose the name to someone else. The reservation is good for sixty days and can be renewed for two additional periods of thirty days each.

The requirement that you state the purpose of the corporation has long been circumvented by simply stating that the purpose is to conduct any business that is legal in the State of Louisiana. This is perfectly acceptable and enables you to try several different businesses under the same corporation without having to amend the articles.

The number of shares that the corporation can issue is not really important. The shares issued determine the percentage of ownership a particular shareholder has. If a shareholder has one of the two shares issued, he owns fifty per cent just as if he owned one thousand of two thousand shares issued. We usually recommend that the corporation be authorized to issue ten thousand shares since this leaves room for expansion in the future.

The duration of your corporation should be perpetual and your shares should be no par value. Par value is only relevant to a public offering of your shares which should not be undertaken without some very specific advice.

The other matters which you may include in your articles of incorporation have to do with such things as how directors are elected and the process for declaring dividends. The sample articles contained in the Do It Yourself Guide show both the required articles and some suggested articles. The required articles are preceded by an asterisk so that you can prepare just the bare bones articles of incorporation if you wish.

The articles of incorporation, duly executed before a notary and two witnesses, are filed with the Secretary of State in Baton Rouge with a filing fee which is currently set at $75. The mailing address for filings or other information is: Secretary of State, P.O. Box 94125, Baton Rouge, LA 70804. You must also include an initial report which states the names and addresses of the incorporators, the office address of the corporation, the names and addresses of the registered agent or agents, and the names and addresses of the directors of the corporation if they have been chosen at the time the articles are filed. The registered agent is the person who is authorized to receive service of process in the event the corporation is sued. The agent must sign an affidavit accepting his appointment. The incorporator, first director, and agent can all be the same person and have the same address.

Forms for the initial report can be ordered from the Secretary of State's office. Also available is a very good book that compiles all of the Louisiana corporation laws. This book can be ordered from the Secretary of State for a nominal price.

You will also have to file an annual report with the Secretary of State which must state any changes in the initial report and must contain the names and addresses of the directors and officers of the corporation together with the number of shares of stock that have been issued. The annual report together with a fee, franchise fees, and corporate income taxes are due the State of Louisiana on an annual basis.

Forming a corporation involves more paperwork, more expense, and may or may not save taxes. So, what advantage is there? Why do so many businesses, large and small, incorporate? The answer is very simple: the individual who incorporates his business insulates himself from personal liability. Unlike the sole proprietorship or even the partnership, the corporation is considered an entirely separate legal person from the individuals who formed the corporation and who own stock in the corporation. If a corporation is sued, only the assets of the corporation are at risk should there be a judgment. The individual shareholder's personal assets and income cannot be seized to satisfy the debts of the corporation.

Let's say that Joe starts Joe's Shoe Store and borrows $30,000 from the bank to pay his initial overhead. Joe also signs a lease with a shopping center, signs a contract with a wholesaler guaranteeing to buy a minimum number of shoes his first year, and hires several salesmen. After the first few months, a customer is injured when she trips over a shoe display and sues Joe's Shoe Store for a million dollars. Joe is forced to go out of business when his creditors find out about the suit and Joe's Shoe Store is also sued by the bank, the wholesaler, the shopping center, and the salesmen who have not been paid. If that is not enough, the IRS is after Joe because he has not made his employee withholding deposits. All of these creditors will be able to go after Joe's personal assets, not just the assets of Joe's Shoe Store.

Now let's say that Joe forms Joe's Shoe Store, Inc. and that he borrows money and signs contracts as president of the corporation, not as Joe the individual. All of the creditors would have to share in the assets of the corporation and could not go against Joe the individual or his property and savings. The only exception is the IRS which can, under some circumstances, proceed against corporate officers personally for taxes owed by the corporation.

As a practical matter, the bank, the wholesaler and the shopping center probably would have required Joe to sign in two capacities —as Joe the president of Joe's Shoe Stores, Inc. and as Joe the individual. If Joe had signed these agreements in both capacities, he would have been personally liable on the lease, the loan and the wholesale agreement. The lady who was injured, however, is going to be able to recover only from the assets of the corporation.

Forming a corporation to insulate yourself from personal liability can be a terrific idea, but if it is not done properly you will find yourself personally liable despite your efforts. The certificate of incorporation that the Secretary of State sends you when you register your corporation is very pretty and suitable for framing. It is also prima facie evidence in any court of law that you are indeed incorporated and that you are entitled to benefit under the Louisiana Business Corporation Law. However, if you do not treat yourself as a corporation, the courts may not either. This is called "piercing the corporate veil" and simply means that the person who operates his business as a corporation may find himself personally liable for what he thought were corporate debts or other liabilities.

As a general rule, if you treat your corporation as a true corporation, the courts will as well. This involves such things as filing annual reports with the state, paying taxes properly, conducting meetings of the board of directors, and, in general, conducting other corporate business in such a way that it is clear that a genuine corporate entity exists. Otherwise, you may be considered just an individual who at one time paid the Secretary of State a filing fee. If the courts decide that you have not operated as a corporation, the corporation may be considered your "alter ego" and you may be personally liable as though there were no corporation at all.

Joe and Lucy bought a new house from St. Mary Construction, Incorporated. Shortly after moving in, the young couple noticed that the slab was beginning to crack. Jerry, the owner and president of St. Mary, told Joe and Lucy that cracks were normal and that nothing could be done. Joe and Lucy hired an engineering firm that discovered the house had been built on the site of a trailer park and there was an old septic tank under the slab. The bill to fix the problem would be $12,000. Jerry refused to fix the problem saying that the one year warranty had expired. When Joe and Lucy sued St. Mary Construction, Incorporated, they found that the corporation had no assets. They also discovered that the corporation did not maintain bank accounts separate from Jerry the individual, the corporation did not file state and federal income tax returns, the corporation did not keep corporate records, and the corporation did not have regular meetings. Joe and Lucy sued Jerry individually for $12,000 and attorney's fees. Jerry asked the court to dismiss the case against him since Joe and Lucy had bought the house from the corporation, not Jerry.

The court found that the identity of Jerry and St. Mary Construction, Incorporated had merged to such an extent that there was no separate corporate existence. The court stated that when a shareholder fails to conduct the business on a corporate footing to such an extent that the identity of the shareholder cannot be distinguished from that of the corporation, the shareholder will become personally liable for the debts of the corporation. Joe and Lucy were awarded the money needed to repair the foundation plus an additional $3,500 for attorney's fees.

When corporations are formed by an individual or by a few family members, there is usually not much disagreement about how things should be run. Problems within corporations usually arise when some of the shareholders are not happy about corporate decisions or about the dividends declared. The corporation is run by the shareholders and, depending on the articles of incorporation, a simple majority may decide on the directors and officers who are responsible for decision making. This leaves the shareholder with just a few shares out in the cold if he is not happy with the way things are going. This shareholder can be frozen out of the corporation and can do little about it. If he holds shares in General Motors he can at least sell out since there is a market for openly traded stocks. The shareholder in the typical small business corporation will quickly find that his stock has no market.

There may be some legal recourse for the minority shareholder to protect him from the majority shareholders. If he has at least twenty per cent of the outstanding stock and has held the stock for at least six months, he can force the involuntary liquidation of the corporation and seek to get his share in the corporation out of the liquidation. Several shareholders can band together to make up the twenty per cent. A shareholder or shareholders with less than twenty per cent have virtually no control over the corporation unless they can prove that some fraud by corporate officers has been perpetrated against them. In forming a corporation or investing in a corporation, therefore, you do not ever want to be in the position of having less than twenty per cent of the stock.

There is another problem that must be considered when more than one person is involved in forming a corporation: you may end up in business with someone other than the person you started the corporation with. This can happen when the other shareholder sells his stock or if he dies and a stranger inherits his stock and shareholder's rights. Or it can happen if the another shareholder divorces and the community is divided. Let's say that when Joe formed Joe's Shoe Store, Inc. he took in Bob as an equal partner with fifty per cent of the stock. The articles of incorporation state that a simple majority of shareholders shall make all corporate decisions. After a few years, Bob dies and his wife Lilly inherits Bob's shares in the shoe store. Bob was a nice guy and did at least half of the work for his half of the profits. But Lilly is something else, knows nothing about the shoe business, and yet is still entitled to her share of the profits. Worse yet, Lilly may decide to sell her shares to a competitor of Joe's who is trying to gain control of the corporation.

This happens all of the time and could have been prevented if Joe and Bob had made stock ownership subject to a buy-sell agreement. This is a contract that makes all stock subject to purchase first by the corporation or other stockholders before it can be sold or transferred to anyone else. The stock certificates themselves must state that they are subject to such an agreement so that third parties can be on notice that the stock cannot be freely transferred. This would have protected Joe from being a partner with Lilly since the corporation would have had the option to buy the stock back upon Bob's death. The buy-sell agreement usually states how payment is to be made for the stock and how a value for the stock is to be determined. Since this type of stock has no market as such, price is usually determined by setting a value on all of the assets of the corporation and may include good will. The agreement would then state that the corporation has a certain amount of time to pay for the stock once the value has been established.

The recent changes in the federal tax laws have put a heavier tax burden on the corporation. The decision to incorporate may not be as attractive now as it was prior to the new legislation. Because of these changes, it is even more important to seek specific tax advice before deciding to incorporate. Existing corporations should also be re-examined to see whether they should now make the election with the IRS to operate as "S" corporations. An "S" corporation generally passes profits and losses to the individual shareholders so that these items can be included on the shareholder's tax return.

Limited Liability Companies

Limited liability companies and limited liability partnerships are a relatively new concept and are now recognized in most states. They became available in Louisiana in 1992 and promise to replace both the partnership and the corporation in many business organizations. The basic concept of limited liability companies is to allow the business owner freedom from personal liability as in a corporation, while still benefiting from individual tax rates as in a partnership.

The limited liability company is extremely flexible in the form it can take. The company is made up of "members" instead of shareholders. The members can run the company themselves, or they can have "managers" who are responsible for the running of the company. If managers run the company, the structure is very similar to a corporation where officers are responsible for running the business. If the members elect to run the company, the structure is more like a partnership where the partners are responsible for running the business.

Like a corporation, the limited liability company must file articles with the Secretary of State and must have a registered agent. These articles are called "Articles of Organization" instead of articles of incorporation. The Secretary of State issues a certificate of organization instead of a certificate of incorporation.

The limited liability company's name must be followed with the designation "limited liability company," or "L.L.C." or "L.C." In other words, "Stan's Hardware Store, L.C." would be an acceptable limited liability company name. The procedure for filing the articles, initial report, acceptance by agent, and filing fees would be the same as for a corporation.

There has been some time lag in determining the tax treatment afforded limited liability companies by the IRS. The limited liability partnership qualifies for favorable tax treatment because it is still, in essence, a partnership. The limited liability company, on the other hand, needs to be prepared by someone who is familiar with the latest requirements by the IRS if the members of the company want to be treated for tax purposes as though they were partners. If this is not done correctly, the limited liability company may be taxed like a non-chapter "S" corporation. There are several elections a limited liability company can make with the IRS for tax purposes that should be explored with a tax expert.

Contracts

Whether your business operates as a sole proprietorship, a partnership, a corporation, or a limited liability company, you should have a basic understanding of general contract law. The most frequent question we are asked in this area concerns whether an oral contract is binding and whether some contracts have to be written.

A contract can be oral and be just as binding as a written contract. There are relatively few instances in which a contract must be in writing. However, some contracts, an agreement to transfer immovable property (real estate), for example, must be in writing. The problem with oral contracts is in proving exactly what the agreement was.

Not reducing an agreement to writing probably results in more law suits than any other single cause. This is not because people are necessarily lying about the terms of the agreement. In nearly every case of a contract dispute that we have handled, the parties probably truly believe their recollections of the agreement. The fact is, each person remembers things differently and generally this recollection is in his own favor. When an agreement is reduced to writing, there is very little chance that one of the parties to the contract will be able to modify the agreement to fit his recollection.

> *Cindy was getting married and her parents decided to spare no expense for her wedding. They held a reception in the Grand Ballroom of a large New Orleans hotel complete with dinners and drinks for 385 people. The hotel sent a bill to Cindy's parents for $13,000. When the bill was not paid, the hotel sued Cindy on open account for the $13,000 and attorney's fees. Cindy answered the suit by saying it was her parents, not her, that contracted with the hotel. The hotel amended their suit to include Cindy's parents. Cindy's parents claimed that they were not liable because there was no written contract with the hotel and because they did not personally benefit from the reception.*

Since there was no written contract and no specific law that covered this situation, the court looked at common custom to decide this case. It is commonly understood that the bride's parents are responsible for the wedding costs. The hotel tacitly acknowledged this custom by not suing the groom or his parents. The court found that Cindy's parents were liable for the bill and Cindy was dismissed from the suit.

All contracts, whether oral or in writing, must satisfy certain basic requirements of law before they will be considered binding. A contract is defined by the Louisiana Civil Code to be "an agreement by two or more parties whereby obligations are created, modified or extinguished."

It follows that there cannot be a contract unless the parties have consented to the creation of the contract. Consent can be explicit, by signing a contract, for example, or it can be implied by a person's actions or inactions. If someone offers to mow your lawn for thirty dollars and you say nothing while he proceeds to cut the grass, you have created a contract because your consent is implied by your lack of action.

There are many types of contracts that are defined by the Civil Code. In Louisiana, the law of contracts comes under the more general designation of "obligations" which includes natural obligations and conventional obligations. A natural obligation may be a moral obligation to do something, like provide support for family members, while conventional obligations are contracts. Conventional obligations, or contracts, are further divided into several types and sub-types. For our purposes only the onerous contract, or a contract in which each party to the contract receives something for his obligation, will be considered.

Contracts can also be nominate or innominate which simply means that some types of contracts are categorized by the type of obligation created and this type of contract is given a specific name. Contracts that are named, or nominate contracts, may be subject to particular laws which vary from general contract law and apply to that type of contract only. For example, the contract of sale and the contract of lease are nominate and have specific laws that apply to them. Other contracts may be innominate which means they fall within no particular category and are therefore subject only to general contract laws.

As you can see from the discussion so far, contract law can be extremely complicated. We have just barely touched the surface of explaining the types of contracts so that you can understand why you should have a lawyer review any contract that you are considering.

A contract that is not carefully prepared can sometimes do you more harm than good. This is because a contract that is unclear or ambiguous is usually interpreted by the court against the person who prepared it. In the course of business, contract issues come up frequently and many can be handled routinely. However, for the preparation of a contract that is not routine or may have a significant impact on your business, you should always have an attorney do the drafting.

Although contracts are formed by the consent of the contracting parties, you should also be aware of some of the situations where consent cannot be legally given or where consent can be withdrawn. Minors who have not been emancipated, people who have been declared incompetent by the court in an interdiction proceeding, and people who are deprived of reason at the time the contract is entered, have no capacity to contract. These people, or their legal representatives, have the right to rescind the contract later, if they choose. A contract can also be nullified because the consent given was tainted by error, fraud or duress. In other words, consent must be freely given by a person who is capable of giving his or her consent to be bound by a contract.

Charlene gave up her infant daughter to Betty and George for adoption. At the same time the act of surrender was executed, Betty and George signed an agreement that Betty would have "reasonable visitation rights." Betty and George later decided that they did not want Charlene to see their new daughter. Charlene sued to enforce the contract.

This is an example of another way in which contracts can be nullified. The court refused to allow Charlene to see Betty and George's new daughter because it would be against public policy. Since a stranger does not have a right of visitation, and since Charlene was legally a stranger to the baby once the adoption took place, the court considered the visitation agreement non-enforceable. If Charlene had sued to nullify the adoption based on Betty and George's false promise instead of suing to enforce visitation, she might have won.

A lesser known reason for nullifying a contract is called lesion beyond moiety or just plain lesion. This terminology is peculiar to Louisiana and simply means that a person who enters a contract for sale, exchange, or division of immovable property should get reasonably close to the actual value of the property sold, exchanged, or divided. If a seller can prove that he received less than fifty per cent of the actual value of the property, he may have an action for lesion and if he is successful, he can require the purchaser to choose between returning the property or paying the difference between what was paid and the actual value. This remedy is only available to the seller and only if the value received is less than one half of the actual value. Also, it only applies to immovable property (generally, real estate). The legal presumption here is that if you receive less than half of the value, you must have been in error as to the value of what you sold and therefore could not have freely given your consent.

Lesion beyond moiety can also apply to partition agreements. A partition agreement is a contract entered into by co-owners for the voluntary division of their property. This type of agreement is a common way to divide succession property among heirs and to divide community property after a separation or divorce. The rules for lesion after a partition are different than for lesion after the sale or transfer of real estate. Since the law assumes equal and fair division as the basic reason for a partition, each party must get at least three-fourths of the actual value of his share.

George and Sally were divorced. George's lawyer prepared a community property settlement which both parties signed. In the settlement, George got the house which was worth a net of $20,000 and agreed to assume the mortgage of $10,000. Sally got $10,000 in cash from a *joint account. Both sides stated in the settlement agreement that they were satisfied with the division and that they had each received equal shares in the community. The settlement was notarized and filed in the conveyance records. A few months later, Sally sued George for lesion claiming that she had not received anywhere near equal value in the community. George argued that it all worked out evenly since he had assumed the mortgage debt and should therefore be given credit for the assumption.*

The court agreed with Sally. Regardless of whether the parties admit in a partition that they are getting equal value, the fact was that Sally did not get at least three-fourths of the value of her share of the community. George had already deducted the mortgage from the total value of the house to arrive at the $20,000 net value. By arguing that he should be given credit for assuming the mortgage debt, George was attempting to benefit twice for the same mortgage. The total net value of the community was $30,000 of which Sally received $10,000 and George received $20,000. Each party should have received $15,000. Sally was entitled to sue for lesion because she received less than three-fourths of what she should have received. Three-fourths of the $15,000 which should have been her share of the community was $11,250. Because she received less than $11,250, she was successful in her suit. An action for lesion must be brought within one year of the date of a sale.

The law generally states that no one can be forced to own property with another. This is true whether the property is real estate, the assets in a partnership, or any other type of property. When a partner in a business wants out of the partnership, it is common for him to file a partition suit demanding that assets be sold to satisfy his interest in the partnership. A partition suit under these circumstances usually means the end of the business. Starting in 1991, owners who hold property in common can agree that there will not be a partition for a specific period of time, not to exceed fifteen years. An agreement that co-owners will not seek a partition must be in writing.

Although much more could be said about Louisiana contract law, if you keep in mind five concepts you will at least have a basic understanding of a few of the fundamentals.

1. The key to the formation of nearly any contract is the consent of the parties to enter into a contract.

2. The law assumes that certain people are not capable of giving consent and will allow them to back out of a contract. Make sure that the person with whom you are contracting is legally capable of entering a contract.

3. Although many types of contracts do not have to be in any particular form, some contracts are not valid unless they meet certain legal requirements. The sale of land, for example, must be an authentic act.

4. If you are the one who prepares the contract, make sure that the terms are clear and precise. Any ambiguities or misunderstandings that result because of the wording of the contract may be construed against you.

5. People are free to enter into any type of contract and the contract they agree to is the law between the parties. However, certain contracts may be considered null because the terms of the contract are against public policy.

It is always wise to have an attorney review any contract that you are considering entering. We have a client who ordinarily would consult us before entering into an important agreement. On one occasion, however, he signed a purchase agreement for a house without taking the time to think through what he was doing. Almost immediately, he found that he was paying far too much and started to suffer buyer's remorse. When he tried to back out of the agreement, the sellers sued him for damages and to demand that he go through with the sale. If he had come to us first, we could have suggested some modifications to the contract that would have given him a way out of the agreement.

Employment Rights

The relationship between employer and employee is heavily regulated by law and the trend is towards further regulation. Discrimination in hiring and firing is subject to both state and federal law, while compensation for injury on the job and unemployment benefits are subject mostly to state law.

Worker's Compensation

The most frequently asked question that employees have about Worker's compensation is "What rights does it give to me?" Well, worker's compensation actually takes away some rights from workers since the law makes it an exclusive remedy.

If you are hurt on the job, or suffer from a job related disease, the worker's compensation laws control the amount and method of your compensation. The employer is immune from virtually any other liability. This can severely restrict the amount an employee might receive for an injury since the amount that can be recovered is largely spelled out in the worker's compensation laws. A back injury received in an automobile accident might be worth considerably more to the injured person than the same injury received on the job.

On the other hand, fault is not an issue in worker's compensation. The worker is entitled to compensation whether the injury resulted from his own negligence or from the employer's negligence. The only circumstances in which compensation is not allowed are when the employee injures himself on purpose, is drunk when he is injured, deliberately fails to use a guard or protection that is provided for him, or is injured when he provokes a fight on the job.

Any employee subject to the worker's compensation laws who receives a personal injury while on the job is entitled to compensation. A few types of employees, such as domestic maids and real estate agents, are specifically excluded from worker's compensation. Also, injury caused to an employee by a third party may still leave open the right to sue the third party. In other words, if Joe is run over while working at his job as a curb painter, he may be entitled to worker's compensation and he may be entitled to sue the person who ran him over. If he recovers against the person who ran him over, he might have to reimburse the worker's compensation carrier for some or all of its payments to Joe.

An employee who develops an disease is also covered if the disease or illness is due to causes and conditions peculiar to the particular trade or occupation in which the employee works. However, the employee has the burden of proving the disease resulted from the job and he must make a claim within six months of either: 1) the disease appearing, 2) becoming disabled because of the disease, or 3) finding out the disease is job related. Failure to make a claim within six months bars the employee from compensation.

Jimmie had worked as a sandblaster for 24 years and began having pains in his chest. A complete check-up showed that Jimmie was suffering from silicosis which is a lung disease that usually results from long exposure to sand particles. Jimmie also was suffering from emphysema as the result of smoking two or three packs of cigarettes daily for thirty years. The doctors told Jimmie that he could no longer work around sandblasting and he was laid off by his employer. Seven months later Jimmie put in a claim for compensation, but the compensation insurance company refused to pay since Jimmie had not filed within six months and since there was no proof that his lung problems resulted from his job rather than from smoking. Jimmie sued, claiming that he was totally disabled.

An employer is required to post a notice that can be seen by all employees setting forth the time limits for filing a claim based on occupational disease. If the employer does not post the notice, the limit for filing claims is extended by another six months. Since there was no evidence at trial as to the required notice, the judge felt that Jimmie had twelve months to file his claim. The testimony of the doctor made it clear to the judge that Jimmie's disability was from the silicosis and not the emphysema. Therefore, since silicosis is related to the occupation of sand blasting, Jimmie won his case.

Other types of diseases, such as heart attack, are very hard to prove as directly related to a particular occupation. The fact that a particular occupation involves more stress than most occupations is probably not enough to show that heart disease is necessarily job related.

The period for notifying an employer of injury on the job is shorter than for job related disease. The employee must notify the employer within thirty days of the injury or he loses the right to recover compensation. The employer, on the other hand, is required to post a printed notice to his employees in some conspicuous place which states substantially: *"In case of accidental injury or death, an injured employee or any person claiming to be entitled to compensation either as a claimant or as a representative of a person claiming to be entitled to compensation, must give notice to (name and address of employer) within thirty days. If notice is not given to the above party within thirty days, no payments will be made under the law for such injury or death."*

If the employer fails to post this notice, the time limit for making a claim is extended to twelve months from the date of the injury. It is obviously in the employer's best interest to make sure that he has posted notice as required by law.

If an employee is so seriously injured that he is not able to notify the employer within thirty days, or if the employee is killed, it is important that a family member or legal representative make the claim within the thirty day limit. All workers should be aware of these limits and should take the time to make sure their families know what to do in case of serious injury or death. Worker's compensation not only pays benefits to injured workers, it also pays benefits to surviving dependents in case of death. These benefits are lost if a claim is not filed in time.

Once the claim has been made to the employer, he is required to make a report to his compensation insurer, if he has one, and to the Office of Worker's Compensation Administration. The Office is then required to send to the injured employee a brochure which summarizes in plain language all of the rights and responsibilities of the employee and employer.

Employers are prohibited from discriminating against employees who have compensation claims and from refusing to hire a person who has filed a compensation claim unless the injury prohibits the employee from performing the duties of his employment. Any employer who wrongfully fires an employee or refuses to hire a prospective employee because of compensation claims, may be liable in damages for the amount the employee would have received in pay up to a maximum of one year.

The amount of benefits the injured employee or his dependents receive is carefully controlled by the worker's compensation laws. The amount of damages you receive as the result of injuries from an automobile accident away from your job may ultimately be decided by a judge or jury. In worker's compensation cases, the amount you receive is set forth in tables and formulas which are keyed to the extent of the injury and whether it is considered as partial or total and whether it is temporary or permanent. The amount of allowable compensation is subject to change from year to year since the Legislature enacts these tables. There is therefore no point in listing all the various types of claims with the prescribed amounts of compensation. However, we will describe a few provisions to give you an idea of the relative amounts that might be expected.

If a worker dies within two years of a job related accident, his dependents who wholly relied on his earnings for support at the time of the accident are entitled to benefits of a percentage of wages paid. The percentage changes depending on the number of children or other dependent relatives. For example, a wife and two children of a deceased worker would be entitled to sixty-five per cent of the wages paid, which is the maximum. If the deceased left no dependents, the parents of the deceased, if any, are entitled to a lump sum payment of $20,000 each. A spouse and children under eighteen, or under twenty-three if attending an accredited school, are conclusively presumed wholly dependent if they were living with the deceased at the time of the accident and at the time of the death. Other parties who claim to have been dependent must prove the relationship and the dependency.

Compensation is usually payable as a percentage of the average wage paid in the State of Louisiana and is payable on the same schedule that the employee received his wages. However, nothing would prevent the parties from agreeing on a lump sum settlement rather than making periodic small payments. This saves the insurance company or the employer from the overhead expense of making many small payments and can give the employee or his dependents a large once-only payment that can be invested. Lump sum payments must be made with the approval of the Office of Worker's Compensation Administration or the court. The amount of the lump sum is usually computed by taking the total of the payments that would be due and discounting the amount to allow for immediate use of the money by the employee. The discount cannot be more than eight percent or the employer will be subject to severe penalties.

The worker's compensation law attempts to categorize nearly everything including the degree of severity of various types of injuries. The category an injury falls into can determine the amount and duration of the compensation. Injuries can be classified as temporary total, permanent total, or permanent partial. The payment for temporary and permanent disability is sixty-six and two thirds percent of wages during the period of disability. The payment for permanent partial disability will depend on exactly the type of injury. For example, the loss of a little toe entitles the worker to sixty-six and two thirds per cent of wages for a period of ten weeks while the loss of a big toe is worth sixty-six and two thirds percent of wages for twenty weeks. The loss of an arm is worth sixty-six and two thirds percent of wages for two hundred weeks while the loss of both arms is considered permanent total disability. The tables of disability benefits cover nearly every conceivable combination of injury and, as you can see, are somewhat arbitrary.

Rose worked at a drug store for several years until she hurt her back lifting a case of soft drinks. The doctor found a ruptured disk and admitted her to the hospital for surgery. After recovery, Rose found that she suffered pain most of the time and the doctor recommended that she not ever try to lift more than ten pounds. After receiving compensation for 115 weeks, the doctor discharged Rose and said she was ready to go back to work. The insurance company stopped her benefits and Rose sued to have them reinstated since she could not find another job, could not do any lifting, and because she was in pain nearly all of the time.

The trial judge found that Rose was at a substantial disadvantage in the job market because of the restriction against lifting and the pain and declared that she was permanently and totally disabled. Because the judge felt that stopping the compensation was arbitrary and capricious, he also assessed penalties and attorney's fees against the insurance company for not paying compensation to Rose. The appeals court overruled the trial judge and said that she was not totally disabled. It used to be the law that you were disabled if you could not perform the job you formerly held or were trained for. Now you are not entitled to compensation for permanent total disability unless you cannot hold any reasonable job. Since Rose was capable of working in a job that did not require lifting, such as a cashier, and since her pain was only moderate, she was not permanently disabled. The appeals court ordered that a new hearing be held to see if Rose might be entitled to compensation for partial disability and revoked the penalties against the insurance company.

Payments of benefits must be made on the same schedule and at the same place as the worker was receiving his wages, although the worker can elect to have the payments mailed to him. The worker is not entitled to compensation for the first week after the accident unless the disability continues for six weeks or more. If the disability continues for more than six weeks, the worker is then entitled to payment for the first week of disability.

There are several miscellaneous worker's compensation law provisions for the protection of workers. Among the more prominent are: the employer or his insurance company must provide the worker with copies of all medical reports and must pay for all reasonable medical treatment; if the worker is killed on the job, the employer is responsible for all burial expenses to a maximum of $3,000; the employer is specifically prohibited from charging the employee, or deducting from his pay, any part of the cost of maintaining worker's compensation insurance.

Effective in 1989, worker's compensation claims are no longer heard by the district courts. This was a major change in our laws apparently in response to the effort to make Louisiana more attractive to business.

The new law requires that your claim be heard by one of nine administrative hearing officers who are appointed by the Governor for six year terms. The hearing officers must be attorneys who have been practicing law for at least five years. The hearing officer has the power to decide the merits of a compensation case and his ruling has the same force as a judgment of the district court. Appeals from the hearing officer must be made within ten days and are to a panel of three hearing officers. Appeals from the decision of the panel are made directly to the appeals court for the district in which the claim was first made.

Job Related Rights

There are other provisions of the law that can cause problems for the unwary employer or go unnoticed by the uninformed employee. For example, employers are prohibited from assessing fines against their employees. A fine can only be levied against the employee if he willfully or negligently damages goods or property of the employer and then only for the actual amount of the damage. Any other type of fine can make the employer himself liable for a fine of up to one hundred dollars and imprisonment for up to three months. One contractor who routinely fined his employees for ordering building inspections before the necessary work was completed, found out about this statute to his regret.

An employer is subject to the same penalties if he requires an employee to sign a contract in which the employee forfeits his wages if he quits or is discharged before the contract is up. In all cases, an employee is entitled to whatever wages he has earned up until the time his employment ends.

An employer should also be very careful about loaning money to an employee. The employer can only charge a maximum of eight percent interest. If he charges more, he is subject to the same maximum three month jail term as the employer who fines his employees.

There is a great deal of misunderstanding as to an employee's rights when he quits or is fired. It is the employer's responsibility to see that the employee is paid in full everything that is owed at the next regular payday or within fifteen days of the termination of the employment, whichever is first. The final payment can be made at the place and in the manner that was customary during the employment or it can be by mail if sent to the address of the employee as listed on the employer's employment records. The payment is considered good when mailed. If there is a dispute as to the amount the employee is owed, the undisputed part must be paid within the three day period.

Most of the misunderstanding comes in trying to apply the penalty sections of this area of the law when the employer fails to make the final payment within the required period. When the employer fails to pay the employee on time, he may become liable to the employee for damages which are figured at the employee's regular rate of pay for every day from the time the employee demands payment to the time the payment is made, but only to a maximum of ninety days pay. Accumulated vacation time is specifically included as an amount owed. The employer may also become liable for the employee's legal expenses.

The law does not specifically say how the employee is to make the demand for payment, but the penalty does not start to run until the demand is made. Obviously, the employee who does nothing for ninety days should not be able to recover damages from the employer who may not be aware that wages are due. This frequently happens when an employee is due commissions, sick leave or vacation time. All of these benefits are considered pay owed the employee and come under the penalty statutes. To be safe, the employee should immediately make written demand for everything he thinks he is owed. The employer should pay the amount demanded unless there is a genuine dispute over the amount owed. Even then, the employer should immediately pay the amount that is not disputed or he will be liable for penalties.

Roberta worked for a telephone answering service until she was discharged on May 14 because of a lack of customers. On May 19, Roberta sent her former employer a written demand for all wages due her and she further stated that if she didn't receive her pay within 72 hours she would turn the matter over to her lawyer. On May 23, two days after the deadline, her employer sent her $97.04 which represented pay for 29.30 hours worked during the pay period. Without any further demand, Roberta filed suit on June 19 asking for unpaid vacation time, penalties and attorney's fees. In December, Roberta received $264 from her employer which represented gross pay for two weeks vacation time. At trial, Roberta claimed that she should have been paid all of her wages immediately and that her employer had no reasonable excuse in waiting so long to pay her. Her employer claimed that she had been paid in full before the trial and that any delays were because it was difficult determining how much vacation time was due. The employer also argued that it had no idea Roberta was demanding vacation pay until suit was filed. After all, it argued, her demand letter only said that she wanted her wages.

The court decided that Roberta was entitled to damages in the sum of $2,376 and attorney's fees of $1,000. The court felt that the employer had the information available as to how much vacation time was due Roberta and was not impressed by the argument that she didn't specifically ask for compensation for vacation time. Since the employer waited more than ninety days to pay her, she was entitled to her full wages for the maximum period of time allowable.

In most of these cases, the courts will look at the employer's good faith in deciding whether to assess damages. If it appears that the employer has made every effort to pay the employee as quickly as possible, the court will probably not assess damages. If the employer has been unreasonable or unfair, damages will probably be assessed.

There are a few provisions concerning job related rights that employers and employees should be aware of:

- Employers cannot require that employees put up a cash deposit to insure the faithful performance of their duties unless the employer pays interest on the deposit.

- Employers cannot require employees or applicants for employment to submit to medical examinations or drug tests unless the employer pays all of the costs of the examination or test, including fingerprinting.

- Employers cannot bring persons from outside the State of Louisiana for the purpose of interfering with strikes or replacing striking workers, although there are some exceptions.

- No employer with more than twenty employees can interfere with the employee's political affiliation or right to be a political candidate.

- Employers cannot require that employees purchase their goods or services from a particular store or supplier.

- Employers cannot fire an employee because that employee testified at a labor investigation.

- No person can bring into the state any person for employment who is not entitled to lawful residence in

the United States, although certain agricultural workers
are an exception.

• No employer with more than twenty employees can
  refuse to hire a person with sickle cell anemia, fire such
  a person, or in any way categorize him or her to limit
  pay or advancement.

• No employer with more than twenty employees can
  reject an applicant based on any age less than fifty
  years.

The penalties for violating some of the provisions listed
can run as high as one year in prison. The employer needs to
seek legal advice if he has reason to believe that he may be in
violation.

A new type of discrimination was made unlawful in
1991: smoking discrimination. The Louisiana Legislature
saw the need to make it unlawful for an employer to discriminate against anyone because "the individual is a smoker or a
nonsmoker." Without getting any more specific about what
action might be considered discriminatory, the statute impos-
es up to a $250 penalty for the first offense and up to $500
for each subsequent offense. Although the employer can have
reasonable restrictions for smoking on the job, the employer
cannot require that the employee abstain from smoking outside the course of employment.

Non Competition Agreements

Is an employment contract that forbids the employee
from competing against the employer binding? This is one of
the first questions that both employers and employees want
to know. The answer used to be generally, no. The answer
today is generally, yes.

The law used to simply state that no contract to restrain
competition against an employer would be enforceable un-

less the employer spent money training the employee. This was amended in 1989, in 1990, and again in 1991, so that the original single paragraph statute is now twenty paragraphs.

The 1989 amendment added a provision to cover the sale or dissolution of a business and the purchase of a franchise. If you sell a business or a franchise, the buyer can require that you agree not to compete in the same business or a similar business. If the seller agrees to this restriction, it will be binding. This was amended the following year to cover employer-employee agreements. An agreement by an employee not to compete with the employer in the same or similar business will be binding on the employee. A non-compete agreement can specifically cover the writing of computer software that would compete with the employer. In all of these cases, the restriction must be for a specific period of time that cannot exceed two years and the agreement must be limited to a specific parish, parishes, cities, or parts of parishes and cities. The non-compete statute was further amended to specifically address franchise situations and computer software design.

Job Related Discrimination

It is often very difficult to determine whether someone has been discriminated against to the extent that state or federal law has been violated. Employers make decisions every day that are by necessity discriminatory in nature. A certain person may not be hired because the employer does not like his or her looks or attitude and this may be legally acceptable. On the other hand, certain classes of people come within protected categories and a presumption may arise that the failure to hire, the treatment of this person while an employee, or the firing of this person, is illegal discrimination.

There are specific provisions in both state and federal law prohibiting discrimination based on status as a handicapped person, race, age, sex, religion, and national origin. The main difficulty comes in proving that a particular person has been discriminated against because that person is a member of the protected class, rather than for some legally acceptable reason.

Another difficulty is in deciding whether to pursue the claim in state court or in federal court. The remedies available overlap to a large extent because Louisiana state law follows the federal statutes in many respects. However, there are significant differences in the procedures that must be followed in the two systems. Federal law requires that you exhaust certain administrative remedies before you can file suit and strict limits are set as to the amount of time you have for filing. Louisiana, on the other hand, has no strict administrative procedure to follow and suit can usually be filed within less restrictive time limits. Only an attorney with experience in this area of law can make the decision as to whether to proceed in state or federal court.

Federal law requires that you file a complaint with the Equal Employment Opportunity Commission before you can begin any proceeding in the federal courts. Federal law also requires that the complaint be made within a certain time period of the occurrence of the discrimination. This time period is normally 180 days. Failure to first file a complaint with the EEOC or failure to bring the complaint within the allowed time period has a drastic consequence: you may no longer have any right to bring the complaint or lawsuit. You may no longer have any federal remedy against the person or company that discriminated against you.

This drastic consequence has caught many a person who waited too long to file a complaint or who filed suit without first going through the EEOC. As a matter of fact, more than a few lawyers have lost cases for their clients because they were not aware of the strict time requirements involved. We know of cases where the lawyer filed suit, saw it dismissed because they did not first file a complaint with the EEOC, and then found that it was too late to file a complaint because time was wasted filing the suit.

If you feel that you have been discriminated against and wish to take legal action, see a lawyer immediately. It is extremely important that you protect your rights and leave open the option as to whether you will proceed in state or federal court. If you let too much time go by, you will lose the option of proceeding in the federal system. You may also lose your only alternative: proceeding in the Louisiana courts.

Louisiana has laws forbidding discrimination against the handicapped, against certain age groups, and against a person because of race, color, religion, sex or national origin. Each of these three groups has its own definition of the persons who may not discriminate and the persons who are in the protected class. For example, an employer for purposes of age discrimination must have at least twenty employees to come under the discrimination law, while an employer for purposes of race, color, religion, sex or national origin must have at least fifteen employees.

Although the Louisiana and federal law on discrimination is very similar, there is one big procedural difference. In the Louisiana system, you do not have to go through an administrative process before you can sue in court. In other words, there is no state equivalent to the Equal Employment Opportunity Commission. Let's take a look at some of the provisions of Louisiana's discrimination laws.

No handicapped person may be discriminated against by any educational establishment, in any real estate transaction, by any person or institution receiving state or local aid, or by any employer with more than fifteen employees. A particular employer might have fewer than fifteen employees yet be subject to the law because he receives state or local financial benefits or in some other way comes under another part of the law. A handicapped person is defined, in part, as anyone who has an impairment which substantially limits one or more life activities. Impairment specifically includes mental retardation as well as physical disorders. The handicapped person is defined by the law and then put in a "class" which the law protects. The law then defines the activities that might be considered discriminatory against this class.

The employer cannot fail or refuse to hire, refuse to promote, or refuse to reasonably accommodate an otherwise qualified individual on the basis of a handicap when it is unrelated to the individual's ability with reasonable accommodation to perform the duties of a particular job. The employer may also be in violation if he limits or classifies the handicapped employee, requires mental or physical examinations prior or during employment when the examination is not directly related to the particular job, or in limiting the utilization of wheelchairs or other adaptive devices needed by the employee.

SueAnna seemed to have anger issues that kept cropping up in her employment. She also seemed to be fond of filing suits against her employer and other employees. In 1988 she was hired as a security inspector. In 1995 she sued her employer, an insurance company, and two employees alleging sexual harassment and racial discrimination. In 1998 she fainted at work and was put on medical leave while testing was done. In 1999 she was allowed to return to work, but was not allowed to carry a gun because of anger management issues. In 2000, SueAnna amended her original suit to include disability discrimination because she was not allowed to carry a gun. She claimed that not being allowed to carry a gun was in retaliation for her various suits and that it would prevent her from getting promotions as a security guard. In 2000, SueAnna was fired for insubordination and in 2005 the merits of the case were finally heard.

The court had an easy time deciding that no discrimination occurred because SueAnna simply was not a handicapped person in the first place. That being the case, it would be impossible for any handicap discriminate to exist. Louisiana law defines "Handicapped person" as meaning "…any person who has an impairment which substantially limits one or more life activities." The testimony of SueAnna showed that she had no physical disability other than a high school track injury that limited her only from running track. So, the court reasoned, her claim boils down to nothing but an attempt on her part to say that not being allowed to carry a gun has *created* a disability. The court said this argument was novel, but flawed. Clearly the law does not equate carrying a gun as a "life activity" that needs protection.

Assuming a person really is handicapped, unlike SueAnna, the main difficulty in determining the point at which the person discriminated against has a valid claim comes down to "reasonable accommodation." Is an employer required to install ramps to his building to accommodate employees in wheelchairs? The question of reasonable accommodation may depend on the financial burden placed on the employer and the relative ability of the employer to make the necessary accommodation. Ultimately, the question may be left to a judge to decide what the Legislature meant by "reasonable."

If a handicapped person feels that the employer or prospective employer has discriminated against him, he must file suit within 180 days of his discovery of the act of discrimination. There is a one year limit from the date of the act of discrimination for filing suit regardless of when he discovered the act. Before filing suit, the handicapped person must inform the employer of his intent to file at least thirty days prior to the filing. Both parties must then make a good faith effort to settle their differences before suit can be filed. If the suit is successful, the person bringing the complaint may be entitled to damages, his attorney fees, and any other relief the judge deems appropriate. However, if he loses he may be ordered to pay the employer's costs and attorney fees.

Discrimination against a person because of race, color, religion, sex or national origin is prohibited by any employer with more than fifteen employees. Labor unions and state or local agencies are included as employers but private schools, nonprofit corporations and religious educational institutions are not included under the law. Discrimination is unlawful if the employer intentionally refuses to hire someone, discharges someone, or in any way discriminates against someone because of that person's race, color, religion, sex, or national origin. The employer is also prohibited from classifying or limiting employees in a way that would deprive an individual of employment opportunities because of color, race, religion, sex, or national origin unless the discrimination is the result of an affirmative action plan.

Agatha worked as a claims representative for a large insurance company. One day, it came to Agatha's attention that there were certain crude remarks about her written on the walls of the men's restroom. Agatha waited until after work, went into the men's room, and saw, to her horror, several obscene cartoons. Some of the cartoons illustrated explicit and perverted acts and were labeled with her name and the names of several men employees. Agatha erased the cartoons that mentioned her name, cleaned out her desk, quit the company, and filed suit for sexual harassment. She also underwent psychiatric counseling because of the incident.

Agatha claimed in her suit that her right to be free of sexual harassment in the work place had been violated. The court acknowledged that there were two types of sexual harassment: harassment that conditions employment benefits on sexual favors and harassment that creates a hostile or offensive working environment. Did the cartoons create an offensive working environment for Agatha? Perhaps they did, but she should have complained to her employer and allowed them a chance to take some action. There was no evidence that the company had any knowledge of the gross graffiti. Also, the cartoons were labeled with the names of both men and women. The court concluded that although an employer has a duty to avoid sexual harassment, it does not have a duty to maintain a pristine work environment. Agatha lost her case.

Louisiana also has some new laws forbidding discrimination against women because of pregnancy and childbirth. Employers with more than twenty-five employees cannot refuse to promote or select for a training program any female employee because of pregnancy, childbirth, or any related medical problem. The employer must make all benefits available to the pregnant worker that are available to other workers including medical, sick leave and disability. The employer is not required to provide disability in a normal pregnancy and birth of more than six weeks. The employer is also required to allow up to four months of leave because of pregnancy and childbirth. The employee can utilize accrued vacation time towards the leave time.

Any party who believes that he has been discriminated against can file suit against the employer and seek damages, lost pay, back pay or whatever is reasonably related to the discrimination. A person who is found to have brought a frivolous claim may be held responsible for the damages and attorneys fees suffered by the employer. Louisiana law does not state a particular time limit for filing suit, so it must be assumed that the general time limit for filing a suit for damages of one year might apply. There is no excuse, though, to let any time go by once you believe that discrimination has taken place. As we said before, you have to do something quickly because your options quickly disappear as time goes by.

Some acts are specifically authorized, like having merit systems for pay and raises, even though some groups may seem to be discriminated against. It is alright for *"An employer to apply different standards of compensation or different terms, conditions, or privileges of employment pursuant to a bona fide seniority or merit system, or a system which measures earnings by quantity or quality of production, or to employees who work in different locations, provided that such differences are not the result of an intention to discriminate because of race, color, religion, sex, or national origin."*

For more information on your remedies in the federal system, or to file a complaint, contact the Equal Employment Opportunity Commission. Since the New Orleans office was closed after Katrina and then re-opened at one point as part of the Houston office, it is probably best to contact the EEOC through their website: *www.eeoc.gov.*

Part 4

Your Rights

As a Consumer

How many times have you bought something only to end up wishing you knew of some way to force the seller to take it back or at least repair it? How many times have you ended up stuck with some product that didn't begin to live up to the claims made about it? Everyone is a consumer and sooner or later faces these questions. In many of these types of cases, the cost of hiring a lawyer is hard to justify compared to the amount that has been lost. It is a sad fact that there is seldom any practical recourse for the consumer unless his brother-in-law is a lawyer or he happens to know a little about his legal remedies. In this section we will discuss the remedies available to the Louisiana consumer and the procedures that must be followed to protect those rights.

The Lemon Law

It has always been the law in Louisiana that any product sold carries an implied warranty that it is fit for the purposes for which it is sold. In other words, if you buy a car there is an implied warranty that the car will run and take you where you want to go. If the car is defective, you could always sue to rescind the sale on the basis of redhibition just as you could for a defective house, as we saw earlier. The Legislature modified the law at one point and added the requirement that you had to give the seller an opportunity to repair before you could demand that the sale be rescinded.

This change in the law caused new problems. What constituted an opportunity to repair? How many times did a consumer have to put up with trying to get a defective product repaired before he could demand that the sale be rescinded? In 1984, the Legislature passed a new law covering warranties on motor vehicles. This law became popularly known as the "lemon law" because it gave new rights to people who bought cars with chronic problems.

The law applies to any motor vehicles sold by a dealer in Louisiana after September 1, 1984 and any vehicle leased after August 30, 1986. The motor vehicle must be subject to an express warranty by the manufacturer and the vehicle cannot be used exclusively for commercial purposes. A person who buys the motor vehicle from the original purchaser while the original warranty is still in effect would also be covered. The lemon law places a duty to repair on the manufacturer when the vehicle does not conform to the express warranty. The consumer must report the problem to the manufacturer or the dealer within the warranty period or within one year of buying the vehicle, whichever is sooner. Once the problem is reported, the dealer must repair the vehicle to make it conform to the warranty.

The original Lemon Law statute provided for 30 days being out of service. This was amended to 90 days, or if the dealer has attempted to repair the same defect on four separate occasions, the lemon law applies. The attempts to repair can extend beyond the warranty period if the problem was first reported during the warranty period or the one year limit, whichever was earlier.

When the lemon law applies to a vehicle, the manufacturer has the option of replacing the vehicle with a new comparable vehicle or refunding the purchase price together with all collateral costs. Collateral costs include sales tax, registration fees, license fees and other costs paid by the consumer at the point of sale. The manufacturer can charge the consumer for the time the consumer had the vehicle before he first notified the manufacturer or dealer of the problem and for any use he had while the vehicle was not out of service for repair.

The manufacturer can, if it wants, provide an informal process to settle disputes if the written warranty contains a description of the process. If this is properly done, the consumer must first rely on the process before he can demand a replacement or refund. Although manufacturers have not yet seemed to take advantage of the dispute settling process, it may become more common in the future. Check the warranty that came with your new vehicle to see if any provisions have been made to require that you first go through a dispute settling process before demanding replacement or refund.

Although it is not part of the lemon law, there is a new statute that requires a car manufacturer to pay rental car fees under certain circumstances. The car must have been purchased after January 1, 1987, it must be subject to an express manufacturer's warranty, and it must be returned to the dealer who sold the car. For the period of the warranty, or for two years, whichever is shorter, the manufacturer must reimburse the owner for the owner's car rental expenses of up to twenty dollars per day. This obligation for car rental fees only comes into effect if the car is in for frequent or long-lasting repairs. What is frequent or long-lasting? The statute applies if the car is in for repairs in excess of ten working days, or, if the car has been in for repairs on two prior occasions for the same complaint. If the manufacturer is liable under the law for these fees but does not reimburse the consumer, the consumer is also entitled to damages and his attorney's fees.

To sum up your rights under the lemon law, you may be entitled to a refund or a replacement if you have brought your car back to the dealer on four separate occasions in an attempt to fix the same problem, or if your car has been in for service a cumulative total of ninety days regardless of the reason. The first complaint must be within one year of the purchase or within the warranty period, whichever is earlier. If you have had to rent a car while the repairs are attempted, you may also be entitled to a reimbursement for your rental car fees.

Consumer Protection

Laws that take more of an interest in consumer protection have been part of a more recent trend. Most legislation in this area has been in response to abuse by sellers and manufacturers rather than an across the board effort to enact pro-consumer legislation. For example, abuses by managers of dance studios in selling lifetime memberships to elderly and gullible clients for exorbitant fees, led in 1979 to laws controlling dance studio contracts.

Contracts cannot require payments or financing for more than two years and cannot be for the life of the client, although the contract itself can extend to seven years. The contract can be rescinded by the client if he gives the studio written notice within three days of signing. It can also be rescinded in the event of the death or disability of the client. All these terms must be in the contract and any studio that does not comply is subject to suit for damages by the client. The studio is required to post a $25,000 bond with the state to be sure there are sufficient funds to pay any judgments.

Similar laws were passed a few years later for the physical fitness services. All facilities for physical exercise or weight control, tanning studios, sport clubs, and health spas come under the law. Any prepaid contract for services of over one month's duration must be in writing and must explain the customer's right to cancel the contract by midnight of the third day after signing the contract. The contract cannot be for more than thirty-six months and it must state all financing charges, if any. Like dance studios, health facilities must post a bond with the state to insure funds for damage suits.

Any person or organization which advertises or offers to find residential rental property is considered a rental referral agency and has its own set of consumer protection laws. Contracts to find apartments cannot charge clients unless they actually secure a place for their client. They can charge a deposit, but it must be returned if they are not successful. In order to be able to charge a deposit, the agency must have a written contract in which the client states what he is looking for and the contract must disclose that the deposit will be returned in ten days if no lodging is found. The agency cannot advertise or represent that space is available unless they have verified this fact within forty-eight hours and they must keep records of the verification for state inspection. The agency must post a bond before they can require deposits and failure to follow some of the requirement can lead to criminal charges.

In 1970 a law was passed in response to a consumer fraud that became popular as direct mail selling became wide-spread. Certain companies would send goods "on approval" and demand payment if the goods were not returned within a few days. The new law provided that any merchandise received by a consumer who did not specifically place an order can be considered an unconditional gift. The consumer can throw the merchandise away or do anything else he wants with it. If the party sending the goods bothers the consumer about payment, the consumer can sue to stop the harassment and, if successful, recover costs and attorney's fees.

Home solicitation is another area that has been fertile ground for fraud. Door-to-door salesmen would talk people into buying anything from encyclopedias to aluminum siding. Using high pressure tactics, the salesman would convince the gullible homeowner to sign a binding contract for goods or services. By the time the homeowner realized that he had been taken, usually right after the salesman left, it was too late. The contract was usually binding and the company would not hesitate to sue for damages if the homeowner refused to pay.

Now the homeowner has the right to back out of a sale under certain circumstances. If the solicitation is made at a place other than the seller's business, the buyer may have the right to rescind if he notifies the seller by midnight of the third day after the agreement to buy is signed. Telephone solicitations are included under this law. The notice must be in writing and is good when mailed to the seller. The seller is required to notify the buyer of this right in the contract and the seller must also provide an address for the buyer to send the notice of rescission.

If you agree to have your brick home covered with vinyl siding, you normally have three days to come out of your moment of weakness. However, if you originally contacted the siding company because of their television ad, you do not come under the three day law. The right to rescind is only good if the salesman first contacted you, either by coming to your home or by telephoning you. The law also does not apply to catalog sales, sales of religious articles, or when the buyer requests that the sale be without delay because of an emergency and the seller makes a good faith attempt to perform.

The Legislature also created the Unfair Practices and Consumer Protection Law. Among other things, this law established the Governor's Consumer Protection Division which set up a full-time office to investigate charges of consumer fraud and to see that consumers are represented on public boards and commissions. The Consumer Protection Division has the authority to investigate claims of unfair practices and to turn over the results of their investigation to the Attorney General.

Under the Consumer Protection Law, "Unfair methods of competition and unfair or deceptive acts or practices in the

conduct of any trade or commerce are hereby declared unlawful." You may have noticed that the statute is vague.
Exactly what practices are unlawful? The Director of the
Consumer Protection Division is given the power to make
rules and regulations consistent with the other laws concerning consumer protection and to have these regulations approved by the Attorney General. If a particular practice is
found to violate the law, the practice can be prohibited and
the courts can assess damages against the party practicing the
unlawful act.

The law also gives a right of action by private persons
against any party who employs an unfair or deceptive method
declared unlawful:

> "Any person who suffers any ascertainable loss of money or
> movable property, corporeal or incorporeal, as a result of the use
> or employment by another person of an unfair or deceptive
> method, act or practice declared unlawful by , may bring an
> action individually but not in a representative capacity to recov-
> er actual damages. If the court finds the unfair or deceptive
> method, act or practice was knowingly used, after being put on
> notice by the director or attorney general, the court shall award
> three times the actual damages sustained. In the event that
> damages are awarded under this Section, the court shall award
> to the person bringing such action reasonable attorney's fees and
> costs. Upon a finding by the court that an action under this
> section was groundless and brought in bad faith or for purposes
> of harassment, the court may award to the defendant reasonable
> attorney's fees and costs."

If the court agrees that a deceptive practice was used, it
may award damages to the successful consumer equal to the
consumer's actual losses. If the court finds that a party
knowingly used a deceptive practice after being put on notice
by the Director or the Attorney General, the court can award
triple the actual damages suffered.

*Walter loved Oldsmobiles. In fact, Walter bought a new
Oldsmobile every two years and spent a great deal of time*

choosing the options he planned to have in his next car. When it came time to buy his next car, Walter went to Gordon Oldsmobile as soon as the new models arrived. Walter spent several hours with the salesman making sure that his new Oldsmobile had all the new gadgets and that it had a 350 V-8 four barrel engine. The chrome air filter had a reassuring decal that said "Oldsmobile 350." Walter bought his new car only to find out several months later that the engine in his Oldsmobile was actually made by Chevrolet. Walter sued Gordon Oldsmobile and General Motors to have his purchase price refunded. Gordon Oldsmobile and General Motors responded by saying that all General Motors engines are basically the same. Walter wanted a 350 V-8 four barrel and that's exactly what he got, the auto giant argued.

The court considered this a perfect example of an unfair or deceptive practice that violated the provisions of the Consumer Protection Law. The court believed that General Motors deliberately took actions, such as putting the decal on the air filter, that were calculated to deceive the consumer. Walter was not only given a refund, he was awarded $2,000 in attorney's fees. In fact, the court made it clear that they would like to have given his attorney more fees if he had only asked for more.

Under the consumer protection statutes, Walter had one year from the date of the unfair practice in which to file suit. Also, since Walter had used the car for quite a few months before he won the case, the court deducted a reasonable amount for his use of the car.

Loretta's Buick had a small problem. The oil pressure light kept going on even though her neighborhood mechanic had checked the oil pressure and found it to be good. The mechanic told her it was probably just a bad switch. Because she was bringing the car in to the dealer anyway for one of the many recalls, Loretta asked that the oil pressure problem be checked. The dealer called her and said that they had stripped down the engine and had not

234/ Louisiana Legal Advisor

found any problem. Loretta authorized the work since the service manager told her the engine was already in pieces. Loretta paid the dealer $1,200 with her credit card. Two days later, the oil pressure light went on again. The neighborhood mechanic fixed the problem by replacing the $7.42 oil pressure switch. Loretta stopped payment on the credit card and the Buick dealer filed suit against Loretta for $1,200 and their attorney's fees. Loretta filed a counter-suit claiming that the repairs were unnecessary. She also sued for mental anguish and her own attorney's fees.

The court found that the Buick dealer had committed a deceptive and unfair trade practice even though Loretta had not specifically made that claim in her suit. Because it was an unfair trade practice, the court dismissed the dealer's suit and awarded Loretta $500 for her attorney's fees.

In a another case, a man bought a supposedly new Ford that had been marked down because the paint wasn't just right. It turned out the car had been repaired and repainted after hail damage. When the paint began to crack and peel, the owner sued for unfair trade practices. He was awarded $3,800 for loss of value, $2,500 for mental anguish, and $3,000 for attorney's fees.

Many types of cases can come under the statutes prohibiting unfair competition or trade practices. If you honestly feel that you have been treated unfairly, there is a good chance that the Governor's Consumer Protection Division or a court might agree with you. You basically have two choices as to how to proceed against the party you feel treated you unfairly. You can make a complaint to the Consumer Protection Division, or you can file suit. But be careful: if you file suit and the court finds that you were in bad faith or filed the suit to harass the defendant, you can be forced to pay the defendant's costs and attorney's fees. It is therefore a good idea to consult an attorney for expert advice before attempting to sue.

It has been largely up to the courts to decide what is an unfair trade practice that is prohibited by the statute. In a recent case the court summed up its definition by saying:

"A practice is unfair when it offends established public policy and when the practice is immoral, unethical, oppressive, unscrupulous, or substantially injurious to consumers."

This language was quoted in a case which found that a former employee was guilty of diverting potential customers away from his employer while he was still employed by that employer. The court decided that this was an unfair trade practice and made the employee pay his former employer all the gross income received as the result of his unfair trade practice. The statute, therefore, can be applied to many situations, not just to consumer affairs.

Consumer Credit

The Louisiana Consumer Credit Law covers most financial transactions that involve consumer loans or credit sales. Mortgage loans for real estate, loans to businesses, and credit sales of automobiles are examples of credit transactions that are not covered by the Consumer Credit Law. However, the parties to a consumer credit transaction can specifically agree that the transaction is subject to the law if they so choose. What is the purpose of this area of the law? To regulate the interest that can be charged and to protect the consumer from unfair practices in the granting of credit and collection of debts.

The law set limits on how much interest the creditor can charge the consumer. In a consumer loan transaction, the maximum runs from thirty-six percent of the first $1,400 through a graduated scale to twenty-one percent of the portion of the loan that exceeds $7,000. Consumer loans are usually made by finance companies and are treated differently than consumer credit sales. Consumer credit sales are made so that a customer can purchase goods from the lender and are typically made with a charge account and credit card. The creditor has the choice of charging interest according to a graduated scale that is lower than the scale for consumer loans, or a flat charge of eighteen percent or less can be made. Most retailers choose to charge the standard eighteen percent on consumer credit sales or one and one-half percent per month on the average daily balance for revolving charge accounts.

There is an exception to the eighteen percent limit for consumer credit sales that consumers should be aware of. If the consumer signs a contract with the seller and agrees to pay an amount of interest that can be as high as a regular consumer loan (thirty-six percent of the first $1,400), the written agreement can then be assigned or transferred to a loan company. For example, if you buy furniture at a department store using their credit card, you would normally be charged a maximum of eighteen percent per year. But if you buy furniture and sign a contract that allows the seller to assign the credit contract to a loan company, the contract can be for as much as twice the interest rate that would have been paid for the usual consumer credit sale. The assignment must be made within thirty-five days or the seller will not be allowed to charge the higher rate. He also must inform the consumer that the assignment was not made and re-compute the interest and payments the consumer must make.

There have almost always been laws controlling the amount of interest that can be charged for a loan. Charging interest in excess of the amount allowed by law is called usury. In the past, usury was considered a crime and punishment could be severe. These days, usury is punished by monetary penalties in favor of the person who paid the usurious interest. In general, Louisiana law considers interest that exceeds twelve percent per year as usury. As you might guess from your own personal experience, there are many exceptions to the twelve percent usury ceiling. As a matter of fact, nearly every transaction has its own usury limit except most loans between private individuals. If you loan your cousin Barney $100 and charge him thirteen percent interest, you are guilty of usury. On the other hand, if you own a finance company, you may be able to charge your cousin Barney thirty-six percent interest.

An exception to the twelve percent usury limit for individuals is made when a person sells real estate and takes a mortgage for part of his payment. In this sort of transaction, the seller can charge as much as the maximum charged by the federally insured lending institutions, but in no case more than seventeen percent. Since very few people are aware that you can charge more than twelve percent when you help finance the sale of your home, many opportunities were lost for owner financing of seventeen percent during past high interest rate years.

There is yet another exception to the general usury limit for transactions between individuals. If the parties specifically agree in the contract that their transaction shall be subject to the Louisiana Consumer Credit Law, the higher interest rates of that law can apply. Suppose a building supply company sells goods to an individual and wants to take a mortgage with 14% interest on that individual's house. The building supply company is not a licensed lender or a supervised financial organization. Nor can a loan on immovable property be considered a consumer loan. For these reasons, the loan would ordinarily have to come under the 12% usury limit. However, the lender and borrower can agree in the contract to be bound by the Louisiana Consumer Credit Law and a higher rate of interest can be charged. However, the lender in this example can only enter into four or fewer of these transactions in a calendar year.

Loans that stipulate that the parties agree to be subject to higher rates should be handled very carefully. Some lower courts have been in disagreement about whether such an agreement is binding. Consult an attorney for specific advice before lending money at a rate higher than 12% interest.

The consumer credit laws also control the maximum charges that can be made for late payments, bad checks, origination fees, and the amounts that must be rebated when the loan is paid early. Loan companies are usually careful to follow these laws since deliberate failure to comply can subject the lender to having to repay to the consumer triple the interest paid and attorney's fees.

> *Robert and Wanda wanted to buy stereo equipment and decided to borrow the money they needed from Jim's Credit Company. The total loan was for $4,400 which included $3,300 for the stereo and $1,100 interest. It was a good stereo, but Robert and Wanda had trouble making the $185 per month payments. When two payments were missed, Jim's Credit imposed a $5 late charge and a $46 deferral fee. After the next two payments were missed, Jim's sued Robert and Wanda for the balance due on the loan less a rebate for the unearned interest. Robert and Wanda answered the suit by claiming that Jim's Credit had violated the Louisiana Consumer Credit Law and sent Jim's Credit a certified letter stating that the late charge was improperly assessed since the payment was not yet ten days overdue and the deferral fee was improper since they had not agreed to it in writing. Two months later, before trial, Jim's Credit refunded the $5 fee and applied the deferral fee to the balance owed.*

The court awarded Jim's Credit $3,225 which was the balance owed by Robert and Wanda. However, the court awarded Robert and Wanda $3,800 which was three times the interest they had paid and their attorney's fees. Jim's Credit ended up having to pay Robert and Wanda $575 because they violated three provisions of the Louisiana Consumer Credit Law. The law provides that creditors can charge a late fee of 5% of the amount due to a maximum of $15 after ten days from the due date. There can be no late fee if a deferral charge is made. Deferral charges, which must be agreed to in writing, are charges made by the creditor in exchange for deferring all or part of the due payments. In this case, Jim's Credit charged a late fee before it was due, charged a late fee in addition to a deferral fee, and charged a deferral fee without a written agreement.

To recover damages from the creditor like Robert and Wanda did, the violation of the Consumer Credit Law must be considered intentional or in bad faith. If the consumer sends the creditor a certified letter pointing out the alleged violation and the creditor does not respond within thirty days, the violation is presumed to be in bad faith. Jim's Credit did not respond to the letter and did not credit the deferral fee until nearly two months after the letter. Therefore, the court found that the violation was deliberate.

There are many rules controlling consumer credit that are specific as to interest rates, insurance, refunds and much more. But there is one general provision of the Consumer Credit Law that was enacted to cover situations where the creditor is just plain unfair when compared to generally accepted business practices.

Virgil wanted to buy a used car and Roy, who worked at Fearsome Finance Company, decided to find a car for Virgil. Roy found a car in the classified ads for $500 and arranged a loan. When Virgil had problems with the car, he sold it to a friend. Roy again handled the financing for a total of $1,600 which include $150 to have the car repaired. When payments were not made on the note, Fearsome Finance sued for the balance on the note.

The court found that the loan was unconscionable and refused to enforce the debt. The court concluded that the loan far exceeded the value of the car and further found that Fearsome had not rebated the unearned interest from the first loan when the car was sold to Virgil's friend. Since Virgil and his friend appeared to have been taken in by Roy's dealings with the used car, the court considered the whole deal unfair and a violation of the Consumer Credit Law.

The Louisiana Equal Credit Opportunity Law was passed shortly after the Louisiana Consumer Credit Law. The equal credit law provides that no extender of credit can refuse credit to any adult because of race, religion, sex or marital status. One purpose of the law was to prevent credit discrimination against women, particularly in light of the increasing number of divorces. The lender can have credit standards, but these standards must be applied equally to all applicants for credit. The creditor must treat the application of an unmarried woman the same as the application of a man.

Credit Repair Services

You have no doubt seen advertisements by companies that claim they can wipe away your bad credit history. Louisiana now regulates these companies by requiring a bond and limiting the claims made in their advertisements. This law applies to any person or organization that claims it will improve a person's credit record, or give advice or assistance to a person regarding improving the person's credit. A credit repair company cannot advertise that it will erase your bad credit unless it also tells you that this can only be done if the credit history is inaccurate or obsolete.

Any contract for services that the credit repair service wants you to sign must disclose that your credit history is available to you directly from the credit reporting agency; that this service is free under some circumstances; that nonprofit credit counseling might be available and where; that accurate information cannot be removed from your credit file; and that the consumer has the right to dispute his credit history directly with the credit reporting agency. In other words, the credit repair agency must make it clear that it is in no position to do anything for you that you cannot do for yourself. The consumer has the right to cancel the contract within five days after signing.

Credit Reporting Agencies

When you apply for a loan, it is the credit reporting agency that usually provides agencies the information about your credit history. Buying on credit is not the only time your credit report is consulted. These files are used by potential employers, the government, and virtually anyone with access to a computer and is willing to pay a fee. The credit reporting agency might be a local company, or it might be one of the large national companies. Whether local or national, credit reporting agencies tend to share information about you with each other. Any glitch in a credit report usually ends up reported in several different files. What can you do if you believe your credit report is inaccurate?

Louisiana's Consumer Credit Law requires the credit reporting agency to mail you a copy of your credit report within five business days of your written request. If you go to their office and request a copy of your report in person, they must provide a copy right away. They can charge you a maximum fee of eight dollars to provide a copy of your credit report. This maximum fee was for 1992 and it can be raised each year by the amount the Consumer Price Index has increased, rounded to the nearest fifty cents. If you have been turned down for credit, there is no fee to provide you a copy if you request it within sixty days of being turned down. Now that you have a copy of your report, what can you do about something in the report that you consider inaccurate?

Any credit reporting agency is required to investigate a written claim by a consumer disputing any item in the credit report. The agency has forty five days to either correct the disputed item or provide the consumer with a written update of the status of the file items after the investigation. If the consumer still does not agree with the credit report, he can make a written statement explaining his side of the dispute and this statement must be made a part of the credit report. Any time the credit agency gives out a credit report, the credit problem must be clearly marked as disputed and the statement or a summary of the statement must be given the creditor. This procedure does not have to be followed if the credit reporting agency has grounds to believe that the dispute is frivolous.

So, if you have problems with your credit record, you need to take advantage of the Consumer Credit Law by making sure your report is accurate. If the report is not accurate, you need to promptly file a written dispute. This is easy, inexpensive, and you can do it yourself.

Payment on Forged Checks

Someone steals your checkbook and writes $20,000 in checks. Your account is wiped out when the forged checks are honored by the bank. Who has to pay, you or the bank?

Oscar and his wife had a joint checking account for many years. Oscar had marital problems and decided to move into an apartment for a trial separation. Oscar's wife kept the checkbook and Oscar came to the house once a week to collect his mail. Oscar noticed that he had not received his monthly bank statement. He called the bank and was told that a duplicate statement would be sent. The following month Oscar had not received the duplicate statement nor the new monthly statement. Oscar went to the bank to inspect the bank's copies of his statements and noticed that there were several entries for large, even amounts. The checks that Oscar and his wife wrote were for bills and were almost always for uneven amounts. Oscar immediately closed the account and requested copies of the checks. When the copies of the checks arrived the following *month, he noticed that all the checks for even amounts were made out to his brother Norman. There were eighteen of them totaling $4,300. Norman was arrested for forgery, but the bank refused to repay Oscar for the loses. The bank claimed that Oscar was negligent in allowing Norman access to the checks and that Oscar should have been reconciling his account monthly so that the forgeries could have been discovered earlier. Oscar sued the bank for the $4,300 that he had lost to Norman.*

Generally, a bank has to pay when it honors a forged check, but there are exceptions. The person who claims that the bank owes for honoring a forged check must not have substantially contributed to the circumstances that led to the forgery. If Oscar was materially negligent, the bank would not be liable if it paid in good faith and in accordance with standard banking practices. In other words, if you routinely leave your checkbook on the seat of your unlocked car where everyone can see it, it is likely that you would end up paying for any stolen checks.

The bank in Oscar's case claimed that Oscar was careless in managing the checkbook. He didn't keep control of it and he didn't keep track of the checks that were written. The court decided that Oscar had done everything reasonable to prevent the forgeries. He had no warning that his brother would steal some of the blank checks and he had done everything he could to get copies of the bank statements. Once he saw that there were some suspicious checks, he closed the account immediately. The bank was ordered to pay Oscar the money that he had lost to Norman.

In another case, a bookkeeper wrote inflated checks to herself and paid personal bills with the company checks. After six months, someone in the company noticed the forgeries and had her arrested. The bank did not have to pay because the bookkeeper was in charge of the checks and

244/ Louisiana Legal Advisor

because the company was negligent in not discovering the problem sooner.

As A Debtor

Someone once said that debt is the certain outcome of uncertain income. A person in debt in Louisiana has certain rights under state law and certain rights under federal law. These laws come into effect once the consumer of credit becomes a debtor. Louisiana law controls the manner in which collections can be made and the manner in which suits can be filed against the debtor. The ultimate protection for the debtor is under federal law through the Bankruptcy Court, which can restructure debts or even eliminate debts entirely.

Collection Agencies

Louisiana law has specific provisions to protect debtors from the unethical practices of some creditors and collection agencies. Creditors, or the collection agencies that are hired by the creditor, are not allowed to contact anyone about the obligation to pay a debt except the debtor or any other person that is present in the debtor's household. In other words, creditors are not allowed to contact your employer or anyone else who does not live with you. As in nearly everything else, there are some exceptions to this.

You can waive the benefits of this law any time after the debt becomes due. However, an agreement to waive that is made at the time the loan is contracted would not be valid. The creditor can contact people without your consent to establish your credit and find out about your general character. The law specifically states, however, that the creditor cannot use this exception to try to collect a delinquent debt.

The creditor is also allowed to contact other people about your debt if he believes that you have changed your address or place of employment. The creditor can also contact a relative if you listed one on the credit application.

What can you do if you are being harassed by a creditor or collection agency? You can send a certified letter to the creditor instructing the creditor to cease further contact with you regarding the debt. Once the creditor receives this letter, he or his collection agency is forbidden to contact you except for one notice by mail per month and four personal contacts per month. The contacts cannot threaten you in any way unless the threat is to do something that the creditor is entitled to do by law. If you find that a creditor is harassing you, send the following letter, it should work like a charm:

Jim's Finance Company
123 Main St.
New Orleans, LA

Re: Account #34554

Pursuant to the provisions of LSA R.S. 9:3562, you are hereby instructed to cease any further contact with me concerning my indebtedness to you except for the limited circumstances allowed by law.

Sincerely,

Dorothy Debtor

If the creditor continues to harass you, you have the right to sue him for damages. If the creditor sues you for the debt and gets a judgment against you, the effects of the letter is canceled and he can make reasonable contacts with you and other parties to find assets to seize.

If you find yourself behind in payments on your debts, you may want to take some action before one of your creditors files suit. One action you can take is through debt counseling. Debt counselors basically work with you in an attempt to set up a budget and re-structure your debt. Any person or organization that manages the assets of an individual and makes distributions of that person's assets to his creditors, comes under the Louisiana Financial Planning and Management Service law. This law requires that the individuals involved in the service be investigated as to their character and that the service be licensed and bonded by the State. Attorneys, banks, employers, non-profit organizations and a few others are generally exempted from this law.

The Family Debt Counseling Service or consumer debt counseling services, which are non-profit and available in most of the larger cities, provide the most help for the least amount of money. These services are usually sponsored by area lenders such as banks and by major area employers. The debt counselors will review your income and expenses and try to determine what must be done to get your debt under control. If you need to be on a strict budget, the counselor will help you drop credit accounts that you do not need and will help you re-structure existing debts. The debt counselor contacts your creditors and, if necessary, may convince some of your creditors to accept partial payments until other debts are paid. The debt counselor may even be able to stop a foreclosure that is in progress.

The family debt counseling service will typically charge a fairly minimum fee for the first meeting, depending on your income. The first meeting may run from one to three hours. Depending on what needs to be done, the counselor may budget your income and make payments to your creditors. There is a monthly charge for this service, but it typically will run about $9. To find out more information, check the Yellow Pages under financial planning or debt counseling. The service will make an appointment for you and will usually send you an application and a schedule of the rates that are charged.

Declaring Bankruptcy

When debts far exceed assets, or when creditors are not willing to agree to a re-structuring of your debt, sometimes bankruptcy is the only solution. Bankruptcy, with some exceptions and depending on the type of bankruptcy you choose, can formulate a re-structuring of your debts or eliminate your debts entirely. There are three types of bankruptcy that are commonly used: Chapter Thirteen, Chapter Eleven and Chapter Seven. Eleven and Thirteen are forms of bankruptcy that allow the debtor to make payments on certain debts under the administration of the bankruptcy court. Chapter Seven eliminates any further responsibility for most debts by distributing certain of your assets to your creditors.

The thing to keep in mind is that an individual may have his choice as to which of the three different types of bankruptcy to take. Each type has advantages and disadvantages depending on the financial circumstances of the debtor and depending on exactly what he wants to accomplish by declaring bankruptcy. It is important to understand bankruptcy and to take full advantage of the opportunities that the Bankruptcy Court has the power to give.

Because bankruptcy can be complicated and because mistakes can leave you worse off than if you had never declared bankruptcy in the first place, you should always have an attorney represent you. There is another reason you should use an attorney rather than try to represent yourself: it will not necessarily cost you any more than trying to do it by yourself. Since most of your debts are going to be discharged or restructured anyway, you may as well pay an attorney a fee to represent you as make that last payment to a creditor.

Chapter Seven is the most common bankruptcy and is the form most people are familiar with. This is the type that discharges you from any further responsibility for the payment of most debts. On the other hand, you do not have your debts extinguished without paying a price: your non-exempt assets are taken to divide among your creditors. This is not as bad as it sounds since many assets are exempt and some assets can be kept by agreeing to keep up payments. In order to decide whether Chapter Seven may be an alternative that you should consider, it is important to have some understanding of which of your debts can be extinguished and which of your assets can be kept. To help you understand the bankruptcy procedure, let's look at the case of John and Marsha.

John and Marsha are a typical couple with two small children. John has a degree in computer engineering and Marsha is a school teacher with six years of experience. Both made good salaries which increased each year. Since income seemed always to increase, John and Marsha always ended up spending all they made in order to afford the things that they wanted. John was offered the opportunity to form his own consulting firm with his friend Bob. This seemed to be the perfect opportunity finally to get ahead of the rat race and allow Marsha to quit teaching so that they could increase the size of their family.

The consulting business did not do as well as John had hoped and the young couple found themselves only paying those creditors that sent the most insistent demands for payment. Finally, with savings spent and the mortgage company threatening to foreclose, John and Marsha decided to consult an attorney to see if they should file for bankruptcy.

John and Marsha were extremely embarrassed even to have to consider bankruptcy. One of Marsha's friends had told her that you lose everything you own in a bankruptcy and that you can even lose your job. John's father told him that only deadbeats and crooks go bankrupt and that he wouldn't be able to borrow money for seven years. The attorney assured them that none of this was true. The purpose of bankruptcy is to give people a new start. The United States Congress recognized this fact when it enacted the bankruptcy laws. In order to have a new start, the lawyer explained, it is necessary to have court protection against creditors. It is also necessary that in filing for protection in the bankruptcy court, John and Marsha be left with enough to continue with their lives.

The attorney asked John and Marsha to supply him with a list of all of their assets and all of their debts. This was necessary, he explained, so that he could see whether bankruptcy was advisable and so that he could prepare a bankruptcy petition if he agreed that bankruptcy was unavoidable. After totaling their assets and liabilities, it was clear that John and Marsha owed much more than they owned. The attorney advised them to file a Chapter Seven bankruptcy after briefly discussing Chapter Eleven and Thirteen.

Chapter Eleven is for people in business. It is a means temporarily to halt creditor pressure and stay in business while a plan for repayment is formulated. A sole proprietorship, partnership or a corporation can file for protection under this type of bankruptcy. John could file for Chapter Eleven bankruptcy because he is in business. Actually, it was John's business that caused most of his problems in the first place. In a Chapter Eleven, a plan is formulated for the repayment or partial repayment of debts while the business is continued and all lawsuits are halted. Although the creditors can demand that someone else be brought in to run the business, in most cases someone like John would still be allowed to operate his business since no one else would be better qualified. The attorney advised John and Marsha that this would not be a good choice for them, however. Most of their debts are personal and, reasoned the attorney, John would be better off getting out of the consulting field and returning to a salaried job.

Chapter Thirteen bankruptcy was also a possibility. This type of bankruptcy is also known as the wage earner's plan and is available to anyone who has a steady income. Like a

Chapter Eleven, the debtor formulates a plan to pay off debts or a portion of debts. Even though John does not have a steady income, Marsha's income is steady and one spouse with a steady income will qualify the couple on a joint petition for a Chapter Thirteen bankruptcy. A repayment plan usually lasts three years and the debtor's salary is budgeted according to the plan. The attorney advised against this type of bankruptcy as well. Since property acquired by the couple in the future, including Marsha's salary, would constitute property of the estate over which the bankruptcy court has jurisdiction, and because it did not appear there would be enough income to come anywhere close to making a reasonable periodic payment towards the debts, Chapter Thirteen was not a good solution to their problems.

The attorney explained that Chapter Seven was probably the best solution after looking over John and Marsha's assets and liabilities. The attorney told them that he would prepare a petition for bankruptcy with schedules showing all of the property owned by John and Marsha, all of their debts categorized by type of debt, all assets that the attorney felt were exempt from bankruptcy and other personal information about John and Marsha. The attorney further explained that the couple would have to sign the petition and schedules and state under penalty of perjury that everything is accurate. As of the day that the petition is filed, all action against John and Marsha would automatically be stayed. This means that creditors are prohibited from contacting John and Marsha and all lawsuits or other actions must be halted.

The attorney explained to John and Marsha that the next step would be a hearing known as the first meeting of the creditors. At this meeting, a clerk of the Bankruptcy Court puts the couple under oath and the trustee is allowed to ask them questions about the petition and their financial affairs. The trustee is appointed by the bankruptcy court to take control of the non-exempt assets of the debtors for eventual distribution to some of the creditors and for payment of costs. Any creditors who wish to appear and ask John and Marsha questions may do so as well. In the majority of personal bankruptcy cases, however, few creditors appear at the meeting of the creditors. John and Marsha were nervous about the prospect of having to attend the meeting of the creditors. Their attorney assured them that the bankruptcy judge would not be there and that the other debtors were more concerned with their own problems then they were with John and Marsha's.

The next and final step is the discharge hearing. At this time the bankruptcy judge explains to John and Marsha the effects of the discharge and, if everything is in order, grants them a discharge which eliminates nearly all of their debts. Debts which cannot be discharged include taxes, child support, alimony and most government insured student loans. Taxes that have been due for more than three years, however, may be dischargeable.

John and Marsha agreed with the attorney's decision and instructed him to go ahead and prepare the papers for them to sign. The attorney collected the filing fee and his own fees after explaining that these fees could be paid in installments if it was really necessary. John and Marsha decided that they might as well use their next car payment towards these fees since they were going to lose the car anyway. The attorney advised John and Marsha that they did not necessarily have to lose their car and explained to them about exempt property and property that can be re-affirmed.

The bankruptcy court allows citizens of Louisiana to keep certain property which the Legislature has declared exempt from seizure. If a creditor is not allowed to seize certain property, the bankruptcy trustee has no right to take that property for the creditors either. John and Marsha will be allowed to keep their living room, dining room, and bedroom furniture; personal clothing, linen, bedding, china, non-sterling silverware, kitchen utensils, and glassware; most major appliances; tools, instruments, and books that are used in a trade or profession; musical instruments actually used by family members; salaries and commissions; and wedding or engagement rings as long as the ring is worth less than $5,000.

Other items of property may not be exempt, but as a practical matter have no real value to the trustee. A used vacuum cleaner, for example, is not exempt but most trustees will not want to bother with it. Since the trustee must go to the trouble and expense of selling non-exempt property, the property must have enough value to make the effort worthwhile. Trustees will often offer to sell non-exempt property back to the debtor if the debtor wishes to keep the property. This frequently happens with television sets and stereo equipment.

John's computer equipment may be exempt as tools of his trade if he stays in the computer business. Also, an automobile can be exempt as a tool if it is used in a business and complies with the Louisiana definition of a business automobile. To be exempt, the automobile must be actually used in a business and not just used solely for transportation back and forth to work. In other words, if John used his car solely to drive to the office it would not be exempt. But if he used his car to make sales calls or to service the computers that he sells, it would be exempt as long as it is not classified as a luxury car. To avoid having to define exactly what constitutes a luxury car, the rule is now that $7,500 of equity in a vehicle is exempt regardless of what type of vehicle.

Also exempt from bankruptcy are pensions and retirement plans. This was a big concern to John and Marsha since John had made the maximum allowable contributions to an individual retirement account (IRA) and to a simplified employee plan (SEP). The attorney explained to John and Marsha that these plans as well as Keogh plans and annuities were exempt from seizure and from bankruptcy. The one exception is for contributions that are made within one year of filing the bankruptcy. Since John made a payment to his IRA just ten months before deciding to file bankruptcy, he would probably lose that one payment.

The fact that property can be claimed as exempt does not automatically mean that you can keep it. If you have voluntarily granted a mortgage or lien on the property, you must either give up the property or re-affirm the debt if you wish to keep the property. John and Marsha want to keep their house which is worth $80,000 and has a $65,000 balance on the mortgage. The day they declare bankruptcy, all assets, including the house, become assets of the Bankruptcy Court under the control of the trustee who is appointed to administer these assets. John and Marsha are entitled to a $15,000 homestead exemption under Louisiana law which is exempt from the bankruptcy. When this is added to the mortgage balance, there is nothing left for the trustee. The mortgage company is then free to foreclose. However, John and Marsha have kept up their payments on the house and have assured the mortgage company that they wish to re-affirm the debt. In other words, they want to keep the house and the mortgage just as though there had not been a bankruptcy in the first place. This is frequently done with houses and automobiles. With automobiles, however, the trustee may require that John and Marsha pay him the equity value in any automobile that they wish to keep.

The attorney was thorough in questioning John and Marsha about their assets. The attorney explained that it was important to list assets that they claimed were exempt since exemptions are not automatic. If the exempt property is not listed specifically on a separate schedule together with the statute that makes the property exempt under state law, John and Marsha will not be able to take advantage of the exemption. The attorney also explained that some types of debts are not discharged by a bankruptcy. These debts include the obligation to pay alimony and child support and the obligation to repay government sponsored student loans.

Assets that belong to the trustee when you file bankruptcy also include deposits you may have with a landlord or utility company, cash and jewelry, and any refunds you may be entitled to on your income taxes. John and Marsha's attorney warned them not to be surprised if the trustee required them to turn over this property prior to a discharge. At the first meeting of the creditors, the trustee asked John and Marsha about their property and also asked whether their parents were living. They might have thought that this was a strange question, but their attorney had explained to them before the hearing that any inheritance rights might also be property of the estate.

The meeting lasted ten minutes and there were no surprises since the attorney was experienced and had prepared John and Marsha for the questions that would be asked. Any creditors who wanted to protest the discharge or file a complaint with the court were given a deadline several weeks before the scheduled discharge date. The attorney explained that creditors rarely had grounds to contest a discharge. If John and Marsha were guilty of any fraud in preparing the bankruptcy or in obtaining credit, a creditor might successfully block the discharge. For example, preparing a false or exaggerated financial statement can give a creditor grounds to object to the discharge of the debt. If the debtors are honest and straightforward, they have nothing to worry about.

The second and last appearance that John and Marsha had to make at the bankruptcy court was for the discharge hearing. There were many more people at this hearing than there were at the meeting of the creditors. Also, this hearing was in the courtroom and the bankruptcy judge was present. The judge explained the meaning of the discharge to everyone present and read a list of discharge conditions which applied to some of the debtors. John and Marsha were required to provide the trustee with copies of their income tax forms when they filed in April. Some of the other people were required to turn over cars and other property to the trustee or to pay the value of the property to the trustee. Some people had no requirements at all. Everyone received his discharge whether there were conditions or not. Failure to later meet any conditions, however, can result in the discharge being revoked. The requirement that the debtors attend a discharge hearing can be waived if none of the debts are going to be re-affirmed.

The decision to file bankruptcy should not be made without giving careful consideration to the possible consequences and certainly not without the advice of an experienced bankruptcy attorney. Bankruptcy should never be used as a simple cure for financial pressure. The fact that a bankruptcy has been filed can be carried on a credit record for ten years and can make it very difficult to get a loan in the future. The decision to file bankruptcy in John and Marsha's case was the correct one and they were given a new start through the discharge of most of their debts. These were debts that they would never have been able to pay. With the pressure of collections and lawsuits removed, they were able to continue with their lives.

As this Edition was going to press, Congress once again was in the process of passing new legislation that would drastically change the bankruptcy laws. As always, you should carefully explore your particular situation with a bankruptcy attorney before taking any action.

Medical Decisions

Medical progress has left a gap between what medicine can accomplish and the legal problems that can result from this progress. It is now possible to keep a person's body alive for months and years past the point of normal death. The machines and drugs that can keep a person's heart beating inside an otherwise dead body are a medical miracle to some or an intrusion into basic rights to others.

This gap has been narrowed in recent years with the passage of Louisiana's medical consent laws and the Natural Death Act. These laws recognize that individuals and families should have some decision making rights when it comes to their own lives.

Living Wills

The term "living will" is unfortunate since it frequently is confused with last will and with living trust. However, "living will" has become the popular name for any document that refuses medical treatment past the point of normal death and we are probably stuck with this term.

Louisiana's Natural Death Act states that *"All persons have the fundamental right to control the decisions relating to their own medical care, including the decision to have life-sustaining procedures withheld or withdrawn in instances where such persons are diagnosed as having a terminal and irreversible condition."* The Legislature further stated that the artificial prolongation of life may not have any medical benefit and may cause a loss of personal dignity. The law then authorizes individuals to make a written declaration directing the withholding or withdrawal of life-sustaining procedures if the person has a terminal and irreversible condition. This declaration can also be made verbally in the presence of two witnesses. However, as a practical matter, you may not be in any condition to say what you want at the time the decision to terminate life support has to be made. If you do not want to be kept alive past the point of normal death when there is little hope of recovery, you should have a living will.

If you are worried about someone using your living will to pull your plug while recovery is still possible, there are safe-guards. For example, two physicians must agree that your condition is terminal and irreversible. Terminal and irreversible is defined to be *"...a continual profound comatose state with no reasonable chance of recovery or a condition caused by injury, disease, or illness which, within reasonable medical judgment, would produce death and for which the application of life-sustaining procedures would serve only to postpone the moment of death."*

The living will has to be witnessed by two persons. The witnesses cannot be related to you by blood or marriage, they must be eighteen or older, and they must not be entitled to any part of your estate.

The living will can be revoked at any time by destroying all copies, by written revocation, or by oral revocation. The revocation of the living will becomes effective when the attending physician is notified.

A living will can be registered with the Secretary of State. If you choose to register your living will, any doctor or hospital can contact the central registry at the Secretary of State's office to confirm that you have a living will. Although the charge for registering a living will is minimal, we see no advantage. If you make sure your relatives and your doctor have copies, registration seems to be unnecessary.

Doris signed a prepared living will form in 2001. Two years later she had a stroke and was admitted to the hospital where two doctors eventually agreed that she was "vegetative" and was only kept alive by feeding tubes. Doris, who was 89 years of age at the time, had three children. Two agreed that she should not continue with the gastric tube feeding. Another child, Betty, disagreed bitterly and filed suit to get a court injunction preventing the removal of the feeding tube. When the trial court

decided against forbidding the removal of the feeding tube,
Betty appealed to a higher court.

The higher court agreed with the trial judge and said:
"The court observed that the case was not about the aspira-
tions that loving children have for their mother; rather, about
Mrs. Doris's right to make her own decisions about health
matters..."

See the Living Will sample in the appendices for the
complete text of a living will suggested by the Louisiana
statute. If you want, you can copy or remove the sample to
use as your living will. Better yet, go to our Website at
La-Legal.com where you can download and print the latest
version of a living will.

Medical Consent

Who has the authority to make medical decisions? Louisiana law sets an order of priority of persons who can decide
whether or not to undergo surgery, autopsy, or any medical
treatment suggested by a physician. First in the order of
priority is any adult who would be undergoing the treatment.
Obviously you should be the first person consulted to decide
about your own medical treatment. It is hard to see, however,
under what circumstances you would need to consent to your
own autopsy. The obvious importance of this statute is in
setting the legal priority of those persons who will make
decisions on your behalf if you are unable to decide. If you
are in an automobile accident, brought to the hospital uncon-
scious, and there are several different surgical options, who
decides what to do?

Assuming you are unable to decide, the person who has
the first priority is any one who has been appointed your
curator. In other words, if the court has appointed someone
to look after your affairs, that is the person who makes your
medical decisions. A curator may be appointed if it appears

you will be unable to handle your affairs because the accident was serious. As a practical matter, emergency medical care could not wait until the court process named a curator.

The next person with priority is the person you name in a power of attorney. This is extremely important if you want someone to make medical decisions for you who is not at the top of the priority list. If you have a power of attorney that specifically gives someone the authority to make medical decisions on your behalf, that person will come before anyone with a lower priority. A simple or general power of attorney will not do. The power of attorney must specifically include medical care decisions or it will be of no use. Therefore, use a lawyer to have this sort of power of attorney prepared for you.

Next in the order of priority is your spouse. A husband or wife, then, has the highest authority to make medical decisions of any person not appointed by a court or named by you in a power of attorney.

After a spouse, any adult child has the authority to make medical decisions. If there is more than one child, the majority of the children can decide. This brings us to a good reason for designating someone in a power of attorney: it avoids family fights among children and others who disagree on what treatment is advisable. If there is someone you would prefer make these decisions, a particular child or even someone not related to you, you should name that person in a power of attorney.

After children, the priority is for brothers and sisters. If there are no brothers or sisters, then any of your ascendants or descendants can decide. In other words, you might end up with a group of parents and grandchildren all trying to decide whether to go with that heart transplant or opt for an artificial heart.

Part 5

Do It Yourself

Can You Do It?

What does it take to represent yourself successfully? Exactly the same thing that it takes for a lawyer to successfully represent a client: being prepared. Next to having a winning case in the first place, the single most important attribute of the successful lawyer is being consistently prepared when he or she goes to court. If you plan to represent yourself, you must make up for your lack of training by being even more thoroughly prepared than a lawyer would be. Before you decide to represent yourself, keep in mind an old saying: court is a machine that you go into as a pig and come out of as a sausage.

Making the Decision

Without doubt, in almost every case you would be better off with a lawyer than without one. A lawyer obviously is trained to practice law and has experience in preparing legal documents and in going to court. However, there is another advantage in having a lawyer represent you that is not so obvious. The lawyer is not usually emotionally involved in a suit or controversy and is therefore better able to see what is in your best interest. The person who acts as his own lawyer usually has a difficult time in playing two roles and in keeping emotionally insulated from the proceedings.

When we see people who represent themselves lose in court, it is usually because they either do not know the procedures or because they cannot dispassionately analyze their case. This happens frequently when one party tries to represent him or herself in a domestic case. We have watched a husband try to cross-examine his wife about her income and expenses in a suit for child support. The issue that must be proved is simply the needs of the children and the means of the parents. It was painfully clear, however, that in the husband's mind the only issue was the fact that his wife left him for another man. It was obvious to everyone in the courtroom, including the judge, that his repeated questioning of his wife about the other man had nothing to do with the case. It was an issue only in his mind and he was completely incapable of seeing it any other way. His wife's lawyer finally objected to the questions, the judge sustained the objection, and the man left the courtroom feeling that everyone had ganged up on him. He had so much wanted to show the world how bad a person his wife was, that he neglected to offer any proof as to his income and expenses.

It is impossible for a book to teach you how not to be emotionally involved in your own case. The plain and simple truth is this: if you have any doubts about your ability to operate in two roles, you do not have any business trying to act as your own lawyer. Try to analyze your case from a different viewpoint. A good lawyer will always try to spot all the weaknesses in a case knowing that the other side will do the same. If you are at least aware of your weaknesses, you will be able to prepare a response should the other side spot them as well. Think your case through completely and then get a friend to analyze your preparation. It is very important to get someone else's viewpoint since you will have a tendency to see things from your own perspective. Even lawyers discuss their cases with each other to get a fresh viewpoint on case preparation and strategy.

The other major stumbling block for non-lawyers is procedure. Legal procedure is like rules for a complicated game. If one player is not familiar with the rules, he simply does not have nearly as good a chance at winning as someone who does know the rules. In describing how to do it yourself, we have tried to make you aware of the procedures that are necessary for each type of case. These procedures must be followed carefully or you will find your case thrown out of court before you even get to first base.

A good example of a procedure that must be followed is the entry of a preliminary default before you can get a judgment on an uncontested divorce. The preliminary default is the first step in getting a judgment against someone who has not filed an answer to a suit. The preliminary default must be entered after the delays for filing an answer have elapsed but at least three full days before the court hearing. We have seen many a person waste his time going to court for a separation or divorce only to be told by the judge that no default had been entered or that it had been entered too close to the court date. Even lawyers will jeopardize a case because they have overlooked some procedure.

You can be sure that if you do overlook some procedure, the lawyer on the other side will be quick to point this out to the judge. After all, a lawyer is defined as someone who earns his living by the sweat of his browbeating.

What if the other side has a lawyer? That brings us to another warning: if the other side has a lawyer, you had better hire one yourself.

We recently observed a case in a city court involving a man who was suing a car mechanic because repairs done by the mechanic were apparently defective. The man represented himself, the mechanic had a lawyer. It was obvious that the man was a fan of one the popular television "real life" courtroom dramas because he brought affidavits with him from several mechanics swearing that the work done on the car was defective. Affidavits can be used on television, but not in Louisiana city courts (although they may be allowed if the suit is in a small claims division and if the judge permits it). The lawyer for the mechanic objected to these affidavits on procedural grounds: in Louisiana you must have a live witness in most circumstances so that the other side has the opportunity to cross-examine. The judge ruled that the affidavits were hearsay and they were not allowed. Hearsay is a writing or testimony by someone who is not present in court. The man had no other proof that the work was defective, and the case was dismissed. The man just stood there waiving his affidavits and protesting that they were notarized as the next case was called.

A lawyer would have known to prepare this case by having the witnesses appear at trial or by taking their sworn testimony in a deposition prior to trial. The man who lost his case could not have been expected to know this. But then, he probably should not have attempted to represent himself without learning a few basics. He should especially have been careful to prepare himself knowing that the other side would have a lawyer.

Many types of cases are not likely candidates for the do-it-yourself lawyer. Cases that are complicated, involve substantial rights, large amounts of money, or possible damage awards to the winning party, are just some of the types of cases you should avoid. A good example of the type of case to avoid was Alfred's attempt to win his own worker's compensation suit.

Alfred was injured on the job when he fell from a ladder. There was no medical proof that Alfred was injured, so his employer and the insurance company refused to pay any compensation. Alfred sued both parties for worker's compensation benefits and the case was scheduled for trial. Alfred was sent a notice of the trial date, but failed to appear. The case was dismissed by the judge without prejudice, which meant that Alfred could refile the suit if he wanted. Alfred appealed the dismissal but lost. He then refiled the suit and started the whole process over again. This time, however, the defendants filed an exception of no right of action since Alfred's second suit was filed more than one year after the alleged injury. Alfred argued that the first suit had stopped the one year period from running

*and that he still had the right to sue. Alfred lost and filed
another appeal.*

*In the second appeal, Alfred admitted that he had made
some mistakes in not appearing for the first trial and in not
filing the second suit soon enough. But, Alfred argued, he
was not a lawyer and should not be held to have the same
procedural knowledge that a lawyer is assumed to have.
Alfred pointed out some cases stating that a non-lawyer's
pleadings should be liberally construed so that he can have
his day in court. Alfred's argument was basically: "Hey,
I'm not a lawyer so don't expect me to know all these little
details."*

Alfred lost. The court summarized the general feeling
among judges about people who represent themselves: "Although we may not always hold laymen to the same standards
of skill and judgment that is required of an attorney, when a
layman chooses to appear for himself, he assumes all responsibilities for his own inadequacy and lack of knowledge of
procedural and substantive law."

You may have noticed that we have not said anything in
this book about representing yourself in a criminal case. This
is because you should never, ever try to go against the
criminal justice system on your own. We are not talking
about traffic tickets here but about any charge in which you
could go to jail or have a criminal record. There is too much
at stake and there is no excuse not to have a lawyer. If you
cannot afford a lawyer, the court will appoint someone to
represent you. In some cities, this will be a full time public
defender. In other cities, this will be a practicing lawyer
chosen at random.

Hiring a Lawyer

An initial consultation with a lawyer can be the biggest
bargain in the world. This is true even if you have already
decided to represent yourself. If you think that you may have

a cause of action against someone, the initial consultation will help you determine whether it is worth pursuing. You should also consult a lawyer immediately if you are ever sued. Remember, legal procedures have built-in time limitations. Don't make the mistake of waiting until it is too late to protect your rights.

Most lawyers will be candid in telling you whether you have a case and whether it is worth the expense of using a lawyer. As a general rule, there probably should be more than $5,000 involved before it is worth the expense of a lawyer. There can be many exceptions to this, including those cases in which money is not the object or in which the principle of the case is the issue. We have had people approach us because the dog next door keeps them up at night and they want to sue their neighbors. They were distressed when we told them that we would have to charge several thousand dollars to go to court. "All that money to shut up a dog?" they said in disbelief, "it isn't worth it." They couldn't understand that it takes just about as much time for a lawyer to prepare and go to court on a little case as it does for a big case. A case like theirs should be settled by other means.

How do you find a lawyer? The best way is through the recommendation of a friend or family member who has had a successful relationship with a lawyer. If you need advice from a lawyer with expertise in a particular field, ask for a recommendation from someone familiar with that field. For example, ask a mortgage banker for recommendations of lawyers knowledgeable in real estate or a bank's trust officer if you need a lawyer for wills and estate planning.

Although it used to be considered unethical for a lawyer to advertise, this has become more relaxed and advertising is at least tolerated by the bar associations. Many lawyers who advertise also list prices charged for services. This is thought to be beneficial by encouraging competition and reducing prices in general. You should be aware of a few things, however. Many people who go to lawyers who advertise low prices for an "uncontested divorce" do not understand what the lawyer means by "uncontested." Uncontested at these prices usually means the filing of a divorce suit against a spouse who does not file an answer. Not included are support, alimony, custody, community property issues or anything else that is not absolutely routine. In many cases, the client will be required to sign a contract which makes the divorce automatically contested and an hourly rate due should anything happen that is not routine. Even if the lawyer is telephoned by the other spouse, it can be enough to convert it to a contested case. By the way, the conversion to an hourly rate is frequently retroactive to the time the client first came in.

Lawyer specialization. We also have reservations about lawyers who advertise more than a few fields of law, thereby inferring that they have some expertise in all these fields. You have probably seen these types of ads in which the lawyer lists "personal injury, family law, divorce, custody, wills, estates, adoption, corporations, contracts, business, criminal, real estate, bankruptcy, worker's compensation, and notary public." We would put about as much faith in this lawyer as we would in a doctor who advertised his expertise as a brain surgeon, cardiologist, and specialist in jungle diseases. The fact is, medical doctors must demonstrate their skill in a specialty before they are allowed to hold themselves out as an expert in any field.

There are now requirements for lawyers in Louisiana before a lawyer can use words like "expert" or "specialist" in certain fields unless they are certified in those fields by the Louisiana Board of Legal Specialization. The specialties currently recognized by the Board are:

- Business and/or Consumer Bankruptcy
- Estate Planning and Administration

- Family Law
- Tax Law

For more information on attorney specialization, visit *www.lascmcle.org/specialization*. On the whole, we cannot recommend that you consult a lawyer solely because he advertises.

Some people expect the initial consultation with the lawyer to be free. This is probably because many lawyers who advertise also mention in their ads that the first consultation is free. This is usually because the lawyer who advertises is mainly interested in personal injury cases. These cases are almost always handled on a contingency basis and no fee would have been charged anyway. The "free" consultation is usually along the lines of "1) were you seriously hurt? 2) was the other guy at fault? 3) does the other guy have plenty of insurance?" If the answer to any of these questions is "no," the free consultation is usually abruptly over.

Some lawyers advertise free initial consultations for any type of case. These free consultations are usually intended to get potential clients in the door because the lawyer has not been able to develop a clientele by other methods. Well, you get what you pay for and in these cases the advice is often worth every penny of what you don't pay. Any lawyer who is worth your time and trust is worth paying a reasonable fee.

Lawyer referral services. If you cannot get a personal recommendation from a friend or business acquaintance, the next best thing is to use one of the lawyer referral agencies that are sponsored by the local bar associations. To be on the recommendation list, the lawyer must have malpractice insurance and he or she must agree to charge a nominal fee for the initial consultation. Most of the larger cities in Louisiana have a lawyer referral service listed in the yellow pages under attorneys or attorney referral services.

A word of warning about the bar referral services: most of the experienced lawyers do not participate. A lawyer who is experienced in a field and has a good number clients typically is not interested in giving discounted consultations or with complying with the red tape of being a member of the referral service.

If you do use a referral service, make sure that it is bar sponsored. There are many private referral services that also advertise in the telephone book. These private services are usually nothing more than a forwarding agency for lawyers that pay the agency a substantial fee. Unlike a bar sponsored service, there are no controls over the qualifications of the lawyer nor over the fees charged to the client. If you have any doubts, call the bar association listed for your city and ask if they have a referral service.

Fees

You can't make a decision about whether or not to hire a lawyer without knowing something about how a lawyer charges fees. Without doubt, lawyers are expensive. A lawyer has been unfairly defined as a one who helps you get everything that is coming to him. Like any professional or businessman, a lawyer must be compensated for years of training and experience as well as expenses and office overhead. The typical lawyer may pay 50% or more of each fee for overhead and there must be enough left over to provide a reasonable income.

Lawyers normally charge fees in one of three ways:

- Hourly rate
- Flat rate
- Contingency

An hourly rate is usually preferred by business clients because they may have several cases that the lawyer is working on at one time. The lawyer itemizes the time spent on each case and presents a bill, usually on a monthly basis. Lawyers will frequently charge a flat rate when the approximate amount of work involved is known in advance or when the client needs to know exactly how much the fees will total. Flat fees are often payable in advance or in installments. Contingency fees are based on a percentage of an award or settlement that the lawyer recovers. If the lawyer does not win the case or obtain a settlement, the client generally does not owe any fees. Contingency fees are usually one-fourth to one-third of the amount recovered. In many cases, the percentage is increased if the case goes to trial or if it is appealed.

Contingency fees have come under attack lately on the theory that they encourage lawyers to file lawsuits that may not have any merit. In actual fact, a competent lawyer is not about to take a case on a contingent basis unless it does have merit. This is because the lawyer ends up spending his time and paying for expenses to prepare a case without any guarantee that he will be paid. If he is successful, he may be well paid for his efforts. If he is not successful, he will have lost a considerable amount of time that could have been used on behalf of a client who is paying by the hour.

The contingent fee is also the only way many potential clients have of hiring a lawyer. If all fees were charged on a flat rate or by the hour, the man who is injured in an accident and loses his job would have no means to obtain the services of a lawyer. Most contingency fee contracts result from personal injury cases. This is because the lawyer can usually expect more of a recovery if he is successful and because the client is usually not in a position to pay any other type of fee. Lawyers will sometimes take other types of cases on a contingency basis, but there usually must be the potential for a large award. As a general rule, the harder the type of case is to win, the more potential there must be for a large recovery.

Once the type of fee is determined, the amount, and how it is to be paid, the lawyer then prepares a contract spelling out the terms of the employment. If your lawyer does not prepare a fee contract, ask for one. This is the only way to avoid misunderstandings when it comes time to pay the bill.

Filing Your Own Suit

Once you have made the determination that you want to represent yourself, you must learn how to prepare and file a lawsuit. Many of these rules are the same whether you are suing someone or handling something simple, like filing for a change of name.

Which Court?

Believe it or not, this is not as easy a question as you might think. There are many city, district and federal courts all with their own rules and procedures. In some cases, you may have a choice of which court to file in. In other cases, you do not have a choice and you will end up with your suit dismissed if you file in the wrong place.

In general, you should file suit in the parish where the defendant is domiciled. There are many exceptions to this, but you are generally safe to file where the defendant lives. If the defendant lives in a city that has a city court, you may want to file in city court since the filing fees are lower and city courts are generally faster than district courts. City courts, however, are limited in their jurisdiction. That means that they cannot hear cases with values above $15,000 or if the case involves the title to land, family matters or a succession.

The exceptions. Although the general rule is that there must be less than $15,000 in dispute before a city court can hear a case, there are many specific exceptions. The City Court of Houma, for example, can hear cases where the amount in dispute does not exceed $20,000. Probably more cities than not have a monetary ceiling other than the general $15,000 limit. It is not always a matter of size, either. Baton Rouge and Springhill both have limits of $35,000 as of 2011. Other cities with a $35,000 limit are the city courts of Slidell, Leesville, Zachary, Winnfield, Baker, and Minden. If you haven't noticed yet, it is an extremely good idea to check with the clerk of your local city court to determine exactly what the limits are where you live.

Evictions in city courts. There are separate rules for evictions in all city courts. Rather than a patchwork of separate limits, the maximum that can be in dispute for evictions is: for a weekly lease, $500 per week or less. For a monthly lease, $3,000 or less. For an annual lease payable by the year, $36,000 or less. You will see some leases that state an annual amount, but payable monthly. If the lease provides for penalties, interest or attorney's fees, those charges cannot be included to calculate the jurisdictional limit of the court.

District courts, on the other hand, do not have a money limit on the cases they can hear. If you have any doubt, it would be safer to file in district court. Federal courts may have concurrent jurisdiction or original jurisdiction. In other words, some types of cases could be filed in either federal or state district court, while others must be filed in federal court. The types of cases that you can file in federal court are beyond the scope of this book and should only be attempted with the advise of an attorney. However, you should be aware that in most cases, assuming the federal court has jurisdiction, there has to be a very substantial amount in dispute as a minimum before the federal courts will accept jurisdiction.

In all cases in district and city courts, you may not state the specific amount of damages you are suing for. You can only ask for damages in an amount that are reasonable. In order to establish that you are suing for enough to qualify for a certain court or for a jury trial, you can allege in the suit that your claim is above or below the amount necessary. Suits for alimony or support, on a contract, promissory note, open account or other negotiable instrument, on a tax claim, or for garnishment, can state the specific amount sued for. In other words, you cannot file a suit against someone for $100 million because they insulted you, caused you to slip in their store, or gave you whiplash in a car wreck. You can only say in your suit for damages that you are entitled to a reasonable amount of damages as may be determined by the court or jury.

Small Claims Courts

Of particular interest to the person who wants to be his own lawyer is the small claims court. These courts are set up as divisions of the city courts with the specific purpose of relaxing rules and making the "judicial system more available to and comprehensible by the public." The grammar used by the Legislature to authorize small claims courts may not be the best, but the idea is terrific. Not only are you allowed to represent yourself as you would be in any court, it is fully expected that nearly everyone who files in small claims court will do so without a lawyer.

All city courts are authorized to establish small claims divisions and even to have court hours in the evenings and on Saturdays. Since city courts are not required to have small claims divisions, it is best to call the clerk of your city court to make sure this procedure is available to you. If you are able to file in small claims court, there are some tremendous advantages for you.

The main advantage is that the rules of evidence are relaxed so that the average person can have access to the legal system without as much risk of being thrown out of court on a technicality. Unlike the other courts of Louisiana, even hearsay evidence can be admissible in small claims court. This means that the judge can consider your statements as to things you were told by others and he can consider affidavits or other written evidence without a witness actually being at the trial. The only requirement is that the judge be satisfied that the evidence is reliable. Another advantage is that the judge is required to be as helpful as possible and to even bring out evidence through his own questioning of the parties and witnesses. Also, the clerk will help you when you file by answering any questions you may have about the small claims procedure.

When you file your suit in small claims court, the clerk prepares a citation and mails it with your claim to the defendant by certified mail. You can request that the service be personally made on the defendant if you feel that it is necessary or if you have a physical address but not a mailing address. The filing fee can be around $50.00 which is intended to cover all expenses as long as the claim remains in the small claims division. In other courts, you can be required to make additional payments to the clerk as costs are incurred. The defendant has ten days to respond to the suit once he is served, but he has the option of requesting that the action be removed to the regular city court if he wants to. Why would he want to do this? Possibly because there is no appeal from the judgment of a small claims court. If you file in small claims court you waive the right to appeal the decision of the small claims court judge. Likewise, if the defendant does not request that the case be changed to the regular city court, he also loses the right to appeal the outcome of the trial.

All courts have limits on the types of cases they can hear and over the people that are subject to their rulings. The small claims courts are no exception to this. First, the general rules of the city courts apply in that small claims courts cannot hear cases involving: 1) title to real estate; 2) the right to public office; 3) any case asserting rights under the federal or state constitutions; 4) any claim for divorce, separation, annulment, alimony, support, or separation of property; 5) successions, interdictions and, certain other types of cases; 6) any suit where the state or other political subdivision is a defendant. In small claims courts there are additional limitations: the amount sued for cannot exceed $3,000 and the court cannot issue restraining orders or give injunctive relief. The City of Slidell is not limited to $3,000 but instead has a limit in the same amount as the local justice of the peace courts

What does all this mean? For many cases small claims court is ideal for the person who wants to handle his or her own case. The clerk will help with preparing the pleadings and with advising you on procedure, the judge will help at the trial, and the whole procedure will be fast with no delays for appeals. If the defendant lives within the jurisdictional limits of a city that has a small claims division, or if a business that you want to sue has its principal operations within the jurisdictional limits, you may be able to sue in small claims court. We say jurisdictional limit rather than city limit because many city courts extend beyond the city limits to parts or even to all of the parish. The Houma City Court, for example, has jurisdiction throughout all of Terrebonne Parish. Other city courts may extend to certain wards beyond the city limits.

Remember, you cannot sue for more than $3,000 in small claims court, not counting interest, costs and attorney's fees. Suits for defective repairs, to recover deposits, to recover borrowed money, for defective merchandise, or nearly anything else you can think of, are perfect for small claims courts. Call to see if your city has a city court and then see if there is a small claims division and whether your defendant is within the court's territorial jurisdiction.

Justice of the Peace Courts

Small claims courts are of no help if they do not have jurisdiction. If the defendant lives outside the city limits, the chances are a city or small claims court cannot help you. You can always file suit in the parish district court, but this may be too expensive and time consuming for a small claim. A good alternative, if it is available to you, is the justice of the peace court.

The jurisdiction of justice of the peace courts is concurrent with the district courts. In other words, the justice of the peace would generally have jurisdiction over a person living within the parish. Many parishes have several justices of the peace, so you would have to find out which justice covers the territory within which the defendant lives.

Justice of the peace courts have most of the same limitations as small claims courts including limits on the amount sued for. They also cannot hear cases involving family matters, probate, title to property, and certain other types of cases. They can hear eviction proceedings and can act as committing magistrates in criminal matters.

The procedures required in justice of the peace courts is extremely relaxed. Written pleading are not even required, although it would certainly be a good idea to submit something in writing that summarizes your claim. You can make a claim orally before the justice and the defendant can present his defenses orally.

We recently had a client who wanted to sue his neighbor. The neighbor left a pile of dirt on the client's property after building a fence. Of course, we could offer no reasonable solution to his problem considering the amount we would charge to go to court. Our client sued in justice of the peace court, a hearing was set the following week, and the justice ordered the neighbor to remove the dirt or pay damages. Justice was sure and swift. However, keep in mind that a judgment of the justice of the peace court can be appealed to the district court. For that reason, be careful to fully present your case and to file any documents or evidence with the justice so that it will be seen on appeal.

Preparing Pleadings

Pleadings are the papers you file with the court in which you ask for some remedy or make an official appearance. In short, you are making a plea to the court by asking the court to do something for you. The term pleadings also includes the answer you file to someone else's suit. Pleadings, at a minimum, must establish certain things: they must have a caption with the name of the court and the names of the parties, they must state a cause of action, and they must be signed by the person who files them. Initial pleadings must also establish the jurisdiction of the court. Let's look at some of the basics that you must know about pleadings before you can be expected to represent yourself in a court of law.

The caption of a pleading is like the title page of a book. The exact format of the caption is not important as long as it contains the required information. The caption must contain: 1) the name of the person or persons filing the suit; 2) the name or names of the defendant or defendants; 3) the judicial district, city court, or family court; 4) the name of the parish or city; 5) the number of the case (or a place for the number if one has not been assigned); 6) the division of the court unless one has not been assigned. One style that would be acceptable in just about every court would be:

```
JOHN J. SMITH              NUMBER _____

                           1ST JUDICIAL DISTRICT COURT
Versus
                           PARISH OF CADDO

ROBERT Q. JONES            STATE OF LOUISIANA
```

Styles for captions vary from area to area and depend somewhat on the local custom. In many small claims courts there is no need to prepare pleading since forms are provided for this purpose. You may want to check with the clerk of the court in which you plan to file to look over some suits. Remember, these suits are public records and you have a right to inspect them.

Some parishes may prefer a slightly different form for the caption. This is really just a matter of custom since the basic requirements of giving the names of the parties, the number, the court, and the parish, are met regardless of the style you use. If you want your pleadings to not stand out, look through several different suits at the clerk's office. Another style of caption used in several parishes is:

```
          STATE OF LOUISIANA - PARISH OF RICHLAND
                    Fifth District Court
       JANE JONES

       Versus                       Filed:

       ROBERT JONES                 Number:
```

The next part of your pleadings is called the title. The title briefly tells the court what you are asking for. For example, if you are seeking a divorce, the title would be SUIT FOR DIVORCE. Or, if you are suing to recover a deposit, you might title your suit PETITION FOR DAMAG-ES. If you are filing an answer to someone else's suit, the title might simply be ANSWER.

The body of your pleading consists of an introduction, a statement setting forth the jurisdiction of the court and brief numbered paragraphs stating your side of the case. The introduction contains your name and your domicile and should look something like this:

> The petition of John L. Smith, who is domiciled in Caddo Parish, Louisiana, respectfully shows the Court that:

The body of your pleading consists of numbered paragraphs and must make the basic allegations of your suit. If you add too much detail, the judge may find your pleading hard to read. If you add too little detail, the defendant may not be able to tell exactly what he is being sued for. The body of a pleading should look something like this:

> 1.
>
> Robert Q. Jones is domiciled in Caddo Parish, Louisiana and owes petitioner the full sum of Two Thousand Five Hundred Dollars ($2,500.00) for the following reasons.
>
> 2.
>
> On or about July 2, 1986, the defendant entered into a written lease agreement with petitioner for a residence located at 123 Main Street in the City of Shreveport.
>
> 3.
>
> [Additional paragraphs showing how the defendant breached the lease and why he owes the money sued for.]

The next part of the petition is called the prayer. This part summarizes exactly what you want the court to do for you. The prayer might look something like this:

> WHEREFORE, petitioner prays for judgment in his favor and against the defendant canceling the lease between the parties, awarding petitioner the sum of $2,500.00 due under the terms of the lease together with legal interest from date of judicial demand until paid, and for all costs of these proceedings.

Remember, you can ask for a specific amount in our example because the suit is over a contract of lease. You cannot mention a specific amount of money anywhere in your pleadings if you are suing for damages other than for a contract or the other exceptions we mentioned earlier. If you ask for a specific amount when you are not supposed to, the other side can have it removed and you will be liable for the other side's attorney's fees and expenses.

John Smith first states that Robert Q. Jones is domiciled in Caddo Parish. This is to establish the jurisdiction of the court. Generally, courts have jurisdiction over persons who are domiciled in the parish or city in which the court sits. If you file your suit in a court that does not have jurisdiction over the person you are suing, that person may be able to have your suit dismissed.

Legal interest. It is important to ask for interest on the amount you are owed because you can't get it if you don't ask for it. The Legislature determines the amount of interest you can get on any amount you are awarded and this rate changes each year. It is therefore best to ask for "legal" interest since the court can then award the maximum amount to which you are entitled.

The final part of the pleading is the signature line. All pleadings must be signed by the person filing the pleading or his attorney. You must also include your current address and telephone number. For more detailed examples of various pleadings, see the sections on specific types of law suits for a specimen of a pleading that is close to what you need to prepare.

In summary, the pleading is comprised of five parts in this order:

CAPTION
TITLE
INTRODUCTION
BODY
PRAYER
SIGNATURE

Pleadings must be typewritten on white paper with at least one inch margins on all sides. They must be double spaced and some state courts require that pleadings by on 8½ x 14 or "legal size" paper. All federal courts, including bankruptcy court, now require that all pleadings be on 8½ x 11 paper. If you are filing in any state or city court, you will be safe if you prepare your pleadings on legal size paper. You are also required to file one copy of your pleading for each defendant so that the copy can be served on each person that you are suing. In small claims court, you may not need to prepare pleadings at all since most pleadings are done by a sort of fill-in-the-blank procedure on forms provided by the clerk.

Procedure

In law, "procedure" means the rules that must be observed to be sure that the case proceeds in an orderly manner. If the proper procedures are not followed, the punishment is sure and swift: your case is delayed or dismissed. Lawyers spend years in law school and still lose cases because some procedural requirement was overlooked. If you plan to act as your own lawyer, you must resign yourself to the fact that your odds of being successful cannot be as good as someone who is fully trained to do what you are attempting to do. Nothing short of spending the required years in law school can put you anywhere close to having an equal chance with someone with the proper training. If you make a procedural mistake, the result may be that the merits of your case will never be heard.

Before filing suit against someone, it may be necessary to put them in default. This simply means that the other party should be informed that you consider them in default of an obligation and that you intend to sue if the default is not corrected. There are many types of cases where this is not necessary. However, it is always a good idea to notify the other party by certified mail that you intend to sue and to give the other party a certain amount of time to correct the default. Sending a certified letter will accomplish three things: it will operate as a formal putting in default if this is required by your type of case; it will give the defendant one last chance to settle the problem before you go to the expense of filing suit; and, it may demonstrate to the judge that you made every reasonable effort to settle with the defendant.

If putting someone in default does not work, the first step in any law suit is the filing of your petition or whatever pleading you have prepared to seek some legal remedy. The defendants in the case generally have fifteen days to file an answer (ten days in city courts). Non-residents of Louisiana may have longer than fifteen days under certain circumstances. If they do not file an answer, you may be entitled to a default judgment against them. However, the defendant may instead file what is known as an exception. If this happens, it will be your first hard lesson in procedure.

An exception, among other things, may mean that the defendant has reason to believe that there is some defect in

284/ Louisiana Legal Advisor

your pleading or that you have no right to sue. For example, there are time limits on your right to sue for certain things. In other states these limits are called statutes of limitation. In Louisiana these limits are called prescriptive periods and different periods of prescription will apply to just about any type of case you might think of filing. In other words, different types of cases may have different time limits within which you have the right to sue. If you have filed your suit past the date that you had a right to sue, the other side may file an exception saying that your right to sue has prescribed. The other side may or may not be correct, but you will be required to prove that your suit was filed within the proper time limit or it will be dismissed by the judge.

There are many other types of exceptions that may require the amendment or dismissal of your suit. Or, as will often happen, the exception may just be a method to delay or confuse you. For whatever reason an exception is filed, you should consult an attorney for specific advice or you should turn the case over to an attorney. Fighting an exception is just too complicated for someone who does not have formal legal training.

The boring stuff. Everything we are talking about here are the things you don't see on television. You don't see them because they are boring. What you see on television is *1) a man is crippled because of a doctor's malpractice,* and *2) the trial.* In other words, you don't see all the stages you must go through before you have your day in court. It is in these stages that most cases are won or lost. Let's continue with the boring stuff.

Once an answer has been filed, it is then up to you to take whatever steps may be necessary to move the case to trial. Remember, the burden is always on you as the plaintiff to take the procedural steps necessary to arrive at your day in court. The defendant is usually in no hurry if he knows you have a good case. If you do not take every opportunity to move your case forward, it will become stale and more difficult to win.

Either side may now use discovery methods. This means that you or the defendant can use certain legal devices to discover the other side's version of the case, to limit the issues which must be proved at trial, and to determine the testimony of possible witnesses. As part of discovery, you can file interrogatories or take depositions. Interrogatories are written questions directed to the other side that must be answered in writing and under oath. Depositions are oral examinations of witnesses taken before a court reporter or other person who can administer oaths.

If the other side files interrogatories, you must file your answers within certain time limits. If you fail to do so, the other side can force you into court to explain your failure to the judge and you may be forced to pay the other side's attorney's fees. In trying to save some money by representing yourself, you may end up paying the other guy's lawyer. If your case is complicated enough to require discovery, you probably need to hire a lawyer.

After the discovery phase, the plaintiff needs to ask for a trial date. Depending on the court you are in and the type of case, this is done either by requesting that the case be set for trial or by requesting a pretrial conference. Each of the many courts in Louisiana have their own local rules that cover the procedure for getting a trial date. Sometimes it is as simple as filing a motion asking that the suit be set for trial. In other cases, there must first be a conference with the judge and you must prepare a pretrial order that summarizes each claim and states all the witnesses and exhibits that each party will use at trial. In small claims court and many city courts, on the other hand, your case may be automatically set for trial as soon as the other side files an answer.

If you are considering filing suit against someone, it is vital that you find out the procedures in the court you will be using. Do not be afraid to ask questions of the clerks and other courthouse personnel. They cannot give you legal advice, but they can help you with the local customs and procedures. The clerk of court may also be able to give you a copy of the local rules which have been adopted by the judges that would hear your case.

As you can see, successfully reaching the point of actually going to trial can be half the battle. It now becomes a matter of using whatever skills you may have to persuade the judge that you should win your case. Although there is no way to teach you how to be a skillful advocate, you should at least be prepared to argue each element of your case in a logical order. This is something that non-lawyers (and even some lawyers) often do poorly. Take a legal pad and make an outline of what your case is about. Put each major element of your case under headings in a logical order. Under each heading, put sub-headings with the details of each major element.

A logical order in many cases might simply be chronological. For example, let's take a case where you are suing an automobile mechanic for defective repairs. Major headings might be: I. How the contract to repair arose; II. When and how the defects became apparent; III. The steps and costs necessary to make proper repairs. Sub-headings under each heading might include the elements of proof to establish each heading. For example, under part I you would want to prove that a contract existed, whether oral or written. Then, as sub-headings, you would want to establish the details of the contract. Under part III, you would want to provide evidence as to what it would cost, or what it did cost, to straighten out the defective repairs.

What is the purpose of the outline? When you go to court you are going to be nervous. If you don't write down what you need to prove, you will forget some important part of your case. Also, if you follow a logical outline, it will be easier for a judge to understand your case. If the judge understands what you are trying to do, and if you include every essential element of your case, your chances of success will be greatly enhanced. Remember, the burden is on you, the plaintiff, to prove your case. If you leave out even one essential element, you may lose.

You may have noticed that we have said nothing about jury trials and that all our references have been to convincing a judge, not a jury. This is because the right to a trial by jury in civil cases is restricted and does not come without cost. If you have pictured yourself making a brilliant argument to a jury of your peers just like Perry Mason, you had better think again. The right to a trial by jury in Louisiana is limited to certain cases. For example, the amount in dispute must exceed $50,000. That is why there are no juries at all in city and small claims courts. Also, many types of cases must be heard before a judge alone. Cases involving divorce, separation, custody, support, successions, and an unconditional obligation to repay a specific sum of money, are just a few examples. Even in those cases where you are entitled to a jury, the party requesting the jury must do so at the beginning of the case and he must put up a bond to cover the expenses of the jury. Jury expenses can exceed $3,000 and the loser usually has to pay.

Whether you win or lose in front of a judge or a jury, that does not mean the case is over. Either side still has the right to appeal the decision. An appeal, whether the other side brings it or you wish to, should never be attempted without an attorney. This is because the ability to research and write briefs for an appeal is specialized. Keep in mind one of the biggest advantages of small claims courts—appeals are not allowed.

How To

We are now at the point of showing you specifically how to prepare certain types of legal documents and certain types of suits. We cannot remind you too often that you would undoubtedly be better off with a lawyer. Even in those limited types of cases where you at least have a chance if you represent yourself, the cases we are about to show you, you would be wise to consider turning to a lawyer for advice before proceeding.

Some types of cases are riskier than others. For each type of case, we will take you through the basic procedures step by step and attempt to foresee the most common problems associated with the type of case you want to handle. It is impossible, however, to anticipate every potential problem and to specifically advise you on local customs and procedures for all the parish, district, city and small claims courts. Also, we can only give generalized advice. Every case is different and has its own unique facts. General advice on how to represent yourself in a type of case may not cover the particular legal problem you are trying to solve.

Before attempting to represent yourself in the types of cases we will discuss, you must do three things: (1) be familiar with the main text of this book which discusses the area you are interested in; (2) familiarize yourself with the customs and procedures of your particular local court; (3) understand that as in any do-it-yourself project, you are on your own and responsible for the problems and mistakes that are likely to arise. Let's start with something that doesn't require a court appearance.

Write a Will

Preparing a proper will that will accomplish what you want and stand up in court can be a relatively simple matter for most people. There is only one type of will that makes sense for the person who wants to do it himself. The formalities that must be observed in this type of will have been well defined over the years by the statutes and by the courts. The best type of will that you can prepare yourself is known as the olographic will. This is generally not as good as a notarial will prepared by an experienced attorney, but it may do well enough for some people. Before attempting to prepare your own will, read the sections on estate planning and successions.

The olographic will is very simply your written statement of what you want done with your property when you die. You can also include instructions as to the person who will be in charge of your estate and the person who will be in charge of your children. There are three very strict requirements for this type of will:

- It must be entirely handwritten by you.
- It must be clearly dated.
- It must be signed by you at the end.

These requirements make many of the fill in the blank type of wills available in other states absolutely useless in Louisiana. Remember, you cannot type and then sign an olographic will, it must be entirely handwritten. Remember also that we have forced heirship laws in this state which require that a portion of your estate go to your children who are incapacitated or under the age of 24.

We will give two examples of olographic wills. The first is for a man with three children who wants his wife to benefit to the maximum extent allowed under Louisiana law.

June 28, 2012

My name is Jonathan H. Jones and this is my last will and testament. I am married to Harriet Jones and we have three children, namely: James, Albert and Susan. I have no other children other than those I have named and I have never adopted anyone. The birth to me of any other children shall not serve to revoke this will.

If I have any forced heirs at the time of my death, I give and bequeath to each forced heir only the forced portion to which each is entitled under Louisiana law at the time of my death. I give and bequeath to my wife Harriet all of my remaining property, whether community or separate and whether owned by me now or acquired later. I also give to my wife a lifetime usufruct over that portion of my property that may constitute the legitime of a forced heir. It is my wish that my wife benefit under the terms of this will to the maximum extent possible. I therefore direct that any ambiguities under this will or changes in the law be resolved in her favor. Should my wife predecease me, or should she not survive me by a period of at least thirty days, I then give and bequeath my entire estate to my children in equal shares.

I name my wife as independent executrix of my will and waive the requirement that she or any other executrix or executor post bond. Should my wife be unable or unwilling to serve as natural tutrix of my children, I then name and appoint my brother Albert Jones as tutor of my children.

Jonathan H. Jones

This will gives the wife the lifetime use of property that might be inherited by any of the children who are forced heirs at the time of death, and gives her outright as much property as is allowed. The wife could prepare a similar will for the benefit of the husband.

Each spouse must have his or her own separate written will. There is no such thing in Louisiana as a joint will. You may have noticed some words in this will that seemed unfamiliar. You may also have wondered why simpler or more common words were not used. This is because certain legal words have very precise meanings that cannot be conveyed by more common words. For example, usufruct means the nearly unlimited right to use a thing and all the profits and advantages of that thing as long as the substance of the thing is not substantially altered. If the usufruct is over money or certain other consumables, the money or consumable can be entirely used up.

To lawyers and judges, the word usufruct has a meaning which has been finely tuned by numerous court decisions. The word "use" might seem like a more appropriate word to utilize when writing your own will. However, "use" is vague and can generally mean that the person with the use is entitled only to enough of the profits of something for daily sustenance. If you use vague words like "use," the judge who reads your will has to decide whether you really meant usufruct but didn't know enough to use the word, or whether you meant something less than a usufruct. Some legal words, even though they seem strange, have to be used because no other words can accomplish what you want.

Other words used in this will with precise legal meanings are legitime, forced portion, executrix and tutor. The legitime is the portion of your estate that Louisiana law says must go to your forced heirs. This amount is currently set at 25% if you have one forced heir or 50% if you have two or more forced heirs. These percentages have changed in the past and will probably change again in the future. That is why we refer to "legitime" rather than leaving a certain percentage to the forced heirs. The forced portion is another way of saying legitime. The executrix (or executor if the office is held by a man) is the person you designate to carry out the wishes expressed in your will. The tutor (or tutrix if the office is held by a woman) is the person you appoint to raise your children. The tutor in Louisiana is virtually the same thing as the guardian in other states.

The Jonathan Jones will gives everything possible to the wife. For example, the usufruct is specifically for her lifetime. If nothing were said about the term of the usufruct, it would end when the wife remarried. The term of the usufruct could also have been for a certain period of time, such as ten years. Having anything less than a lifetime usufruct, however, can result in adverse tax consequences for larger estates. If you have an estate anywhere close to being "large" you have no business writing your own will. Mr. Jones could have given less to his wife and he could have made specific gifts to other people in his will with his wife receiving the remainder. If you are clear in your will as to who gets what, there should be no problems. Another example of an olographic will is written for someone who is not married and has no children:

June 8, 2005

My name is Agatha Johnson and this is my last will and testament. I have never been married and I have no children.

I give and bequeath the sum of $10,000.00 to my nephew Ralph Johnson. I give and bequeath the sum of $5,000.00 to my niece Mary Smith. I leave my house, which is located at 123 Main Street, Shreveport, Louisiana, to my sister Regina Wilbert. I leave the rest of my estate to the Fund For Cats, a non-profit corporation located at 4545 Feline Way, Chicago, Illinois.

I name my sister Regina as independent executrix of my will and waive the requirement that she post bond.

Agatha Johnson

As you can see, Agatha's will is short and to the point. In some places she leaves people property; in other places she gives and bequeaths her property. It does not matter how she words her will in disposing of her property as long as it is clear that she intends that the person receive it.

Both wills waive the requirement that the executor or executrix post a bond. If you do not have this provision in your will, your executor or executrix (other than a spouse) will have to put up a bond equal to a percentage of the value of your estate. This can be a considerable financial hardship and might cause the executor or executrix to refuse the appointment. Waiving the bond will avoid this problem.

The wills also name the executrix as "independent" which is a relatively new provision of Louisiana law that allows the executor to perform certain acts without having to get court permission. For example, an independent executor can go ahead and pay bills without having to seek court authority in advance.

The problem with olographic wills. One final warning about doing your own will: it will be more trouble to probate than a notarial will. A notarial will is self-proving. That is, no testimony or evidence needs to be given the court to probate a notarial will. With an olographic will, either someone will have to testify as to the handwriting, or there will need to be affidavits from people attesting that the handwriting is that of the testator. For the cost of getting a notarial will, this can be avoided. There is also the obvious problem of an olographic will being easier to contest than a notarial will. A notarial will is done in front of a notary and two witnesses. It it therefore much harder to claim incapacity on the part of the testator when three people are watching the signing.

Anyone can write his own will as long as it is dated, signed at the end, and entirely handwritten. The will must also be clear as to what is desired or it may do more harm than good. If your estate has enough assets to be worth protecting, you should have an attorney prepare your will. If you do not feel that you need a lawyer, or if you want to be covered by a will until you "get around" to seeing a lawyer, the olographic will may be the best answer to your needs.

✓ WILL CHECK LIST

- ☑ Make a careful inventory of your assets.
- ☑ Decide who is to get your assets.
- ☑ Decide who should care for your children.
- ☑ Decide who you want to be executor.
- ☑ Write your will.

  Your will must be handwritten by you.

  You should use an ink pen on white paper.

  You must clearly date your will.

  You must sign your will at the end.

- ☑ Tell your executor where the will is kept.

Change Your Name

The procedures required to legally change your name are relatively uncomplicated and can be successfully managed by nearly anyone without the help of a lawyer. To change your name, you must sue the district attorney in the parish where you live. This must sound strange, but the law requires that a legal change of name be made through a contradictory hearing. This means that you must file a petition against the district attorney and he must file an answer to your petition. Don't let this procedure intimidate you. Having to sue the district attorney is just a formality to insure that the purpose of your change of name is not illegal.

JANE PLAIN   NUMBER _____

                 19TH JUDICIAL DISTRICT COURT

VERSUS

                 PARISH OF EAST BATON ROUGE

JOSEPH SMITH   STATE OF LOUISIANA

Petition for Change of Name

The petition of Jane Plain, who is domiciled in the Parish of East Baton Rouge, Louisiana, respectfully shows the Court that:

1.

Petitioner wishes to change her name from JANE PLAIN to JANE BEAUTIFUL pursuant to the provisions of LSA R.S. 13:4751.

2.

Petitioner wishes to change her name for the following reason: she prefers the last name Beautiful to the last name Plain.

WHEREFORE, petitioner prays that the district attorney for this parish be served with a copy of this petition and that he be cited to appear and answer same, and after all due proceedings, there be judgment changing petitioner's name from Jane Plain to Jane Beautiful.

You prepare the petition just as you would with any type of suit and you name the district attorney as the defendant. In some districts, the defendant is your new name. In our example, the caption would read "Jane Plain versus Jane Beautiful" rather than "Jane Plain versus Joseph Smith." You must file the suit in state district court, it cannot be filed in a city court. Unlike other types of suits, in some parishes you also must prepare the answer for the district attorney. The law requires that your petition state your present name, the name you want to adopt, and the reason you want to change your name. Your petition and the judgment you prepare should also contain your date of birth, your sex and your address. If you want the Bureau of Vital Statistics to change your birth certificate, the judgment must also contain your place of birth, your father's full name and your mother's maiden name.

The petition is short and simple and would be followed by the signature, address and telephone number of Jane Plain. Although you are required to state a reason for requesting that your name be changed, it is perfectly acceptable to simply say you prefer one name over another.

JANE PLAIN	NUMBER _____
VERSUS	19TH JUDICIAL DISTRICT COURT
	PARISH OF EAST BATON ROUGE
JOSEPH SMITH	STATE OF LOUISIANA

Answer

Now into court comes Joseph Smith, District Attorney of East Baton Rouge Parish, who for answer to the petition of Jane Plain respectfully states:

1.

Joseph Smith has no objection to urge against the change of name of Jane Plain to Jane Beautiful.

WHEREFORE, Joseph Smith prays that there be such judgment as the law and the evidence may warrant.

Joseph Smith

By:_____
John Jones, Asst. District Attorney

The next step is the answer. In most districts you will have to file your petition and bring a copy together with the answer and judgment to the district attorney's office. The district attorney will then check to be sure that you have no illegal reasons for requesting the change. After this check, he or his representative will sign the answer and you can bring all your papers to a judge for his signature. This can usually be done in the judge's office without a court hearing, but you should make an appointment.

[Caption]
Judgment

Considering the petition and the answer filed herein, the law and the evidence being in favor of petitioner;

IT IS ORDERED, ADJUDGED AND DECREED that petitioner's name Jane Plain be, and hereby is, changed to JANE BEAUTIFUL and that she henceforth be known by this name as her true and lawful name.

Petitioner's name at birth: Jane Plain
Petitioner's date of birth: 9/15/46
Petitioner's address: 123 Main St., Baton Rouge, LA
Petitioner's sex: Female
Petitioner's place of birth: New Orleans, Louisiana
Petitioner's Father's name: Arthur C. Plain
Petitioner's Mother's maiden name: Bertha Ann Smith

JUDGMENT RENDERED AND SIGNED at Baton Rouge, Louisiana, on this ___ day of _____, 2012.

JUDGE

A certified copy of the judgment, after it is signed, must be recorded in the conveyance records of the parish in which the suit was brought. In some parishes the clerk may do this automatically, in others you will have the responsibility of doing this. Be sure you find out whether you need to file your judgment because it has no legal effect until it is filed. After filing, the clerk is required to send a copy to the registrar of voters in your parish so that your voting registration can be changed. It is usually a good idea to take a certified copy of the judgment to the registrar yourself if you want to be sure your registration is changed.

Many district attorney's offices have sample forms of the petition, answer, and judgment that they prefer you use. Also, some districts require additional information such as social security numbers. Check with your district attorney to find out their particular procedure and whether they have any forms you can use.

The information as to your place of birth and your parents' names is not necessary unless you want your birth certificate changed by the Bureau of Vital Statistics in New Orleans. If you want your birth records changed, you must send a certified copy of the judgment together with a small fee.

If a person under the age of eighteen wants a change of name, the procedure is basically the same. The parents must sign the petition or, if one parent is dead, the surviving parent must sign. If the parents are divorced, the parent with custody can file for a change of name if the parent without custody has refused to pay child support for a period of one year after a court order for support. If the non-custodial parent does not live in Louisiana, the parent with custody can petition to change the name of the child if the other parent has not contributed any support for a period of one year after the award of custody even if support was never ordered.

✓ CHANGE OF NAME CHECK LIST

☑   Check with your district attorney's office.
See if they have forms that you can use.
See if you must prepare the answer.
Must there be other information in the petition?

☑ Check with the clerk of court's office.

    Look at other change of name suits.

    Ask about the filing fee.

☑ Prepare the petition, answer and judgment.

    Make sure the caption has the correct district.

    Make sure you give a reason for your change.

    Add any other details required in your parish.

☑ File the petition.

    Bring petition, answer and judgment to D.A.

    Make sure you have several copies of all papers.

☑ If you want to:

    Provide certified copy to registrar of voters.

    Send certified copy to Bureau of Vital Statistics.

Make a Marriage Contract

Louisiana is a community property state. This means that all income and property accumulated during a marriage belongs to each spouse regardless of the actual earnings of each party. If this concept is not to your liking, it is very easy to avoid Louisiana's community property laws by entering into a marriage contract prior to the marriage. After marriage, a marriage contract has to be by petition to the court and by approval of a judge. Read the sections on marriage and marriage contracts for the details on community property and ways to terminate the community.

Most marriage contracts simply state that the parties wish to renounce the community regime established by Louisiana law. The effect of this is to make all income and property the separate estate of the spouse who earned the income or accumulated the property. A marriage contract can also be limited. For example, a contract could state that only the income from a certain investment is to be separate while the rest of the property is to remain community.

Although marriage contracts without court approval must be executed before the marriage, there are two exceptions. If you are married in another state and move to Louisiana, you have one year to file a marriage contract without needing to petition the court. Also, if you want to file a marriage contract that re-establishes a community regime, you do not need court approval. In other words, if you at one time filed a marriage contract renouncing the community property laws but now want to establish a community, you can file a marriage contract without having to go to court.

Here is an example of a marriage contract that renounces the community regime so that all property and income of the spouses is separate.

The marriage contract has to be an authentic act. That means it must be signed by both spouses in front of two witnesses and a notary public. For the marriage contract to be effective against third parties, it must be recorded in the parish where the spouses are domiciled and in each parish where either of the spouses own real property. Unless emancipated, someone under the age of eighteen cannot enter into a marriage contract unless the parents give their written consent.

This marriage contract would then be filed in the conveyance records of the clerk of court where the couple will reside and in any other parish where the spouses own real estate. If you wanted to limit the property that is going to be separate, you would modify this agreement to make it clear which property will be community and which property will be separate.

MARRIAGE CONTRACT

STATE OF LOUISIANA
PARISH OF IBERVILLE

Before me, the undersigned notary public, personally appeared JANE SMITH and JOHN JONES who did both declare that they are domiciled in Iberville Parish and that they intend to be joined in the bonds of matrimony on or about December 25, 2012, and in order to fix certain rights between them, they do contract as follows, to wit:

1. The said intended husband and wife shall be separate in property. Accordingly, they do hereby formally renounce those provisions of the Louisiana Civil Code which establish a community of acquets and gains between husband and wife.

2. All property and effects of the said husband and wife, whether owned by him or her at the time of the celebration of said intended marriage, or acquired during said marriage, are hereby declared to be separate property, and they and each of them do hereby expressly reserve to themselves individually the entire administration of their respective particular movable and immovable property, and the respective free enjoyment of each of their revenues.

Thus done and passed on this 1st day of November, 2012, before me, notary, and the undersigned competent witnesses.

_____   _____
Witness   Jane Smith

_____   _____
Witness   John Jones

_____
Notary Public

✓MARRIAGE CONTRACT CHECK LIST

☑ The contract must be signed before the marriage.

    Unless you moved to Louisiana within one year.

    Unless you have court approval.

    Unless you are re-establishing the community.

☑ The contract must be an authentic act.

    It must be witnessed and notarized.

☑ Be sure you are clear in what you want.

    A marriage contract can reject the community.

    Or, it can do anything less than a rejection.

☑ The contract must be recorded.

    It is not effective against others unless it is.

    Record the contract where the spouses live.

    Also record in every parish where there is realty.

Collect a Debt

What do you do when someone owes you money and doesn't want to pay you back? If it is not a large amount of money, you might have to forget about it because the cost of an attorney may not make the recovery worth while. If this is your situation, you have nothing to lose by trying to represent yourself.

A debt can arise for many reasons. Regardless of why someone owes you money, the procedures are basically the same. We will assume that you have a city court available to you and that Joe Smith skipped out on two months rent that he owes you. In small claims court you might not have to prepare any pleadings. We will assume that you are filing in the regular section of city court and that a written petition is required.

FRED FRIENDLY   NUMBER

VERSUS

THE CITY COURT

CITY OF LAFAYETTE

JOE SMITH   STATE OF LOUISIANA

PETITION

The petition of Fred Friendly, who is domiciled in the City of Lafayette, respectfully shows the Court that:

1.

The defendant, Joe Smith, is domiciled in the City of Lafayette and owes your petitioner the sum of Eight Hundred Dollars ($800.00) for these reasons:

2.

On March 1, 2011 the defendant rented from petitioner a two bedroom home located at 4545 Ferguson Street, Lafayette, Louisiana. The defendant agreed to pay petitioner the sum of $400 per month rent and, in fact, paid that amount for the three month period March 1, 2004, through May 30, 2004.

3.

The defendant failed to pay the rent due on June 1, 2004 and the rent due on July 1, 2004. The defendant moved out of the rented property on July 16, 2004 and refuses to pay rent for the months of June and July, or a total of $800.00.

WHEREFORE, petitioner, Fred Friendly, prays for judgment in his favor and against the defendant, Joe Smith, in the full sum of Eight Hundred Dollars ($800.00) together with legal interest from date of judicial demand until paid and for all costs of these proceedings.

Fred Friendly

[Fred's full typed name, address and phone number should be added]

The petition would be served on Joe and he would have ten days to file his answer. Remember, in most cases it's ten days in city courts and fifteen days in district courts. If Joe doesn't answer, Fred can enter a preliminary default. If Joe does file an answer, Fred needs to set the case for trial. In many city courts a trial date is set automatically when the answer is filed. At the trial, Fred would present his evidence to prove that Joe rented the property and that two payments were not made. It may be just Fred's word against Joe, or Fred might have a neighbor or other witness who could verify the fact that Joe occupied the house.

An important piece of evidence that Fred could introduce would be canceled rent checks from Joe or receipts showing how much had been paid. If Fred had only prepared a written lease, he would have less trouble proving that Joe rented the house and that Joe agreed to pay $400 a month. Another important advantage that a written lease could give Fred is an agreement that whoever breaks the lease will be liable for attorney's fees. However, a judge is probably not going to award enough attorney's fees to pay for a lawyer on a debt as small as $800.

There are other types of debts that may entitle you to attorney's fees so that you do not have to represent yourself. Two common debts that can include attorney's fees are notes that specify attorney's fees and suits on open account. Most standard promissory note forms provide for an additional 25% in attorney's fees if the note is not repaid. If you ever loan any money, be sure that you get a promissory note in return since the procedures for filing suit are much simpler and attorney's fees can be included. If you provide goods on open account, you can also recover attorney's fees if you follow the correct procedures for collection. For promissory notes and for suits on open account, let a lawyer handle the work for you. There really is no reason to represent yourself.

In our case, Joe filed an answer and the case was set for trial. Fred didn't have a lease and is not entitled to recover attorney's fees. However, he did win his case and the judgment he prepared looked like this:

FRED FRIENDLY   NUMBER

                       THE CITY COURT
VERSUS
                       CITY OF LAFAYETTE

JOE SMITH   STATE OF LOUISIANA

JUDGMENT

    This cause came before the Court on the 2nd day of January, 2012 by regular assignment. Present in court were Fred Friendly and Joe Smith. Having considered the pleadings, testimony and evidence, and finding the same to be in favor of petitioner, for the reasons orally assigned;

    IT IS ORDERED, ADJUDGED AND DECREED that there be judgment in favor of Fred Friendly and against Joe Smith in the sum of $800 together with legal interest from date of judicial demand until paid and for all costs of these proceedings.

    Judgment read, rendered and signed at Lafayette, Louisiana, this ___ day of _____, 2012.

_____
JUDGE

Any other sort of suit to recover a debt would be similar to the suit filed by Fred Friendly. If Joe Smith does not file an answer to the petition, Fred would need to enter a preliminary default. A preliminary default can be entered if the defendant fails to file an answer within the time limits. The procedure for entering a preliminary default varies from one parish to another. Usually, it is done by filing a motion. In some parishes it can be done by letter or even orally. Once the default is entered, it can than be confirmed after three days from the preliminary default. Even if the defendant fails to answer and you enter a preliminary default, you must still go to court to confirm the default. This means that there must be a hearing and that you must present enough evidence to the judge to show that the debt exists and is unpaid. If you end up with a defendant who does not file an answer, you must find out the procedures in your parish for entering a preliminary default, and then the procedures for confirming the default.

The judgment specifies that interest is due from "judicial demand" which is the date the petition is filed. The judgment also makes Joe responsible for costs which includes the filing fee that Fred had to put up to file his suit.

Some local court rules require that the person who prepared the judgment also sign underneath the judge's signature. If that is the case, Fred would need to sign the judgment, together with his address and telephone number.

✓COLLECT A DEBT CHECK LIST

☑ Check with the clerk of court.

  Look at other collection suits.

  Find out about filing fees.

☑ Watch some collection cases in court.

☑ Make sure you are suing for the right amount.

  Small claims courts have a maximum of $3,000.

☑ Prepare your petition.

  Make sure your caption has the right district.

  Be sure you allege how the debt arose.

  Be sure you sign the petition with your address.

State on the petition directions for service.

☑ Find out the exact date the defendant was served.

It is best to find this out from the sheriff.

☑ Enter a default if there was no answer.

Find out how this is done in your parish.
You must wait a full 10-15 days after service.

☑ Schedule a trial date.

Find out the local procedure for this.
Trial must be more than 3 days after default.

☑ Plan your evidence and witnesses.

☑ Before the trial:

Make sure the record has the sheriff's return.
Make sure the record has the preliminary default.
Find out whether you must bring record to trial.

☑ At the trial:

Bring your witnesses, if you have any.
Be sure to state you live in the parish.
Have the judgment ready, with copies.

Form a Corporation

Forming a corporation is easy. The hard part is in deciding whether your business should be in the form of a corporation or in some other form. We assume that you have reviewed the section on starting a business and that your tax advisor has recommended that your business be incorporated.

The Louisiana corporation starts its existence the day the articles of incorporation are signed and notarized, as long as the articles are then filed with the Secretary of State within five days. The articles are the essential part of the corporation. Although you can have as much information as you want in the articles, we usually recommend that the articles only contain the bare minimum that the law requires. This is because the less you say, the less chance there is that you may have to amend the articles later on. For example, the articles must state the purpose of the corporation. It is perfectly acceptable to state only that the purpose of the corporation is to engage in any lawful activity. This will leave you free to change the type of business you do under the corporation or to expand without having to file an amendment to the articles.

The articles should be typewritten and can be on 8 x 11 or legal size paper. They must be signed by at least one incorporator in front of two witnesses and a notary. It is then your responsibility to file the original with the Secretary of State, get a certified copy, and file the copy with the clerk of court in the parish where the corporation is domiciled. You must also prepare and file an initial report with your articles. In our sample articles of incorporation, the paragraphs marked with an asterisk are required. The other paragraphs are suggested but can be left out if you choose.

Your articles have to be witnessed and notarized. Since there probably is a presumption that the notary also prepared the articles, you had better find out in advance whether a notary would be willing to sign articles prepared by someone else. You might avoid this problem by adding "These articles were not prepared by the undersigned notary" to the last paragraph.

This corporation was formed by John Jones who is also the only stockholder, sole incorporator, chairman of the board and president. If you are considering forming a corporation with other parties, you should consult an attorney. There can be much more to incorporating than preparing and filing the articles. When you share the corporation with other stockholders, you should also have by-laws and a stock ownership agreement. Remember, if you find yourself with less than a majority of the stock, you may lose control of the corporation.

ARTICLES OF INCORPORATION OF
MAMMOTH INDUSTRIES, INC.

STATE OF LOUISIANA
PARISH OF EAST BATON ROUGE

BE IT KNOWN, that on this 14th day of July, 2012, before me, the undersigned notary public, personally appeared the subscriber hereto, John Jones, of the full age of majority and domiciled in Caddo Parish, Louisiana, who did declare before me and the undersigned competent witnesses that availing himself of the provisions of the Louisiana Business Corporation Law, he does hereby form a corporation under and in accordance with the following articles of incorporation.

* Article I. Name

The name of this corporation shall be MAMMOTH INDUS-TRIES, INC.

* Article II. Purpose

The purpose of this corporation is to engage in any lawful activity for which a corporation may be formed under the Business Corporation Law of the State of Louisiana.

* Article III. Duration

The duration of this corporation shall be in perpetuity or such maximum period as may be allowed and authorized by the State of Louisiana.

* Article IV. Corporate Office

The location and address of the registered office of this corporation is:

    5454 Milky Way
    Shreveport, Louisiana

which shall continue as the corporate office until changed by the Board of Directors in the manner required by law.

* Article V. Registered Agent

The full name and address of the registered agent of this corporation for the service of process is:

John Jones, 5454 Milky Way, Shreveport, Louisiana

* Article VI. Capital

This corporation has the authority to issue an aggregate of ten thousand (10,000) shares of capital stock, all of which are designated common stock having no par value per share. The Board of Directors shall fix the terms and conditions of sale and the time for payment of all stock sold.

Article VII. Voting Rights

All voting rights at the stockholders' meetings are vested in the shareholders of this corporation and each stockholder shall be entitled to one vote either in person or by proxy for each share of stock standing in his or her name on the books of the corporation.

Article VIII. Shareholder's Consent

Whenever the affirmative vote of the shareholders is required to authorize or constitute corporate action, the consent in writing to such action signed only by shareholders holding the proportion of the total voting power on the question which is required by law or by these Articles, whichever requirement is higher, shall be sufficient of the purpose, without the necessity for a meeting of the shareholders.

Article IX. Directors

The number of directors of this corporation shall be such number, not less than one or more than ten, as shall be elected by the shareholders. Any director absent from a meeting of the Board of Directors or of any committee thereof may be represented by any other director according to the written instructions, general or specific, of the absent director.

* Article X. Incorporators

The name and address of each incorporator is:

John Jones, 5454 Milky Way, Shreveport, Louisiana

Article XI. Amendment of Articles

The Article of Incorporation of this corporation may not be amended except by an affirmative vote of at least 51% of the shareholders so entitled to vote on any such amendment.

THUS DONE AND PASSED on the date first mentioned above in presence of the undersigned competent witnesses and me, Notary, after due reading of the whole.

[Signatures of John Jones, Notary, and witnesses]

Blank stock certificates are available at some stationery stores, but it is easier to just create certificates with a laser printer. The certificates are proof of ownership of shares in the corporation. You also need to file an initial report with the articles. These forms are available from the Secretary of State. See the section on incorporating for the address and telephone number. It is perfectly acceptable to prepare your own initial report instead of using the form provided by the Secretary of State.

INITIAL REPORT
MAMMOTH INDUSTRIES, INC.

State of Louisiana
Parish of _____

Complying with R.S. 1950, 12:101, Mammoth Industries, Inc. hereby makes its initial report as follows:

Municipal address of registered office: 5454 Milky Way, Shreveport, Louisiana.

Name and municipal address of each registered agent: John Jones, 5454 Milky Way, Shreveport, Louisiana.

Name and address of the first directors (if elected when articles are filed): none at this time.

Tax ID number: _____

Dated at Shreveport, Louisiana, this 14th day of July, 2012.

John Jones, Incorporator

The registered agent of the corporation must file an affidavit with the articles of incorporation stating that he has accepted the appointment as registered agent. The affidavit form is available from the Secretary of State or you can prepare your own affidavit:

AFFIDAVIT OF ACCEPTANCE OF APPOINTMENT
BY DESIGNATED REGISTERED AGENT

State of Louisiana
Parish of_____

On this ___ day of _____, 20__, personally appeared before me, the undersigned authority, [name of agent], who is to me known to be the person, and who, being duly sworn, acknowledged to me that he does hereby accept appointment as the Registered Agent of [name if corporation] which is a corporation authorized to transact business in the State of Louisiana pursuant to the provisions of Title 12, Chapter 1, 2, and 3.

_____
Registered Agent

Sworn to and subscribed before me on ____ 20__.

_____
Notary Public

✓ INCORPORATION CHECK LIST

☑ Always seek tax advice before incorporating.

☑ The corporation is a separate tax paying person.

☑ Decide whether to be a regular or "S" corporation.

☑ Find out if the name you want is available.

Call the Secretary of State to check on the name. Reserve the name if you want to be sure.

☑ Prepare the articles of incorporation.

Make sure the minimum information is included.

They must be signed by each incorporator.

They must be witnessed and notarized.

☑ File the articles and initial report.

Also file the affidavit of registered agent.

This can be done by mail.

Include the filing fee.

☑ You will receive a certified copy by return mail.

File this with the parish clerk.

☑ Be very sure to keep up corporate books.

☑ Have regular meetings with minutes.

☑ Promptly file annual reports and tax returns.

Recover a Rent Deposit

Nothing is more frustrating than being required to put up a deposit and then having to fight to get it back. It used to be a losing proposition since the cost of recovery would usually be more than the deposit. Certain landlords, who understood this, would routinely keep deposits knowing full well that there was nothing you could do about it. Well, things are different now. If you know how to do it, you can force the return of your deposit and additional damages. Review the section on tenant's rights before you attempt to recover a deposit.

The landlord has one month to return your deposit, if you did not abandon the premises. If the deposit is not returned, the landlord must give you an itemized statement showing why the deposit or part of the deposit was not returned and what it was used for. You must give the landlord a forwarding address to send the refund or statement.

If you make written demand for a refund and the landlord still fails to refund or send you a statement within thirty days of your demand, he may also be liable for damages and attorney's fees. The trick here is to make a written demand as soon as you suspect there may be a problem. The sooner you make the demand, the sooner your thirty day waiting period will be over. If you wait until the end of the thirty day period that the landlord has to refund your deposit and then make a written demand, you will be giving the landlord sixty days to refund or give a statement.

The written demand can be mailed or hand delivered. Since the burden will be on you to prove that a written demand was made, be sure you can prove the date you made your demand. Send the demand by certified mail or hand deliver it with a witness present. However you make your demand, it should look like this:

May 1, 2012

Mr. Larry Landlord
123 Ghetto Road
New Orleans, LA

Re: Apartment 205

Dear Mr. Landlord:

Written demand is hereby made for the return of my $250 deposit which was made to you on September 1, 2011.

Sincerely,

Terry Tenant

As you can see, the written demand does not need to be complicated or threatening. It only needs to put you in compliance with the requirements of the law so that you can add damages, attorney's fees and court costs to a suit if your deposit is still withheld.

If the landlord sends you a statement showing why the deposit was withheld, you can still sue if you do not agree with his reasons. If the statement is totally groundless, you may still recover your damages and attorney's fees. If there is some justification to withhold, you may only be entitled to a part of your deposit and no damages. The judge will have a great deal of discretion in deciding whether the landlord has dealt fairly with you. In any event, some landlords have gotten into the habit of not returning deposits unless a written demand is made. Once the demand is made, this type of landlord will refund your money because he knows you understand how to go through the procedures.

If you do not receive satisfaction from your written demand, you must file suit. Hopefully, the landlord or the rental premises are within the jurisdiction of a small claims court. At this point, if you have a good case, you might find a lawyer willing to take over and handle the suit for the small amount of fees that might be awarded. You have to understand, however, that most judges will not award a completely adequate amount of attorney's fees for a $250 liability. The attorney's fees to take your case to trial might run many times what is owed you and a judge will hesitate to make the landlord pay that much. There is also the possibility that the judge will feel that the landlord's failure to return the deposit was justified.

If you represent yourself, the court cannot award attorney's fees. So, by being your own lawyer, you may reduce the amount that the landlord has to pay for not returning your deposit. Before trying to file your own suit, make a real effort to find a lawyer willing to represent you for whatever might be awarded. Your best chance would be with a young lawyer who is just out of law school and is looking for experience.

If you end up filing suit for yourself, use the same procedures that we explained in the section on collecting a debt. Try to file in a city court or, better yet, in a small claims division of a city court. You must be able to prove that you gave a deposit, that the deposit was not returned, that you gave the landlord no cause to withhold the deposit, and that you gave written notice demanding a return of the deposit.

✓RECOVER A DEPOSIT CHECK LIST

☑ Make sure you are entitled to a refund.

Did you abandon before the lease was up?

Did you leave the premises in good condition?

Did you leave a forwarding address?

☑ Make a written demand for your refund.

Do this as soon as you see a problem.

Make sure it is witnessed or by certified mail.

☑ If the deposit is still not returned:

Try to find a lawyer willing to handle your case.

File suit and ask for damages.

Settle a Small Estate

Some types of estates can be settled without having to open any court proceedings. Review the section on small successions to see if the estate you want to settle will qualify. If it does, you merely have to prepare an affidavit that contains certain facts, have the affidavit signed by all the heirs, and then record the affidavit if any real estate is part of the succession.

To qualify, the deceased must not have had a will. Also, all the heirs must be closely related, and the total estate must be valued at $75,000 or less. The affidavit must be signed by the spouse, if any, and at least one other heir if there is a spouse or by at least two heirs if there is no spouse. The heirs must sign in front of a Notary Public.

SMALL SUCCESSION AFFIDAVIT

State of Louisiana

Parish of East Baton Rouge

Before me, the undersigned authority, personally appeared Jane Davis and John Davis, both domiciled in Jefferson Parish, Louisiana, who did depose and say:

That they are respectively the surviving spouse and son of George G. Davis, deceased, and as the sole heirs of the deceased, they do hereby make this affidavit pursuant to the provisions of Code of Civil Procedure Article 3432:

1. George G. Davis died September 1, 2010, at his home in Kenner, Louisiana. The deceased was domiciled in Jefferson Parish at the time of his death.

2. The deceased died intestate and owned no immovable property at the time of his death.

3. The deceased was married to Jane Davis, 123 Shady Lane, Kenner, Louisiana, at the time of his death and was survived by one son, namely: John Davis, 4040 Elm Street, New Orleans, Louisiana. The deceased had no other children and never adopted anyone.

4. The deceased owned the following movable property at the time of his death (values shown are the deceased's community interest):

    a) 2007 Oldsmobile VIN JAB3434CD, value: $1,950.00

    b) United Savings and Loan certificate of deposit number 566687 dated June 1, 1988, value: $2,400.00

    c) Personal effects and clothing, value: $400.00

    d) Bayou Bank checking account #345-0098, value: $1,200.00

    Total value of the deceased's estate: $5,950.00

Jane Davis   *John Davis*

Sworn to and subscribed before me on this __ day of May, 2012.

_____
Notary Public

✓ SETTLE A SMALL ESTATE CHECK LIST

☑ Make sure the estate qualifies.

Was there a will?

Are all the heirs closely related?

Is the total value $75,000 or less?

☑ Prepare the affidavit.

All the heirs must sign.

There must be an address for each heir.

The relationship of each heir must be listed.

All the property and values must be listed.

The total value must be listed.

It must include the domicile of the deceased.

It must include the date of death.

It must be notarized.

If there is real estate, the full description must be included and the affidavit must be recorded.

Frequently Asked Questions

I have custody of my three children but my former husband keeps calling and threatening to leave the state with them if I don't agree to reduce my support award. He always denies that he makes these threats. I would like to record the telephone conversation so that I can prove that he is doing this. Would I be breaking the law if I tape record my former husband when he calls?

The Legislature enacted a law in 1985 which made the taping of telephone conversations illegal even if you are one of the parties to the conversation. In 1988 this law was declared unconstitutional by the Louisiana courts. At the present time, you may record telephone conversations with your husband without his knowledge or permission. It would be advisable, however, to seek legal advice before you make any recordings just to be sure the law hasn't changed yet again.

I am very close to my niece and nephew and have been a second father since they were born. My brother and his wife went through a messy divorce recently, she was awarded sole custody, and she has declared that no one in my family will be allowed to see the children again. Do I have any visitation rights as an uncle?

There is a Louisiana statute that provides a procedure for the award of visitation rights to any relative who does not have custody. The only requirement is that a judge find that it is in the best interest of the children to allow the visitation. You might be able to get visitation, but you must do it through a court proceeding.

I moved here from another state several years ago. My mother is dead and my father was never any help when I was growing up and going through college. My father remarried someone much younger and I doubt that I am in his will. Now that I live in Louisiana, what rights do the forced heirship-Forced heirship laws give me against my father's estate?

Assuming your father does not live in Louisiana, you have no forced heirship rights against his estate. Forced heirship only applies to citizens of Louisiana. Since your father lives in another state, the laws of that state would control inheritance rights.

When my husband and I divorced, he agreed to pay the mortgage note on our house. He filed bankruptcy a few months ago and the bank is now insisting that I make the payments or they will foreclose. How can they do this? What was the point in settling with my husband if he can now get out of his obligation?

You obligated yourself to the bank when you first bought your house and signed the mortgage. Any agreement you later make with your husband does not change your obligation to the bank. His obligation under the settlement agreement is a personal commitment to you and it can be extinguished in a bankruptcy. People frequently enter into community property settlements with the belief the problems are over only to find that they are not if a former spouse goes bankrupt. This will often force the other spouse to declare bankruptcy as well.

I have a grown son and a daughter. My son was constantly in trouble and ran away from home when he was eighteen rather than face theft charges. I have not heard from him in five years. I know we have forced heirship laws in this state, but it does not seem right that my son should get part of my estate when my daughter is much more deserving.

Forced heirs can be disinherited under certain circumstances. For example, you could disinherit your son if he struck you or attempted to strike you; if he has been guilty of cruel treatment towards you; if he has attempted to take your life; if he has refused to support you if you are in need and he has the means; or if he has been convicted of a crime that is punishable by death or life in prison. There is an additional ground for disinherison: if the child has refused to communicate with the parent for a period of at least two years after reaching eighteen. The child must know how to contact the parent and the child cannot be in the military during this time. You probably have the right to disinherit your son. This can only be done in a will. You must prepare a valid will and you must state the reasons you are disinheriting your son. Your son would then have no forced heirship rights unless he could show that you and he reconciled after you wrote the will, or that the reasons stated in the will for the disinherison were untrue.

I have been paying child support for many years for my two children. When my oldest child turned eighteen last year, my former wife agreed to allow me to cut my payments in half. I have heard that this type of agreement is not binding and that my ex-wife can sue me for back support. Did I make a mistake in trusting her?

You have to first look at the support judgment to see how it is worded. For example, if the judgment is for $150 per child for a total of $300 per month, the support obligation for the older child would automatically end when that child turns eighteen. If, on the other hand, the judgment was simply $300 for the support of the two children, the obligation would not change until both children were eighteen. An agreement to modify an award of support can be binding in certain circumstances. However, you face the problem of proving whether there really was an agreement and the exact terms of the agreement. What if your former wife sues you for back support and contempt? Can you prove that she agreed to the reduction? Did you both put the terms of the reduction in writing? The only safe way to modify any type of judgment is to go back into court and have the original judgment

322/ Louisiana Legal Advisor

changed. If both parties agree to the change, this can be a simple procedure that may not require a court appearance. If you do not want to go to the trouble of changing the judgment, you should at least have a written agreement signed by your ex-wife. There is no guarantee, however, that a judge will necessarily recognize the agreement if it creates a hardship on the children.

A car ran into me while I was stopped at a red light. I was taken to the hospital for x-rays. There was no serious injury, but my neck has been sore for weeks. My car was probably a total wreck and I am without transportation. Am I entitled to a rental car? The other guy's insurance company has offered to settle the case for the book value of the car but I can't possibly buy a car in the same condition for the book price. Do I have to accept their offer? Should I press my claim for the injury to my neck? Should I have a lawyer, or can I do this myself?

The insurance company has to either pay to repair your car or pay you the local fair market value of the car. The "book" price of the car might approximate the fair market value, but you are not obligated to accept the book price. You can visit local car lots to see what similar cars are selling for and make your own case as to the local fair market value of your car.

The insurance company will probably owe you a rental car, but only until they either repair your car or decide that it is a total wreck. There are usually restrictions on the maximum daily amount they will pay for a rental car. Therefore, you should have this arranged before making any personal commitments to pay the rental. If you decide to accept their offer to settle the damage to your car, make sure that any releases you sign or any checks you endorse release the insurance company only for the property damage. Do not sign anything that releases all claims.

You have one year from the time of the accident to sue for personal injuries. It would be advisable to wait and see about the problems with your neck. It is not uncommon for this type of injury to suddenly become worse weeks or even months later. If you do not feel that you want to press a personal injury claim, you can probably represent yourself to recover the property damage. The insurance company should also settle with you for the hospital and any medical bills and they should be willing to pay you something for the pain and inconvenience that you have suffered. If you are satisfied with an offer, you do not need a lawyer. If you are not satisfied, you should hire a lawyer to represent you. In any event, do not let anyone rush you into signing something that you do not understand or feel right about. If you have any doubts, see a lawyer.

I have gotten way behind on all my bills and it doesn't seem like there is any chance of catching up. I see advertisements by lawyers who charge $450 for bankruptcies. Should I consider declaring bankruptcy? What are the disadvantages?

The decision to go bankrupt should not be undertaken lightly. You should first make every attempt to satisfy your creditors by debt consolidation and debt restructuring. In other words, you should try to convince your creditors that you want to satisfy your obligations. Many creditors, if they think you are doing your best, will work with you. You should also consider debt counseling. There are many non-profit debt counseling agencies that can assist you in negotiating with your creditors and with setting up a budget for you and your family. Bankruptcy should be an alternative only if your attempts to satisfy your obligations fail and there is no other reasonable solution.

The major disadvantage to you in going bankrupt is the blemish to your credit record. The fact that you have declared bankruptcy can be carried on your credit record for as long as ten years. Some lenders will never extend credit to someone with a bankruptcy on his or her credit record. A bad credit record can make it very difficult to get a loan. For example, you may find it impossible to buy a house. Another disadvantage is that you may lose some of your assets in a bankruptcy. This can be especially true if you have equity in a house or automobiles. An attorney can explain to you which assets can be kept and which assets may be lost.

My father died several years ago but I have never heard anything about his estate. My mother still lives in the house, which is fine with me, but I know my father had a lot of money in savings. Shouldn't I have received some of this money? I don't want to upset my mother by discussing this with her, but it seems like I should have heard something by now.

There could be two reasons why you have heard nothing about your father's estate. It is very possible that a succession was never opened. If your mother is living in the house and has access to the bank accounts, it may not have occurred to her that there is any reason to take the legal steps necessary to settle your father's estate. Another possibility is that the succession was opened but you have no immediate rights to estate property. Although you are a forced heir, your mother might have a usufruct over the portion of your father's estate that belongs to you. This would make you the naked owner of a portion of the estate without any right to actually possess the property while your mother has the usufruct. This usufruct would end if she remarries, unless your father had a will that made different arrangements. There are too many variables that would determine exactly what rights you have. For example, was there a will? Was a succession opened? Was your father's property community or separate? You need to discuss these questions openly with your mother.

When I went to court last month, my wife was awarded $400 per month child support. I have a friend like me with one *child who makes about the same amount of money. He only has to pay $250 per month to support his child. It seems clear to me that my lawyer blew it and that I am now stuck having to pay more support than I should have to. Do I have any recourse against my lawyer?*

People frequently compare notes on their support obligations and feel that they are paying too much because someone else is paying less. The fact is, your friend has a different set of facts that were presented to the judge. No two cases and no two judges are identical. The judge has the job of looking at what you make and your expenses, what your wife makes and her expenses, and what your child needs. The judge is then supposed to take into account all these factors and arrive at an amount of support for your child. The factors that the judge considered in your particular case probably boiled down to the affidavits and testimony as to you and your wife's income and expenses. It is impossible to guess why the particular judge in your case arrived at the figure $400, although it is certainly within the normal range for this state. It might very well be that you "blew it" when you testified on the stand. Judges are usually pretty good at setting support that comes as close as possible to being fair to everyone, including the child. Stop trying to find someone to blame for what you imagine is an unfair amount of child support.

I am considering selling my house. A neighbor is interested and suggested that we could save a real estate commission by arranging the sale ourselves. We have tentatively agreed on a price, but don't know what to do next. Should we be trying to do this ourselves?

There is nothing wrong with trying to save money. The problem is, many people lose a great deal of money trying to save money. The major function of a real estate agent is to find a buyer for your house. Since you have already found a buyer, it would seem that you do not need an agent. However, have you stopped to consider whether the price your neighbor wants to pay is fair? Would you perhaps get more on the open market? Enough to more than make up for a commission? A real estate agent, among other things, would also screen potential buyers, prepare a purchase agreement, and help arrange financing.

Assuming you do not use an agent, the next step is to prepare a purchase agreement. Any agreement for the sale of real estate must be in writing. Also, the buyer is going to need a copy of the purchase agreement if he intends to apply for financing. At this point, you or the buyer should consult an attorney. It is customary for the buyer to pay the closing costs, so let him look into financing and let his mortgage company recommend the closing attorney.

I have been separated from my husband for over a year. We have never gone to court to make it official, but just decided to not live with each other for a while. I let him use my car recently and he wrecked it. I have no collision insurance and he has refused to pay for the damages. Can I sue my husband for the money I am out?

Louisiana's "doctrine of interspousal immunity" prevents you from suing your husband. This doctrine is supposed to promote harmony in the marriage by forbidding law suits by husband against wife and wife against husband. Obviously, it was not intended to apply to cases where there is little or no harmony anyway. If you had been judicially separated or divorced at the time of the accident, you would have the right to sue him. If you are certain that neither your insurance nor his will cover the damages, you might consider going ahead and getting a judicial separation. You could even get a divorce since you have been apart long enough. You would then have the legal right to sue your husband once you were divorced. In accident cases, suit must be filed within one year of the date of the accident or you lose the right to sue.

My daughter is over eighteen and attending college. I have heard that my ex-husband is responsible for child support past the age of eighteen if the child is still in school. What can I do to make him help with my daughter's education?

The idea that the responsibility for child support is extended if a child goes to college is a common misunderstanding. There is a statute that would extend the obligation for support until the age of nineteen, but only if the child is attending a secondary school and only after a court order. In other words, a child who is still eighteen and in high school may be entitled to support—not a child who is in college.

I bought a house recently and got a very good deal. We went through all the formalities of a sale and I paid the seller in cash after getting a bank loan. The seller now says that he talked to a lawyer and he wants more money or he will take the house back. I told him that I thought he was crazy. A deal is a deal. Is there some way he can do what he threatens?

Whether you may have to pay more or return the house depends on what you paid. If the price you paid was less than one-half the value of the property, Louisiana law considers this lesion. Lesion means that a seller received so little for his property that he must have been mistaken and therefor not freely given his consent to the sale. The point at which a sale may present a lesion problem is when the seller receives less than one-half the actual value of the property. In other words, if the property was worth $50,000 but you paid only $20,000 for it, the seller can claim lesion. If he is successful, you would have the option of returning the property or making up the difference between what you paid and the actual value of the property.

Lesion is a remedy that is available only to the seller and only for the sale of immovable property (real estate). Lesion can also apply to the division of property among co-owners. In division cases, lesion can apply if the sale is for less then three-quarters of the actual value. Community property settlements are an example of a division among co-owners that can raise the problem of lesion.

I recently moved here from Wisconsin. I have a will that my wife and I made several years ago. Is my will valid in Louisiana? Should I make a new will?

If your will was valid in the state of your domicile at the time the will was executed, it can be recognized as valid in Louisiana. This would be true even if the form of your Wisconsin will would be invalid under Louisiana law. However, the burden would be on your heirs to prove that your will was valid under Wisconsin law at the time you lived there. This involves getting certified copies of the Wisconsin statutes and proving to the judge's satisfaction that everything was done properly. The best way to avoid this potential problem is to have a new will prepared. Also, a new will can specifically address issues that are peculiar to Louisiana, like forced heirship and collation.

I have a problem that I know should be handled by a lawyer. I should have done something about it years ago, but I have been putting it off because I don't know any lawyers. There has been a lot of advertising by lawyers recently, but frankly I am put off by what I have seen —especially the television and billboard ads. What is the best way to find a lawyer?

If you do not personally know a lawyer that you have faith in, the next best method of finding a lawyer is through the recommendation of a friend or business associate. If the lawyer does not handle the sort of problem you have, he or she may be able to refer you directly to someone that does. If you do not know anyone that can recommend a lawyer, the next best choice is to call a referral service that is sponsored by your local bar association. Be very careful that the referral service is connected with a bar association. There are many referral services that are nothing more than profit making companies that charge certain attorneys a large fee to belong to the service. These services have absolutely no requirements as to competency and there is no regulation as to fees charged. There are even "referral agencies" that are actually owned by the lawyer to whom referrals are made. Most major cities in Louisiana have bar sponsored referral services. Look in the business white pages of your telephone book under the name of your city for a bar association. For example, "New Orleans Bar Association." Call and ask whether they sponsor a lawyer referral service. The referral service will ask you what type of problem you have and will refer you to a lawyer who handles your type of problem.

I have been married for twenty years. My husband has always worked and I have stayed home taking care of the children. Every month, my husband takes a part of his paycheck and puts it in a savings account in his name. I do not have access to this money and only he can withdraw funds. That money has always been a sore point with me. There have been many times that we have gone without because he refuses to touch a cent of "his" money. I would very much like to know exactly how much money there is. Do I have any right to the money in that bank account?

Assuming you have no marriage contract and that there is no judgment terminating the community, you own an undivided one-half interest in the savings account. You have an interest in the account because your husband's income is community property. The fact that he arranged an account with the bank to which only he has access, does not alter your right to your share of the money in that account. There are several methods you could use to find out how much is in the account. Short of filing for a separation and then seeking a division of the community, you could demand an accounting from your husband of all community property and debts. There are other legal remedies that would also force your

330/ Louisiana Legal Advisor

husband to disclose the assets in the account and distribute your share to you. You would need to consult with an attorney for specific advice on how to force this information from your husband. However, we have found from experience that these actions frequently end up as separation suits. If you could convince your husband to consult an attorney, he would be advised that he has no right to keep this "separate" account from you.

What is a title opinion, who does them and where can I find copies of them? An oil land lease agent has contacted me in reference to drilling on property that I supposedly own, stated that 3 title opinions had been done, and that I in fact do own it. I am very hesitant about signing a lease, without knowing for certain that I in fact do own this property.

A title opinion is a form of legal opinion rendered by an attorney who specializes in such matters. The crux of the title opinion is the attorney's legal opinion that title to the property is vested in certain persons whose names appear in the public records, less and except (or subject to) certain claims, leases, debts, obligations, sell-offs, etc. Typically a title opinion excludes all matters not expressly shown by the public records of the parish where the immovable is located, and all things that might impact title that would or could be shown by a competent boundary and/or encroachment survey, a wetlands survey, and an environmental impact assessment. Also excluded are such things as zoning classifications, flood classifications, mineral valuations, and current appraisal (FMV) information. Supporting documents to a title opinion typically include: (1) a mortgage certificate from the clerk of court, (2) tax certificates from the sheriff going back at least 3 years, and (3) an abstract of title consisting of all recorded documents affecting title to the property in any way going back at least 55 years. Full title opinions tend to be expensive, given the amount of time and professional liability at stake. They are typically rendered at the request of a lending bank and are property of the party paying for them.

Are there situations where probate is not necessary? For example, my grandmother was in a nursing home and died with some money in an account. There was probably not more than a few thousand dollars. Will we have to hire a lawyer and go through probate for this?

The probate process in Louisiana is called a succession. A succession is not necessary under certain circumstance: 1) when the estate has a gross value less than $75,000; and 2) there was no will; and 3) a spouse and/or close relatives are able to sign an affidavit as to the facts and amount of the estate. Keep in mind that all three of these conditions must exist. If all of the factors are present, then instead of a succession the heirs can provide an original copy of the executed affidavit which operates as a release of estate property to the heirs named in the affidavit.

Glossary

A MENSA ET THORO. A separation "from bed and board."

A VINCULO MATRIMONII. A divorce "from the bonds of matrimony." A Complete dissolution of the marriage.

ABANDONMENT. The withdrawal or denial of marital obligations without justification or cause. It is more commonly understood to be one spouse leaving the matrimonial domicile without cause and refusing to return.

ABSTRACT. A condensed history of the chain of title to land based on courthouse records.

ACKNOWLEDGMENT. To admit something is genuine. When used in connection with paternity, it is a formal recognition that a child is one's own.

ACQUETS. Property acquired by gift, purchase, or otherwise than by succession (also acquets and gains).

ACT OF SALE. In Louisiana it is an original record of a sale of property made by a notary.

ADMINISTRATOR (female: Administratrix). The person who has court authority to manage a deceased's estate.

ADOPTION. The act of taking another person as one's own with all the rights and responsibilities that would have existed between parent and child.

ADULTERY. Voluntary sexual intercourse of a married person with someone other than that person's spouse. May also include oral intercourse.

AFFIDAVIT. A voluntary written statement that is signed and sworn under oath by the person making the statement before an officer having authority to administer the oath, usually a notary.

ALIMONY. The right of either spouse to receive support from the other. Now called spousal support.

ALIMONY PENDENTE LITE. A right for support that is temporary pending a final divorce.

ANNULMENT. Act of rendering something void retrospectively as well as prospectively.

ANSWER. Usually a pleading in response to a lawsuit which alleges facts to deny or avoid the allegations made by a plaintiff.

APPEAL. The removal of a case from an inferior court to a superior court for review.

ATTORNEY. One who is authorized to act for or in stead of another.

AUTHENTIC ACT. An act executed before a notary and two witnesses.

BAD FAITH. Generally a deliberate fraud or a design to mislead others for one's own benefit.

BEQUEATH. To give personal property by a will.

BIGAMY. Contracting a marriage while a prior marriage is still valid.

BULK SALES ACTS. Class of statutes to prevent the defrauding of creditors by a secret sale of most or all of a merchant's stock.

CHATTEL. Article of personal property. Property other than real estate.

CODICIL. A modification or addition to an existing will.

COLLATION. The return to a succession by an heir who received more than his share during the deceased's lifetime.

COMMUNITY PROPERTY. Property owned jointly by a husband and wife in a marital partnership.

COMMUTATIVE CONTRACT. A contract in which each contracting party gives and receives an equivalent, e.g., the contract of sale.

CONCUBINAGE. Living together or cohabiting without the authority of marriage.

CURATOR (female: Curatrix). Person appointed to be a guardian of a minor or other person not regarded as able to manage his own affairs.

DATION EN PAIEMENT. The giving by a debtor to a creditor of something other than money to cancel a debt. Usually a dation is made of mortgaged property to the mortgage holder in exchange for canceling the debt.

DEVOLUTIVE APPEAL. An appeal that does not suspend the execution of a judgment.

DIVORCE A VINCULO MATRIMONII. An absolute divorce that totally releases the parties from their matrimonial obligation.

DOMICILE. A place of permanent residence in which a person always intends to remain and to return when traveling elsewhere.

EARNEST. A payment of part of the price for the purpose of validating the contract.

EMANCIPATION. Surrender of parental duties with the concurrent granting to a minor of the legal status of adult. Some types of emancipation can be partial.

EVICTION. The removal of a tenant from an owner's property through judicial process.

EXCEPTION. A pleading that is filed to delay or dismiss a suit without necessarily making a legal appearance before the court.

EXECUTOR (female: Executrix). Person appointed in a will to carry out the deceased's instructions and dispose of the property in accordance with the deceased's wishes.

FORCED HEIRS. Those persons who must receive a portion of a deceased's estate in a proportion set by law.

FORCED PORTION. The amount a forced heir must receive. Can be used interchangeably with "legitime."

HEIR. One who is entitled to receive the property of a deceased either by will or by operation of law. The more technical definition in Louisiana is one who inherits when the deceased had no will, as opposed to a legatee who inherits through a will.

INCEST. Sexual intercourse between parties related by blood in the degree prohibited by law.

INJUNCTION. A court order forbidding a defendant from doing something or allowing a plaintiff to do something.

INNOMINATE. Having no classification. In the law of contracts, a type of contract that falls under general contract law since it is not classified under a particular statute.

IN SOLIDO. An obligation where several obligors may each be individually liable for the whole obligation.

INTERDICTION. A court proceeding to declare a person incapable of managing his own affairs because of physical or mental disability. The person interdicted is called an interdict and the person appointed is called a tutor.

INTERLOCUTORY. A temporary judgment or decree which decides some point but is not final in nature.

INTERROGATORIES. A set of written questions propounded to an opposing party to gain information or to force admissions that can be used at trial.

INTESTATE. Without a will. When a person dies intestate, Louisiana law determines who will inherit his property.

LAWYER. A person licensed to practice law. Commonly used interchangeably with attorney.

LEGITIME. The portion of an estate that a forced heir is entitled to inherit. This can also be called the forced portion.

LESION. The harm suffered by a seller who does not receive a fair amount for the property which he has sold.

LESION BEYOND MOIETY. The harm suffered by a seller who does not receive at least one-half the value of the property he has sold.

MAJORITY. Age at which a person has all the rights of an adult.

MALPRACTICE. Unreasonable lack of skill or care by someone who practices a given profession.

MARRIAGE CONTRACT. An agreement between married persons, or those who intend to be married, usually as to their respective property rights.

MYSTIC WILL. A will that is written by hand, sealed in an envelope, and then the envelope is signed by the maker, witnessed and notarized.No longer recognized in Louisiana.

NE VARIETUR. "It must not be altered." Phrase placed on a note by a notary to identify the note in connection with an act of mortgage. Also used in other types of legal documents.

NOTARY PUBLIC. An officer authorized to administer oaths and certify signatures. In Louisiana, the notary has many other powers, such as preparing wills.

OLOGRAPHIC WILL. A will written by the testator. To be valid it must be entirely written, dated and signed in the hand of the testator.

PAROL EVIDENCE. Evidence given by mouth. Often not allowed in court when used to dispute written agreements.

POWER OF ATTORNEY. A written authorization giving another person power to do specific or general acts for the person giving the power.

PRELIMINARY DEFAULT. A judgment that is entered into the court minutes reflecting a request or motion by a plaintiff to recognize that a defendant has not filed an answer or opposition within the time period allowed.

PRESCRIPTION. A time period the running of which creates or terminates rights. For example, a suit for wrongful injury usually must be brought within one year or the right to sue is lost.

PRO SE. "For himself." Applies to a person who is representing himself without an attorney.

PUTATIVE MARRIAGE. A marriage contracted in good faith where one or both parties are ignorant of an impediment which makes the marriage unlawful.

QUANTUM MERUIT. "As much as he deserves." A right to receive payment for services even when there is no express contract.

RECIPROCAL WILLS. Wills made by two or more parties that make similar provisions in favor of each other. In Louisiana, the wills must be separate documents.

RECONCILIATION. The renewal of relations between married people after a separation. A reconciliation after a judicial separation acts to void the judgment of separation.

REDHIBITION. The avoidance of a sale because of a defect in the thing sold which renders the thing useless or so imperfect that it can be presumed that the buyer would not have bought the thing had he known of the defect.

SETTLOR. One who creates a trust.

SIMULATED SALE. A sale which appears to be genuine but which in fact is intended to defraud creditors or other parties.

SMALL SUCCESSION. A succession that has a gross value of less than $50,000.

SPENDTHRIFT TRUST. A trust that is created with certain provisions that prevent the beneficiary from selling or mortgaging his interest in the trust.

STATUTORY WILL. A will which is dated, signed by the testator on each page, executed before a notary and two witnesses, and which is attested by the testator, witnesses and notary.

SUCCESSION. The estate of the deceased as well as the act of determining and transferring the estate and rights to the heirs or legatees —the successors.

TESTAMENT. A written disposition of property to take effect after the maker's death. It is used interchangeably with the term "will," but the strict definition is that of a will of personal property only, not real estate.

TESTATE. A succession in which there is a valid will.

TESTATOR (Female: Testatrix). The person who makes a will.

TORT. A wrong done by one person to another.

TRUST. A right or property held by one party, the trustee, for the benefit of another, the beneficiary.

TUTOR (Female: Tutrix). One who has the care of a minor and the administration of his estate. Can be used almost interchangeably with the word "guardian."

USUFRUCT. The right to enjoy and use a thing that belongs to another and to take all the income and utility of the thing as long as the substance of the thing is not altered. The usufruct of money or consumeables implies the right to use the thing entirely up.

WILL. The written wishes of a person as to the disposition of his property after his death, as to the appointment of his executor, and as to the tutor of his children.

WORKER'S COMPENSATION. A set of statutes that provide for payments to workers and their dependents when the worker is injured as the result of his employment.

Judicial Districts

1st DISTRICT:
Caddo

2nd DISTRICT:
Bienville, Claiborne, Jackson

3rd DISTRICT:
Lincoln, Union

4th DISTRICT:
Morehouse, Ouachita

5th DISTRICT:
Franklin, Richland, West
Carroll

6th DISTRICT:
East Carroll, Madison, Tensas

7th DISTRICT:
Catahoula, Concordia

8th DISTRICT:
Winn

9th DISTRICT:
Rapides

10th DISTRICT:
Natchitoches

11th DISTRICT:
DeSoto, Sabine

12th DISTRICT:
Avoyelles

13th DISTRICT:
Evangeline

14th DISTRICT:
Calcasieu

15th DISTRICT:
Acadia, Lafayette, Vermilion

16th DISTRICT:
St. Mary, Iberia, St. Martin

17th DISTRICT:
Lafourche

18th DISTRICT:
Iberville, Pointe Coupee, W.
Baton Rouge

19th DISTRICT:
East Baton Rouge

20th DISTRICT:
East Feliciana, West Feliciana

21st DISTRICT:
Livingston, St. Helena,
Tangipahoa

22nd DISTRICT:
St. Tammany, Washington

23rd DISTRICT:
Ascension, Assumption, St.
James

24th DISTRICT:
Jefferson

25th DISTRICT:
Plaquemine

26th DISTRICT:
Bossier, Webster

27th DISTRICT:
St. Landry

28th DISTRICT:
LaSalle, Caldwell

29th DISTRICT:
St. Charles, St. John

30th DISTRICT:
Vernon

31st DISTRICT:
Jefferson Davis

32nd DISTRICT:
Terrebonne

33rd DISTRICT:
Allen

34th DISTRICT:
St. Bernard

35th DISTRICT:
Grant

36th DISTRICT:
Beauregard

37th DISTRICT:
Caldwell

38th DISTRICT:
Red River

CIVIL DISTRICT COURT:
Orleans

Index